PACIFIC COAST

LEAGUE STARS,

VOLUME II

Ninety Who Made It In The Majors, 1903 to 1957

BY JOHN E. SPALDING

Other Books by the Author:

"Always on Sunday, The California Baseball League, 1886 to 1915"

"Pacific Coast League Stars, 100 of the Best, 1903 to 1957"

"Sacramento Senators and Solons, Baseball in California's Capital, 1886 to 1976"

Copyright 1997 by John E. Spalding

ISBN 0-89745-983-0

FIRST PRINTING – By Ag Press, Manhattan, KS

INTRODUCTION

If I had known when I published "Pacific Coast League Stars" in 1994 that there would be a second volume, I'd have done some things differently.

Like the earlier book, this one features biographies of many of the greatest players who appeared in the Coast League before the National League moved west in 1958. Many of the men described in the first volume had long careers in the PCL, but never achieved much fame in the Big Leagues. All played a minimum of three seasons in the Coast League.

Since I didn't envision a "Pacific Coast League Stars, Volume II," at that time, biographies of a number of players who could have been saved for this book were included in the first. Specifically they were Ping Bodie, Dolph Camilli, Joe DiMaggio, Ernie Lombardi, Lefty O'Doul, Earl Sheely and Gus Suhr.

All of them meet the criteria I set down when scanning the list of stars who might fill this second volume: each played at least one year in the PCL before rising to the majors and each appeared in the big leagues for a minimum of seven seasons. Exceptions to the latter rule were made for Luke Easter, a black who was prevented from playing in Organized Baseball for years because of his race; Swede Risberg, whose career was shortened by his participation in the Black Sox conspiracy, and Jimmy O'Connell, who was banned from baseball after two seasons in the majors for offering an opposing player a bribe.

There were many fine players who didn't qualify for a spot in the first volume because they didn't meet my three year minimum rule. I considered 120 players for this book. Among those selected are Hall of Famers Dave Bancroft, Mickey Cochrane, Stan Coveleski, Lefty Gomez, Harry Heilmann, Dazzy Vance and Ted Williams, plus many oth-

ers who were promoted from Coast League rosters quickly because of the high level of their skills on the diamond.

Those in the latter category during the 55 seasons between 1903 and 1957 range from Hal Chase, the Pacific Coast League's first great star in the majors, to Easter and Minnie Minoso, two of the black players who entered the league after the color line was broken in the late 1940s.

In a departure from the first volume, which pictured most of the players only in a Coast League uniform, this book shows every one in major league attire and more than two-thirds in a second shot taken while he was in the PCL. The task of finding Coast League photos was a daunting one, because a third of these men appeared in the league for only one or two seasons.

Photos came from a variety of sources. Most are from my own collection, but friends also helped out. You'll find their names in the photo credits. My thanks to them all.

Friends in the The Society for American Baseball Research answered questions that helped fashion some of the stories. These always helpful researchers are Carlos Bauer, whose thorough study of the 1903 season and several players provided me with statistics never available before; Bob Hoie, Larry Zuckerman and Pacific Coast League Historian Bill Weiss.

Once again, players of all types are discussed. There are powerful sluggers, great hitters, fleet-footed runners and players who could hold their own with the glove. I hope you enjoy all their stories.

John E. Spalding
1409 Beringer Court
San Jose, CA 95125-5993

PHOTO CREDITS

CONTENTS

DEDICATION

To the memory of my boyhood sports hero, Jackie Jensen

(1903 -1909)
THE EARLY YEARS

HAL CHASE

Hal Chase's first brush with authority over a baseball game came when he was 12 and his father disciplined him for accepting 50 cents to play in a Sunday game.

His last came 25 years later when no team in Organized Baseball would hire him following a career marred by drinking, gambling and repeated accusations that he offered bribes to other players and threw games.

Chase was the first great star to rise from the Pacific Coast League, going from Santa Clara College to the Los Angeles Angels to the New York Highlanders in one year.

A left-handed second baseman and pitcher in college, Chase made three hits in a game in Los Angeles against St. Vincent's College early in March, 1904. The umpire was Los Angeles owner James Morley, who needed a first baseman and signed Hal for $75-a-month.

Although he went hitless in his first game on March 27, the *Los Angeles Times* reported, "(Chase) plays first base as well as anyone would care to see."

Chase showed that he had some talent as the season progressed. "Chase has been hitting the ball and pulling off sensational fielding stunts like he did when he first joined the team, " said the *Sporting News* in June. "He has scored men from second so regularly that the fans appear to expect him to do it every time."

By year's end, Hal had a .279 average with 39 stolen bases and was drafted by New York for $750. Morley was furious, because the draft violated the PCL's peace agreement with the majors. Years later, Morley told the *San Francisco Bulletin* he had rejected a $6,000 offer for Chase before the draft stole him away.

When Chase reported to the Highlanders, Willie Keeler watched him for a few minutes and told manager Clark Griffith, "if that kid can keep on doing this stuff, he will be the greatest first baseman I have ever seen."

It was the first of many similar assessments. Hal was idolized by the fans, who were awed by his catlike quickness, his ability to field bunts in front of the mound, tag the batter and throw out the lead runner. The mild-mannered Chase seemed to be well-liked by players. He was generous and had a quick wit.

Although he was one of the most graceful first basemen in baseball history, Chase habitually posted substandard fielding averages, led the league in errors six times and

Hal Chase

showed frequent fielding lapses. His critics said these were clues that Chase was a crooked ball player, whose play suffered when he was in the pay of gamblers bent on fixing games for profit. Opposing bench jockeys shouted, "what are the odds today?"

Shortstop Roger Peckinpaugh recalled throwing balls to Hal that would get away from him while runs scored. "I'd think the throw wasn't that bad," said Peckinpaugh. "Then I'd think about his reputation and recognize he was tangling up his feet and making a fancy dive after the ball so it would

9

look like a wild throw."

This escaped many fans, who saw only a quick and mobile infielder making sensational plays while hitting well in the era of the dead ball. He batted .291 in 15 major league seasons. Analyst Bill James described it as an empty .291 average, arguing that Chase had little power, was an impatient hitter who drew few walks and never drove in as many as 90 runs in a season.

Hal was sought by many teams, including Stockton in the outlaw California State League, where he played after the

---

"(Hal Chase) plays first base as well as anyone would care to see."
— Los Angeles Times

1905 and 1906 seasons. He threatened to stay in California in 1907 if New York wouldn't pay him $4,000. Hal got his money and came back to Stockton after the American League season ended.

Under pressure from the Pacific Coast League, the National Commission declared anyone who played with the outlaws would be blacklisted. Chase changed his name to Schultz and continued playing, although the ruse fooled no one. He was reinstated with New York in 1908, but jumped the club in September to play in California again. He was reinstated after paying a $200 fine.

In 1910, manager George Stallings accused Hal of trying to throw a game and threatened to resign if Chase wasn't released. Instead, Stallings was fired and replaced by Chase, who finished the season with a 10-4 managerial record.

Hal hit .315 in 1911, but the ball club wound up sixth with a 76-76 mark. Chase's career as manager was over, but he stayed with New York until early in 1913, when he was traded to the Chicago White Sox.

Chase jumped to the outlaw Federal League in 1914 and White Sox owner Charles Comiskey obtained an injunction to prevent him from playing. Another court vacated the injunction and Chase hit .347 in 75 games with Buffalo. In 1915, he led the Feds in home runs and averaged .291.

Reinstated in 1916 as part of the Federal League peace agreement and apparently blackballed by the American League, Hal went to Cincinnati and led the National League with a .339 average. In August, 1918, Reds manager Christy Mathewson suspended Hal for indifferent play.

Closed hearings on the charges were held early in 1919. A number of players testified that Chase offered them

bribes, but Hal denied the allegations and said he had bet on only two games, a post-season Cincinnati exhibition and another as a spectator. League President John Heydler ruled Chase had acted carelessly, but said the evidence and record of the games refuted the accusation.

The Reds traded Chase to the New York Giants, where he played 110 games and hit .284. Chase did not return to Organized Baseball in 1920. During the furor over the conspiracy by Chicago White Sox players to fix the 1919 World Series against Cincinnati, Giants manager John McGraw revealed he had cut Chase loose when Lee Magee confessed that Hal had bribed him to throw games.

Magee later filed suit against the Chicago Cubs to recover back pay. During the trial it came out that Magee and Chase each bet $500 against Cincinnati in a 1918 game with Boston. The Reds won the game.

In California, Chase was banned by local leagues and from Coast League ballparks after being accused trying to bribe Salt Lake City pitcher Spider Baum.

When the Black Sox scandal erupted, Chase was indicted by the Cook County Grand Jury. Pitcher Rube Benton told the jury that Chase and Heinie Zimmerman tried to give him $800 to throw a game when all three were with the Giants. Benton said Chase told him about the Black Sox fix in advance and claimed Hal had won $40,000 betting on Cincinnati. California refused to extradite Chase and he never stood trial with the others.

Hal played outlaw ball in the Southwest, wandered from place to place drinking too much and eventually eating so poorly that he contracted beri beri and was hospitalized in Colusa, California. Chase gave his side of his life's story in a 1941 interview by *Oakland Post-Enquirer* reporter Lester Grant that was published in the *Sporting News*.

Chase admitted that his life had been "one big mistake after another," but he denied any part in the Black Sox fix. Hal claimed Sleepy Bill Burns told him about it and said he regretted not reporting the fix to Heydler.

Chase contended the Giants were ready to give him a raise in 1920, but he preferred to go back to the West Coast to play ball and mend his failing second marriage.

Chase claimed to have written Baseball Commissioner Kenesaw Mountain Landis in 1931, asking about his status. He said that Landis replied, "as far as I know, you are in good standing in Organized Baseball. You mention a certain mistake you have made. I should like to know more about this." Chase said his attorney tore up the letter and advised him not to elaborate on his original statement. Landis later declined another reporter's request for information about the letters, referring him to Chase.

Less than a month before Hal died in 1947, the *Sporting News* ran an interview Chase had given the *Woodland Daily Democrat*. "I could have made a million dollars out of baseball on bets and gambling," Chase said. "I used to bet on games (but) I never bet against my own team."

Chase made no death bed confession, but one of his remarks might have made a suitable epitaph:

"I am an outcast and I haven't got a good name. I'm a loser, just like all gamblers are."

HAROLD HOMER CHASE
Born: 2/13/83, Los Gatos, CA, BR/TL, 6-foot, 175 pounds

		G	AB	R	H	2B	3B	HR	RBI	SB	AVG.
1904	LA	190	702	78	196	33	5	2	—	39	.279
PCL	1	190	702	78	196	33	5	2	—	39	.279
Majors	15	1919	7417	980	2158	322	124	57	942	363	.291

CHICK GANDIL

Everything in Chick Gandil's background is consistent with his role as the chief instigator and ringleader of the conspiracy to fix the 1919 World Series between the Chicago White Sox and the Cincinnati Reds.

Gandil had a reputation around baseball as a hard guy who was ready to take advantage of any opportunity to improve his livelihood. He was a renegade player at the beginning of his career and he was outlawed at the end.

Charles Arnold Gandil ran away from home when he was 17. Baseball was what he did best so, after a brief trial with two PCL teams in July, 1906, Chick rode a freight train to Texas, where he heard he could get a job playing with a semi-pro team in Amarillo.

Gandil bummed around the Southwest, eventually winding up in Cananea, Mexico, a wide open town mining town near the Arizona border, where he played ball for an outlaw team.

Chick was a big, rough hewn man, tall and muscular with deep set, brooding eyes. Baseball didn't provide enough money for Gandil to live the way he wanted so Chick worked in the copper mines and picked up extra money as a heavyweight fighter for $150-a-bout.

Married at 19 and tired of the grind in the mines, Gandil entered Organized Baseball in 1908, playing under the name of "Chick Arnold" with Shreveport in the Texas League. He performed reasonably well at first base and batted clean-up, compiling a .269 average in 116 games. Arnold disappeared from the lineup in late August, but it is unclear whether he was injured or left the club as the result of some dispute.

The *Sporting News* reported a month later that Arnold had been drafted by the St. Louis Browns, but he was listed on Shreveport's reserved list later in the year and apparently never had any contact with the American League team.

Shreveport officials and Gandil differed about how much he should be paid in 1909 and Chick refused to report. The following spring he went to California, where — once again as Chick Arnold — he won a place on the Fresno team in the outlaw California State League.

The Pacific Coast League was in a fight to the finish with the outlaws, who had employed many PCL contract jumpers. Sacramento club secretary J. M. Inman went to Fresno to pirate Gandil and outfielder John "Indian" House away from the outlaws.

Gandil broke into the Fresno clubhouse the night he left to recover his suitcase which contained a Raisin Growers

Chick Gandil

uniform. He went to Sacramento, but was arrested the next day and charged with defrauding the Fresno team of $250 transportation and advance money. Before the Senators could put Gandil on the field they had to bail him out of jail and pay off Fresno's claim.

Gandil was slow afoot but a good target at first base, which he held down through the early stages of the campaign. When the Senators acquired speedy and hard-hitting Hap Myers from the outlaw league in August, Chick was moved to the outfield, where he acquitted himself well considering his lack of experience there.

His .282 average and league-leading 214 hits attracted the attention of the Chicago White Sox, who bought him in early July. Chicago promised to send a replacement first sacker immediately, but Sacramento owner Charlie Graham said they couldn't take Gandil until the end of the season.

Everyone assumed Gandil was Sacramento property. But, a note from the *Shreveport Times* in the July 8 *Sporting News* set the record straight.

Oakland and Des Moines were bidding for Chick Arnold, it said, but Shreveport directors announced his sale to the White Sox for $3,000. "Arnold is at present playing with the Sacramento team . . . under the name of Gandil and Chicago will have to arrange matters with that club." After he jumped to the outlaws, the story explained, Shreveport

---

CHARLES ARNOLD GANDIL
Born: 1/19/87, St. Paul, MN, BR/TR, 6-foot-1.5, 190 pounds

		G	AB	R	H	2B	3B	HR	RBI	SB	AVG.
1906	LA-Fr	2	5	1	0	0	0	0	—	0	.000
1909	Sac	206	758	95	214	30	16	7	—	27	.282
PCL		2	208	763	95	214	30	16	7	—	27	.280
Majors		9	1147	4245	449	1176	173	78	11	556	153	.277

Hal Chase (third from left, top row) played on the 1903 Santa Clara College team.

Jack Graney

Chick Gandil

Roger Peckinpaugh

Vean Gregg

loaned him to Sacramento, "in order that he remain in organized ball."

Chick didn't show much with the White Sox in 1910. After hitting .193 in 77 games, he was sent to Montreal in the International League where he revived major league interest by batting .304.

Washington acquired Gandil and he spent four seasons in the nation's capital. He hit .291 or better three times with a high of .318 in 1913. Chick's work at first base was first rate and he set a league record of 143 assists in 1915 — a mark that was not broken until 1942, when Detroit's Rudy York registered 146.

Cleveland bought Gandil for $7,500 in February, 1916. He hit .259 and led the league in fielding percentage, chances accepted and assists, but the Indians let him go to the White Sox a year later for $3,500.

ChiSox owner Charles Comiskey was a tightwad who kept player salaries at a minimum. Gandil was making $4,500 on a club where the only big money was the $14,500 paid to Eddie Collins, probably a carryover from his days with Philadelphia's "$100,000 Infield."

Chicago won the pennant and took the World Series in 1917. Gandil hit .273 in the regular season and .261 in the post-season where he batted in a team high five runs.

In 1919, the Sox met Cincinnati in the ill-fated World Series. Chick had his best year at first base with a record .997 and only three errors and a .290 batting average.

When he was approached by gamblers to throw the World Series, Gandil didn't hesitate and recruited six teammates to join him in the fix. A seventh, Buck Weaver, attended meetings where the conspiracy was formulated, but he did not participate in throwing games or take any of the $20,000 that was distributed.

The favored White Sox lost the series five games to three amid rumors something funny was going on. Gandil, who had hit .233 with one error that led to a run in the series, asked for $10,000 the following season and played semi-pro ball in Bakersfield after Comiskey refused. The story of the fix broke near the end of the 1920 season and by then Comiskey's detectives had discovered that Gandil was the only player whose lifestyle had changed visibly when he bought a quantity of diamonds, a new house and a new car.

Gandil, who claimed he never received any of the tainted money, and the others were cleared by a Chicago grand jury, but were banned from baseball for life by Baseball Commissioner Kenesaw Mountain Landis.

Gandil played outlaw ball in the Southwest for awhile and returned to California where he worked as a plumber.

JACK GRANEY

Jack Graney might have had an inkling that his days as a pitcher were numbered one day in spring training when he beaned Cleveland manager Nap Lajoie with a pitch.

Lajoie called off the contest and told Jack he would be playing with the regulars from then on, because, "if some player is going to the hospital, it will be a rookie." Jack pitched batting practice and coached the bases for the Naps until Lajoie decided to farm him out to work on his control. Columbus refused to take him, so Cleveland sent Graney to Portland in 1908.

Graney was stocky and left-handed all the way. Buffalo manager George Stallings first spotted Jack on a team in his hometown of St. Thomas, Ontario, Canada, and dispatched him to Erie in the Inter-State League. He lasted only one game, which he won, as he recalled, "13-12 and I walked 15 batters."

Graney may have exaggerated, although he had a considerable wild streak. Jack joined Fulton in the Empire State League. While no records exist, Jack reported winning so many games that Chicago Cubs signed him to pitch for Wilkes-Barre in the New York State League. Pitching statistics again are not available, but Graney said he went 20-4 on the mound. He hit .280 in 37 games. Cleveland pitcher Bill Barnhard was scouting the minors while recovering from a broken finger and liked Graney's speed, despite his inability to find the plate regularly.

At Portland, Graney showed why Cleveland thought he needed more work as he walked 111 and struck out 146 while posting a 12-13 mark. His inordinate wildness won Graney the nickname "Three and Two Jack" in honor of his most frequent count on the batter.

In the winter of 1908, Jack was a member of the Reach All-American team which toured the Far East for three months. It recorded 14 wins and no defeats in Japan. The squad, made up mainly of Pacific Coast League players and managed by former PCL team owner Mike Fisher, also played games in the Philippines and Hawaii and finished 37-3.

Graney returned to Portland in 1909 and pitched in 31 games with a 17-9 record and a 122-165 walk to strikeout ratio. The *Portland Oregonian* called him, "the star of the staff" and "the premiere southpaw of the Pacific Coast League." In June, Graney pitched an 18-inning, 1-1 tie against Sacramento and showed decent control with only five walks and seven Ks.

It was apparent to manager Walt McCredie that Graney had value far beyond his strong arm and Jack appeared in 106 other games, including 98 as an outfielder, hitting .252 with nine triples.

When he returned to the American League in 1910, Cleveland officials decided his talents as a batter, base runner and outfielder exceeded his potential as a pitcher and he never worked from the slab again.

Jack never hit .300 in 14 years at the top. A .299 mark in 1921 when he played part-time was his highest batting average on the way to .250 lifetime. But, he was a patient batter with a great eye and drew 712 walks while heading the league in that department in 1917 and 1919. He also topped the league with 41 doubles in 1916.

Graney was popular around the league, but his pet bull terrier, "Larry," was an even bigger favorite of spectators. Larry traveled with Cleveland and performed acrobatic tricks on the diamond before games until he died in 1917. During a 1914 game at Washington, the dog retrieved a ball in foul territory and refused to relinquish it to umpire Bill Dineen. The fans were delighted, but American League president Ban Johnson barred Larry from any more appearances in the Washington ballpark.

Before his lengthy career was over, Graney played 1,402 games in the majors, more than any other Canadian-born player. Graney's career included two firsts of note. He was the first batter to face Boston Red Sox rookie pitcher Babe Ruth in 1914. Jack hit a single. In 1911, Jack was the first player to go to bat with a number on his uniform when Cleveland had numerals sewn on one sleeve of each jersey.

Another baseball first would come after his retirement as a player. Graney ran an automobile agency in Cleveland until he was wiped out in the 1929 stock market crash. Jack

JOHN GLADSTONE GRANEY
Born: 6/10/86, St. Thomas, Ont., Canada, BL/TL, 5-foot-9, 180 pounds

		G	AB	R	H	2B	3B	HR	RBI	SB	AVG.
1908	Port	46	105	7	24	1	1	0	—	4	.229
1909	Port	137	385	48	97	14	9	3	—	12	.252
PCL	2	183	490	55	121	15	10	3	—	16	.247
Majors	14	1402	4705	706	1178	219	79	18	420	148	.250

		W	L	PCT	G	IP	H	ER	BB	SO	ERA
1908	Port	12	13	.480	—	—	—	—	111	146	—
1909	Port	17	9	.654	31	—	—	—	122	165	—
PCL	2	29	22	.569	31*	—	—	—	233	311	—
Majors	1	0	0	.000	2	3	6	2	1	0	6.00

*incomplete

Jack Graney

Duffy Lewis

was selling used cars when he was hired as the announcer for Cleveland's games, becoming the first former big leaguer to do radio play-by-play.

His crisp and dramatic delivery was laced with anecdotes from his playing days and analysis of the game's action. When Baseball Commissioner Kenesaw Mountain Landis banned him from calling the 1934 series on grounds he might be biased in favor of the American League, Graney wrote to Landis. "My playing days are over," he said. "I am now a sportscaster and should be treated as such." Jack was permitted to broadcast the series the following season.

Graney was heard over the airwaves for more than 20 years and ended his career with the World Series in 1954.

DUFFY LEWIS

Duffy Lewis played left field in the Boston Red Sox outfield often called the greatest of all time. Duffy's not in the Hall of Fame but the other two outfielders — Harry Hooper and Tris Speaker — are enshrined there.

This "greatest outfield ever" label was hung on the trio by sportswriters. They included one whose respect for them ran so deep that he penned this verse:

"I'd like to be a pitcher
　　"Amid the baseball fight,
"With Duffy Lewis out in left
　　"And Hooper out in right;
"With Speaker out in center field
　　"And with no fences near,

"I'd like to pitch upon that club
　　"For sixty cents a year."

Baseball writer Fred Lieb said Hooper was quiet, unassuming, superb on defense and did everything so easily fans were inclined to overlook the fact he performed wonders. Speaker was unsurpassed, he added, but not hungry to win and Duffy Lewis was similar to Tris, " a careless, good fellow type who . . . had few equals in playing the position."

At the start of his career, Duffy was sought for his bat as much as his skill at patrolling the outfield. A graduate of Alameda High School, Duffy was attending St. Mary's College in Oakland when he joined the Alameda Grays in the outlaw California State League in 1907 and hit .170 in 16 contests.

He was batting .282 with Alameda the following season when Oakland manager George Van Haltren offered him a position with the Coast League team. Lewis joined the Oaks near the end of August, played left field and produced a .253 average in 50 games while batting well down in the lineup.

Appearing in 200 of Oakland's 213 games the following season, Duffy's .279 batting average was eighth among league regulars in a year when batting champion Henry Melchoir of San Francisco hit only .298.

Duffy's fielding was poor in his rookie year, but it improved greatly in 1909 when he was third in average and fourth in assists. The *Oakland Enquirer* called him, "the sweetest little fielder in the Coast League." A sensational play that demonstrated the strength of Duffy's arm was described years later by Abe Kemp in the *San Francisco*

Bulletin.

Vernon trailed Oakland by a run at Recreation Park in San Francisco in the ninth inning, Kemp said. The Tigers had Brick Devereaux at third base with one out when Drummond Brown belted a long drive that Lewis chased down and caught. Thinking it was the final out, Duffy continued running toward the club house in deep center field.

"Devereaux, alive to the humorous possibilities of the situation, refused to run," said Kemp. "He stood a few feet away from third base, hollering at Lewis. The frantic howls of his teammates caused Duffy to stop. He realized the situation . . . (and) cut the ball loose toward the plate." Certain he had scored the tying run on Duffy's mental mistake, Devereaux raced home and slide across the plate.

Umpire Bull Perrine bellowed, "you're out." When Devereaux asked why, the ump replied, "because the throw beat you to the plate." Kemp said the call was correct, but the amazing part of the story was that Lewis was in the shadow of the clubhouse more than 350 feet from the plate when he made the peg.

Lewis was drafted by the Red Sox where he joined Speaker and Hooper, who came out of the California State League in 1908 after batting .344 with Stockton. The great outfield was intact until 1916, when Speaker was traded to Cleveland.

Duffy hit .286 with a high of .307 in eight years at Boston and played left field so well that a troublesome outfield incline at Fenway Park was dubbed "Duffy's Cliff." The Sox won pennants in 1912, 1915 and 1916 and took three World Series. Lewis was the batting star of the last two, hitting .444 against the Phillies in 1915 and .353 against Brooklyn a year later.

Following the 1915 series, Duffy cashed in on his popularity on the California vaudeville circuit. His 15-minute conversation, "Tales of the Ballfield," earned him $5,500 for a 10-week run, the equivalent of about two-thirds of his Red Sox salary.

After spending 1918 in the Navy, Duffy was traded to the Yankees the following season. After hitting .272 and .271 with New York, he closed his major league career with 27 games at Washington in 1921 and a lifetime batting average of .284.

GEORGE EDWARD LEWIS
Born: 4/18/88, San Francisco, CA, BL/TL, 5-foot-10.5, 165 pounds

		G	AB	R	H	2B	3B	HR	RBI	SB	AVG.
1908	Oak	50	186	11	47	9	0	0	—	4	.253
1909	Oak	200	748	72	209	—	—	—	—	—	.279
1921	SLC	105	424	88	171	42	6	14	—	3	.403
1922	SLC	164	566	111	205	52	2	20	108	5	.362
1923	SLC	145	478	99	171	28	8	28	115	4	.358
1924	SLC	154	528	128	207	55	5	28	154	7	.392
1925	Port	130	442	65	130	17	2	15	71	5	.294
PCL	7	948	3372	574	1140	203*	23*	105*	448*	28*	.338
Majors	11	1459	5351	612	1518	289	68	38	793	132	.284

* incomplete

Lewis joined Salt Lake City after his release by the Senators. To celebrate his return to the Coast League and show he still could swing the bat — particularly at high altitude — Duffy opened with a 32-game hitting streak. He batted .403 with 42 doubles and 14 homers in 105 games to finish far ahead of the pack. But, he only had 424 official plate appearances and the batting title went to Oakland's Hack Miller, who hit .347 in 726 trips to the plate.

Lewis was named Salt Lake City's manager the following season. The Bees, usually a middle-of-the-pack team, finished fourth and fifth twice during his reign. His PCL managerial record of 290-311 was outstripped by his hitting.

Duffy batted .362 to finish as runner-up to teammate Paul Strand's .384 in 1922, was sixth with a .358 mark the next year and won the title in 1924 with a .392 average, edging teammate Lefty O'Doul by .0002 percentage points. Lewis took unusual steps to insure he'd top the league, picking his spots and pitching opponents to give himself every advantage.

"Duffy Lewis kept nursing his batting average by staying out of both games yesterday," Ed Hughes reported in the *San Francisco Chronicle* in early September. "Duffy is determined to finish the season as the league's leading hitter if he has to miss all the remaining games."

He resigned from the Bees in 1925 and took over at Portland, where he had purchased some shares of stock. Without the assistance of Salt Lake City's altitude, Duffy's average fell to .294, although he assigned himself to the bench against many left-handed pitchers. With the Beavers headed for a fifth place finish, Lewis quit in early September and was replaced as manager by Truck Hannah

Lewis was a playing manager at Mobile in the Southern Association and Portland in the New England League the next two seasons. After managing the latter for two more years, Duffy was a Boston Braves coach from 1931 to 1935 and later was the team's traveling secretary for many years.

HARRY LUMLEY

It its inaugural year in 1903, the Pacific Coast League was a shadow of the powerful minor league it would become.

Few of its stars went on to successful big league careers. One of the exceptions was Seattle outfielder Harry Lumley, who won the PCL's first batting championship.

There's a difference of opinion about the title. It lies in the fact that Lumley — called "Chub" by Seattle newsmen — didn't arrive in the Northwest until July 8 and appeared in only 109 of Seattle's 198 games.

The first PCL record book published by the Helms Foundation in 1941 gave the batting title to Portland outfielder Edward "Deacon" Van Buren, who averaged .361 in 205 games. Official record books designate Lumley as the batting champion with a .387 mark on 180 hits in 465 at bats.

Even Lumley's figure remains in dispute. According to a

recent study of every 1903 box score by baseball researcher Carlos Bauer, Lumley actually batted .383 on 180 hits with 23 doubles and 13 triples in 470 plate appearances. Statistics about the 1903 season in this biography come from Bauer's detailed and thorough study.

Lumley played like a winner after arriving in Seattle in spite of going hitless and looking bad in the field in his first game. "Lumley . . . made one error and did not do anything with the stick," reported the *Seattle Times*. "However, he carries himself like a ball player and should make good."

Before the month was over, San Francisco newspapers were touting Lumley "as a fine sticker" and the *Times* agreed that, "there is not a better one on the coast." This opinion would not have surprised baseball observers who had watched Lumley's brief development.

Lumley was 20 when he hit .350 for Rome in the New York State League and went to St. Paul of the outlaw American Association in 1902. A free-swinging slugger, he was banged up and on crutches part of the year, but batted .299 with 14 triples in 114 games. However, his fielding average of .871 was near the bottom and throughout his career he was never more than a mediocre outfielder.

The following season, St. Paul dispatched Harry to Colorado Springs in the Western League, where he hit .314 in a dozen games before disappearing from the lineup. There appears to have been a dispute over his contract, but by July it had been resolved and Lumley was in Seattle, ready to take the Coast League by storm.

Lumley started slowly and by September was hitting .341. On Sept. 5, he began an 18-game hitting streak in which he batted .458 and elevated his average to .374.

On the final day of his hitting rampage, Seattle beat Oakland, 8-1, after losing the day before. With Harry leading the way with a .446 average, the Siwash juggernaut set a league record of 19 straight wins plus one tie. Los Angeles matched the win streak record in 1939 and broke it with a 21-game skein in 1943.

Lumley cooled off late in the campaign, hitting .337 in his final 22 games. Seattle had climbed into second place behind Los Angeles, but also faltered by losing seven of its last eight to drop to third behind L. A. and Sacramento.

Lumley was drafted by Brooklyn. The Superbas were in decline after being National League champs in 1899 and 1900 and had fallen out of the first division with a fifth place finish in 1903. Brooklyn was never better than fifth during Harry's stay with the team.

Harry was the senior circuit's rookie sensation in 1904, batting .279 and leading the league in triples (18) and home runs (9). His extra base total of 136 was second only to Honus Wagner's 146. Lumley's home runs accounted for 60 percent of Brooklyn's total of 15, which was lowest in the league.

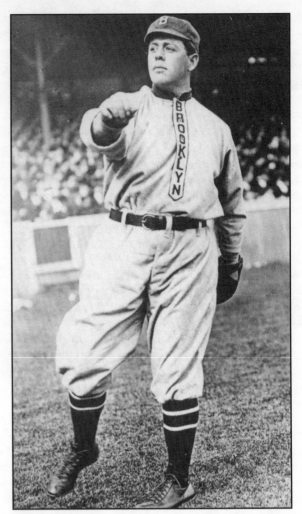

Harry Lumley

"The Brooklyn right fielder is the only redeeming feature of the Superbas these days," Abe Yager wrote in *The Sporting News*. "His steady batting and mighty swatting (are) proving a bright spot right among the continual string of defeats." Yager's only criticism was that Harry struck out a lot.

In late July, manager Ned Hanlon tried to get pitcher Frank Corridon from the Cubs. When Chicago owner Frank Salee demanded Lumley as part of the deal, Hanlon refused, saying Lumley was, "a $10,000 man and I couldn't part with him under any circumstances."

Lumley hit .293 with seven homers the following season and in 1906 batted .324 with nine home runs, second in the league to teammate Tim Jordan's 12. Harry led the circuit in slugging average at .477 and Brooklyn reportedly turned

HARRY G. LUMLEY
Born: 9/29/80, Forest City, PA, BL/TL, 5-foot-10, 183 pounds

		G	AB	R	H	2B	3B	HR	RBI	SB	AVG.
1903	Seat	109	470	106	180	23	13	5	—	23	.383
PCL		1	109	470	106	180	23	13	5	—	23	.383
Majors		7	730	2653	300	728	109	66	38	305	110	.274

down $30,000 from the New York Giants for Lumley and Jordan.

A broken ankle limited Harry to 127 games in 1907 and, while his power numbers continued at career highs in doubles (23) and home runs (9), his average dropped to .267.

Although the fans still liked him as a player, they roasted Harry's apparent indifference as field captain and he seemed to lose interest when his average dipped to .216 and the team slumped to seventh place. Still, owner Charles Ebbets hired Lumley to replace Patsy Donovan as manager, but he was discharged at the end of the 1909 season and a sixth place finish.

Harry played and managed at Binghamton in the New York State League from 1910 to 1912 and ran a restaurant there after his retirement from baseball following the 1913 season.

ORVIE OVERALL

When the Sacramento Senators relocated to Tacoma after the 1903 season, owner Mike Fischer took most of his everyday players along. The transplanted Tigers won the first half of the 1904 Coast League schedule and knocked off second half co-champ Los Angeles in a playoff.

Key additions to the Tigers roster were first baseman Lou Nordyke, who hit .304, and a pair of pitchers, veteran southpaw Jim St. Vrain and rookie right-hander Orval Overall.

St. Vrain went 19-14, while Jack Fitzgerald was 17-13 and Bill Thomas finished 27-24. Regardless of his inexperience, the 23-year-old Overall was the staff workhorse, winning 32 games and losing 25. No other pitching statistics were published by the league.

Overall was an unusual ballplayer for his time because he was a college graduate. In four years at the University of California at Berkeley, Orvie starred on both the diamond and the gridiron.

A tall 200-pounder, Orvie played guard on the California football teams from 1900 through 1903, creating the winning play in the traditional Big Game against Stanford as a sophomore when he blocked a punt for a safety and a 2-0 Golden Bears victory. Orvie also was a kicker of note, averaging 52.5 yards punting in one game and kicking two field goals to help Cal beat Stanford in 1902, 16-0. George Trevor of the New York Sun named Overall to the fourth team on his six all-time college football squads in 1927. Cal end Brick Muller (second team) and Stanford fullback Ernie Nevers (third team) were the only other West Coast players selected.

As a senior, Overall teamed with tackle Heinie Heitmuller to lead Cal to a 6-1-2 record. Heitmuller was an outstanding outfielder who played briefly with the Philadelphia Athletics and established an unique record with Los Angeles in the Pacific Coast League in 1912 when he won the batting title several weeks after dying of typhoid fever.

Orvie and Heinie played together on Cal's nine, but

Orval Overall

Overall's most notable college baseball teammate was Nick Williams. Orvie and Nick alternated as battery mates, pitching one game and then switching positions to catch the next. Williams had a long PCL baseball career as a pitcher and catcher with Seattle and San Francisco and as the Seals' manager.

Few pitchers were making more than $200-a-month in the Coast League, but Fisher hired Overall for $300. Orvie had spotty success in spring training and an early season report in the *Sporting News* summed him up this way: "Overall, the California collegian, gives much promise and has phenomenal speed, lack of control being his chief weakness."

Fortunately for Overall, his catcher was the experienced Charlie Graham, the team captain who later owned the Sacramento Senators and San Francisco Seals. Graham was a great handler of young pitchers and it showed in Orvie's success as the Tigers grabbed the first half title over Seattle.

In two typical performances near the end of the first half, he blanked L. A., 1-0, with 10 strikeouts and two walks, then struck out 10 and walked five in a one-run loss to Portland. The Tigers supported him with only one hit in the first game and five in the second.

Orvie continued to produce big strikeout totals in the second half race, fanning 16 in a 15-inning win over Portland. But, he remained inconsistent. After shutting out Seattle twice in succession on three and four hits, he surrendered 14 hits to the Siwashes in his next outing and lost,

12-4.

The Tigers had a big lead when they left Tacoma in late October to finish the season in the warmer climate of California. On the season's final day, Overall lost to Portland and Los Angeles took two from Seattle as the teams tied with identical .571 percentages. The Tigers won the playoff in nine games with Overall capturing two.

Cubs manager Frank Chance played a few games in the PCL late in the year, went hitless in four tries against Orvie and recommended Chicago buy him. But, Cincinnati outbid the Cubs and Orvie went 18-23 in a personal high of 318 innings for the fifth place Reds in 1905. Chance thought Overall was overworked and that judicious scheduling of his mound appearances would make him more effective.

Cincinnati changed managers in 1906 and new skipper Ned Hanlon swapped Orvie to the Cubs for $2,000 and pitcher Bob Wicker. Only 4-5 with the Reds, Orvie won 12 of 15 decisions with the pennant-bound Chicagoans. The powerful Cubs lost to the White Sox, but took the 1907 and 1908 World Series from Detroit. Overall was undefeated in three post-season decisions.

Overall developed a lame arm in 1910 and declined to leave California for 1911 spring training after a bitter salary dispute with Chicago owner Charles Murphy. Orvie pitched in Angel's Camp near his mining operation and returned to the Cubs for what turned out to be a futile comeback in 1913. After a 4-5 start, the Cubs sold him to San Francisco.

It was a sad state of affairs for Overall, who had won 108 games in seven big league seasons with a 2.24 ERA,

the eighth best of all-time. Orvie went 8-9 for the fourth place Seals, but showed renewed arm strength by averaging better than seven strikeouts per nine innings pitched — best in the league.

Seals owner Cal Ewing received a letter in November from Overall, who had been offered a two-year sales job by Los Angeles brewery magnate Ed Maier. Orvie said he'd return to the Seals in 1914 for a $1,000 bonus.

This angered Ewing, who paid big money to buy Overall for just half a season and then gave him a high salary. Chiefly he was indignant because Maier owned the Venice ball club and there seemed a clear conflict of interest.

Maier said Overall had worked for him before and was free to play with the Seals if he wanted to. In February, Overall quit baseball. Eventually he left the brewery job and became a banker in Visalia, where he had large orchard holdings. When he died in 1939, Overall was manager of a Fresno bank. He advised many ballplayers to save their money because, "the money you make playing ball will be the easiest money you ever receive."

ORVAL OVERALL
Born: 2/2/81, Visalia, CA, BB/TR, 6-foot-2, 214 pounds

		W	L	PCT	G	IP	H	ER	BB	SO	ERA
1904	Tac	32	25	.561	—	—	—	—	—	—	—
1913	SF	8	9	.471	19	147	—	—	31	118	—
PCL	2	40	34	.541	19*	147*	—	—	31*	118*	—
Majors	7	108	71	.603	217	1532	1230	—	551	933	2.24
* incomplete

THE LEAGUE GROWS UP

DAVE BANCROFT

The man John McGraw described as, "the best shortstop in baseball without a doubt," was left behind when big league scouts came calling early in his career.

Some of the men chosen over Dave Bancroft were good ones such as Harry Heilmann and Carl Mays. Others were highly regarded minor league prospects, including Bill "Raw Meat" Rodgers and Art Kores, who never lived up to their press clippings.

Aside from Heilmann, "Beauty" Bancroft outshone them all and was taken into Baseball's Hall of Fame in 1971.

The trip to baseball immortality began for the little switch hitter in 1909, the first of his of three seasons in the Wisconsin-Minnesota League.

Wearing the tiny fielder's glove in vogue and playing on poorly tended infields, Bancroft made nearly one error in every two games. But, he showed a great arm and range with nearly six chances per game and 80 more assists than his closest competitor the first year. These characteristics carried over to his major league career, where he set the single season record of 984 chances in 1922.

After hitting .273 playing for Superior in his third year, Portland drafted him. *Sporting News* correspondent Lou Kennedy wrote glowingly of Dave's "light agility" during spring training, adding his every move "is a dream." Manager Walt McCredie gave Bancroft the "splendid chance" to succeed that Kennedy predicted, but he failed to take advantage of it. Dave averaged .213 and McCredie sold him to the Portland Colts, the Beavers farm club in the Northwestern League.

The Colts were loaded with talent in 1913 — Heilmann and Mays were Bancroft's teammates — and finished second. Detroit bought the other two, but left Bancroft to be taken by the parent Portland team, where he was expected

Dave Bancroft

to fill a utility role in 1914. Instead he helped Portland take the championship.

The possibility Bancroft could win a starting role depended on how well he hit. His opposition for shortstop was Bobby Davis, described as a player, "who has a world of speed and looks like an exceptionally sweet hitter."

Dave broke into the starting lineup in May, leading off at shortstop with Davis moved over to third base. Dave went four for four with two triples. Bancroft outhit Davis by thirty points and out fielded him at shortstop. He finished with a .271 average and showed power with 35 doubles. Dave led the league in put outs and the fans compared him with Roger Peckinpaugh, who had starred at shortstop for the 1911 Beavers.

Cleveland had the first pick of Portland players and took Rodgers, a consistent .300 hitter. The Indians hoped to grab Bancroft later in the player draft. The New York Giants selected Kores over Bancroft in the draft because they said Dave wanted too much money and feared he would jump to the Federal League.

DAVID JAMES BANCROFT
Born: 4/20/91, Sioux City, IA, BB/TR, 5-foot-9.5, 160 pounds

		G	AB	R	H	2B	3B	HR	RBI	SB	AVG.
1912	Port	166	565	68	120	29	8	0	—	29	.213
1914	Port	176	664	97	180	35	9	2	28	29	.271
PCL	2	342	1229	165	300	64	17	2	28*	58	.244
Majors	16	1913	7182	1048	2004	320	77	32	591	145	.279

* incomplete

McCredie wanted to keep Bancroft, but couldn't afford to pay Dave what he wanted — reportedly $5,000-a-year — so he was sold to the Philadelphia Phillies. Others thought the National League club made a mistake by not buying Roy Corhan, the vaunted San Francisco shortstop, who had hit .293.

Whatever the Phils paid, Bancroft was a bargain. He was regarded as a key to the infield on defense and batted .254 as Philadelphia won its first National League pennant. Bancroft hit a resounding .294 in the World Series, but the team averaged only .182 and lost to the Boston Red Sox in five games.

The sophomore jinx stifled Bancroft's bat in 1916 and his average slipped to .212. It rose annually for the next six seasons, peaking at .321 in 1922. With the livelier ball of the 1920s now in play, Dave continued to hit well, going above the .300 mark three more times and completing his career with a .279 average.

Bancroft's fielding continued to improve. He was a three time leader in put outs and assists and topped the National League in fielding average once. His 5.98 chances per game is second on the lifetime list at shortstop.

After five seasons with Philadelphia, Dave was traded to the Giants in mid-1920. He was outstanding as the Giants won three straight pennants from 1921 to 1923, but his hitting fell off badly in the World Series.

As a favor to long-time New York favorite Christy Mathewson, then general manager of the Boston Braves, McGraw sent Bancroft and outfielders Casey Stengel and Bill Cunningham to Boston for pitcher Joe Oeschger and outfielder Billy Southworth.

Matty wanted Bancroft as player-manager, a role Dave filled through 1927. Dave played well, but the Braves did not, finishing eighth, fifth, and seventh twice. Bancroft was released and played two more years with Brooklyn before returning to New York as a coach with the Giants from 1930 through 1932. He later managed in the minors.

STAN COVELESKI

If Pacific Coast League sportswriters had taken a vote for the circuit's best rookie pitcher in 1915, Stan Coveleski would have been high on the list, although he was hardly a neophyte at the game.

While it was his first year in the league, Coveleski had been making his living as a pro player for seven seasons, including a three-game trial with the Philadelphia Athletics in 1912. He was 24 years old when he showed up a week late for the Beavers' spring training camp in Fresno.

Coveleski came to Portland with credentials as a pitcher who could throw regularly every fourth day. The question was whether he or one of five other newcomers in camp could win a spot on the seven-man pitching staff which had six holdovers.

It wouldn't be easy, but Coveleski was no stranger to adversity. He was born in the heart of Pennsylvania anthracite coal country, where he dropped out of school

Stan Coveleski

after a year. By the age of 12 he was toiling in the mines from 7 a.m. to 7 p.m., six days a week for 5 cents an hour.

Stan didn't have time to play much ball, but he threw rocks at cans every night at home just for something to do. Coveleski joined the Shamokin team in the outlaw Atlantic League when he was 18 and contributed six wins to its 1908 pennant-winning drive.

This performance led to a contract with Lancaster in the Tri-State League where his older brother, Harry, had pitched before being purchased by the Philadelphia Athletics. When Stan and Harry played for opposing teams in the American League, they refused to pitch against one another.

Coveleski escaped the mines for good when he joined Lancaster. He won 73 games in four seasons in the league and was purchased in 1912 by the Athletics, who saw he needed more experience after he went 2-1 with the A's late in the year.

Sent to Spokane in the Northwestern League, Stan

STANLEY ANTHONY COVELESKI
Born: 7/13/89, Shamokin, PA, BR/TR, 5-foot-11, 166 pounds

	W	L	PCT	G	IP	H	ER	BB	SO	ERA
1915 Port	17	17	.500	64	293	279	87	82	171	2.67
PCL 1	17	17	.500	64	293	279	87	82	171	2.67
Majors 14	215	142	.602	450	3081	3055	982	802	981	2.89

PCL PICTORIAL

Duffy Lewis

Dave Bancroft

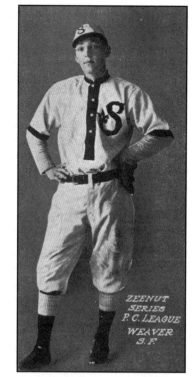

Buck Weaver

Irish Meusel

Bob Meusel

Dazzy Vance

worked on his spitball and pitched 316 and 314 innings while posting 17-20 and 20-15 records. He led the league in strikeouts in 1914 and was drafted by Portland.

Coveleski was badly out of condition when he arrived in camp and his pitching was spotty. Stan took a terrible beating in a contest against the American Colored Giants, giving up 14 hits in a 9-1 loss. Giants manager Rube Foster still thought Coveleski showed potential. "Of all the (Portland) youngsters, I like Coveleski the best because he

has all the natural requirements," Foster said.

Stan also had many unnatural requirements. Over his career, Coveleski liked to doctor the ball with a piece of sandpaper glued to his pants and he threw the spitter constantly. He gripped the ball loosely and loaded it up after inducing saliva with alum or slippery elm bark. A knuckle ball also was part of his repertoire.

Even with all these trick pitches, Stan showed amazingly good control. He threw seven innings without putting the ball out of the strike zone in one major league game.

Coveleski's first appearance for Portland came in relief as the Beavers lost to Los Angeles in early April. Manager Walt McCredie used him mainly as a reliever and he pitched in 64 games to tie Salt Lake City's Lefty Williams for the most appearances.

The Beavers finished last, but Coveleski outshone the veterans with a 17-17 record that made him Portland's only regular pitcher to finish as high as .500 percent. He topped the club with 171 strikeouts and a 2.68 earned run average.

Cleveland bought his contract. Coveleski spent the bulk of his 14-year Hall of Fame career with the Indians before joining Washington for three seasons and finishing with the New York Yankees in 1928. In his 11 seasons as a full-time performer, Coveleski averaged 271 innings pitched and nearly 19 wins.

Coveleski won 20 games four years in a row with Cleveland (1918-1921) and took three complete game victories against Brooklyn in the 1920 World Series.

Stan had a fine year near the end of his career with Washington's 1925 pennant winners. He won 13 straight games in a 20-5 season and led the American League with a 2.84 ERA. Coveleski lost two decisions to Pittsburgh in the World Series.

Coveleski's record was 215-142 and his percentage of .602 is 65th all-time. He gave up only 66 home runs in 3,082 innings and was elected to the Hall of Fame in 1969.

HOWARD EHMKE

Scoring decisions in successive games in 1923 gave Howard Ehmke one no-hit game and then prevented him from beating Johnny Vander Meer to the record by taking away a second no-hitter four days later.

Howard no-hit the Athletics, 4-0 on Sept. 7. The crucial play was a line drive which outfielder Mike Menosky reached, but fumbled. The scorer called it a hit, but before the inning ended reversed himself and ruled it an error. Ehmke chalked up a one-hit win over New York in his next outing four days later when lead-off batter Whitey Witt was credited with a questionable hit in the first inning after first baseman Joe Harris flubbed the throw. Ehmke retired the next 27 batters for a 3-0 victory.

Umpire Tom Connolly was so infuriated by the call that he wrote a letter to American League President Ban Johnson, protesting the scorer's decision and declaring if he "had ever seen a no-hit game that was it." Johnson refused to intervene and in 1938 Vander Meer became the only major league pitcher to toss successive no-hitters.

The best-remembered win in the sidearmer's 15-year big league career came near the end when Connie Mack made Ehmke Philadelphia's surprise starter against the Chicago Cubs in the 1929 World Series opener. The tall and slender Ehmke had gone 7-2 with the Athletics, but Mack told him in late September that his major league career was over and that he wanted to send Howard to Portland as manager.

At 35, Ehmke took the news gracefully, but told Mack

Howard Ehmke

he regretted missing the opportunity to play in a World Series. Knowing the Cubs would be expecting Lefty Grove or George Earnshaw to start the first game, Mack sent Ehmke to scout Chicago for several weeks at the end of the year.

Everyone was stunned when Ehmke warmed up before the first World Series game. All but one of the Cubs hit from the right side and they couldn't handle Howard's array of right-handed fast balls and sweeping curves. He sent a series record 13 Cubs back to the dugout on strikes in a 3-1 win — his last major league victory.

If Ehmke was amazing as a baseball senior citizen, he was no less sensational in his 1914 debut as a pro with the Los Angeles Angels. Howard found his way to the Coast League in a somewhat round-about fashion.

Ehmke was attending high school near Buffalo and hoped to enter Brown University, where four older broth-

HOWARD JONATHAN EHMKE
Born: 4/24/94, Silver Creek, NY, BR/TR, 6-foot-3, 190 pounds

		W	L	PCT	G	IP	H	ER	BB	SO	ERA
1914	LA	12	11	.522	40	232	228	72	91	89	2.79
PCL		1	12	11	.522	40	232	228	72	91	89	2.79
Majors	15	166	166	.500	427	2821	2873	1142	1042	1030	3.75

PCL PICTORIAL

Harry Heilmann

Stan Coveleski

Swede Risberg

Ken Williams

Ossie Vitt

Jimmy Johnston

ers had played baseball. But when his brother, Frank, secured a coaching job at Glendale High School, Howard went along and attended the school.

Frank had written to Connie Mack requesting a tryout for Howard and the Philadelphia manager said he would be in touch. When Frank never heard from Mack again, he contacted Los Angeles officials and Howard joined the Angels after the season had begun.

Harry Williams, baseball writer for the *Los Angeles Times* who later became PCL president, described Ehmke as, "the Glendale High School phenom," and said one

Southern California scout thought he might be, "a second Walter Johnson."

Ehmke's first appearance came in six effective innings of relief work against San Francisco in mid-April. Manager Pop Dillon used the young and inexperienced pitcher as a starter and reliever and Howard responded with eight straight wins, including three shutouts, over the next two months.

The batters began to take aim at Howard's low slung fast ball the second time around the league, but he appeared in 40 games and recorded 12 wins and 11 losses as the

Angels finished second to Portland.

The Angels peddled Ehmke to Washington for a reported $7,500 before the season concluded. Ehmke balked at the terms of the sale, saying he wanted to stay on the West Coast to gain more experience. Before the Senators ever got a look at him, Howard jumped to the Federal League's Buffalo team for $700-a-month. A spring training elbow injury limited Ehmke to 53 innings in 18 appearances and an 0-2 record with the last place Buffeds.

Back in L.A., Williams wrote about rumors that Ehmke's failure in Buffalo was a result of not being able to throw the emery ball. Williams said Howard was reluctant to go to the American League, which had banned use of the trick pitch before Washington took him, but the Federal League did not make the pitch illegal until after he had signed with the Buffeds.

When the Federal League folded following the 1915 season, Washington did not claim Ehmke under the peace agreement. He returned to Los Angeles, but was cut and went to Syracuse in the New York State League. With a healthy arm, Ehmke posted a 31-7 record and league-leading 195 K's and 12 shutouts. Again, he was accused of using the emery ball, but the complaints were not upheld by umpires.

Detroit purchased his contract for $3,000 and players. He finished 1916 with a 3-1 record in Detroit and went 10-15 the following season before enlisting in the Navy in 1918.

Back from the war, Howard had four good seasons with the Tigers (62-59) and was traded to the Boston Red Sox. Durable and a hard worker, Ehmke pitched more than 300 innings with eighth and seventh place teams the first two years in Boston, going 20-17 and 19-17. The Sox finished eighth again in 1925, but Howard's record fell to 9-20 and he was traded to Philadelphia the following year.

With the A's, Ehmke's use declined annually until his retirement in 1930, the season after his World Series masterpiece.

VEAN GREGG

Vean Gregg may have been the best sore-armed pitcher in baseball during his peak years, but problems with his salary wing eventually got the best of him in the majors and the Coast League.

A southpaw with a dazzling fast ball and a sharp-breaking curve, Gregg had outstanding years at both ends of his Pacific Coast League career and won 20 or more games three straight seasons with Cleveland after rising to the American League in 1911. His other performances in a 15-season career spread over two decades ranged from strong to dismal as the aching arm took its toll.

Vean began his career with Spokane in the Northwest League in 1908. No record is available for his rookie season but the following year with same team Gregg posted a 6-13 mark and showed enough potential that Cleveland bought him.

Gregg refused to report because of a low salary offer by the Indians and was purchased by Portland. It was one of the best deals the Beavers ever made and Vean led the ball club to the championship over Oakland. Portland's strength was a formidable four-man rotation that figured in 84 percent of its decisions: Gregg (32-18), Gene Krapp (29-16), Bill Steen (23-17), and Tom Seaton (17-17).

Vean was the PCL strikeout king with 376 in 320 innings. In a September game against Los Angeles, he pitched a no-hitter and fanned a record eight straight batters. Gregg also pitched a record three one-hit games.

Gregg tossed the most shutouts in PCL history, 14, including three in early October as the Beavers chalked up 88 straight scoreless innings against Sacramento and L. A. The Coast League was a pitcher's league in 1910. Its teams posted a composite batting average of .218 as San Francisco's Hunky Shaw took the batting title with a .281 average, lowest in league history.

Gregg was sold to Cleveland for $4,500 and the Indians also purchased Krapp, shortstop Ivan Olson and catcher Gus Fischer. All four stuck with the Tribe, but Gregg was the best of the recruits. He struck out Detroit's Sam Crawford twice in his first appearance in relief. When he became a starter, Vean was the league's acknowledged rookie pitching sensation as he compiled a 23-7 record and topped the junior circuit with a 1.80 earned run average.

Near the end of 1911, Gregg showed the first signs of arm problems and did not pitch in the post-season Ohio championship series against Cincinnati. He held out for a $5,000 paycheck in 1912, but the lame arm made him a question mark. Since playing ball beat his off-season job as a plasterer, Gregg eventually agreed to return without any apparent raise in pay.

Vean complained of a sore arm again in 1912, but managed a 20-13 record averaging a career high six strikeouts per game. Peeved by fan complaints that he was not trying to win the pennant, manager Harry Davis sent Gregg into action twice in three days against the champion Athletics in August and Vean won both games. With a six-run lead over Detroit in September, Gregg told catcher Steve O'Neill to stop using signals. He cut down his windup and threw the ball over the plate as Cleveland won, 12-2.

Gregg had signed his 1913 contract and was allowed go home a week before the season closed to rest his arm. In March, the *Sporting News* reported that, "Gregg condi-

SYLVEANUS AUGUSTUS GREGG
Born: 4/13/85, Chehalis, WA, BR/TL, 6-foot-1, 185 pounds

		W	L	PCT	G	IP	H	ER	BB	SO	ERA
1910	Port	32	18	.640	53	320	262	—	141	376	—
1922	Seat	19	20	.487	46	327	338	122	74	150	3.36
1923	Seat	17	15	.531	47	281	259	86	71	173	2.75
1924	Seat	25	11	.694	49	326	341	105	75	175	2.90
1927	Sac	0	0	.000	2	3	—	—	—	—	—
PCL	5	93	64	.592	197	937	1200*	313*	361*	874*	3.01*
Majors	8	92	63	.594	239	1393	1240	257*	552	720	2.70

* incomplete

Vean Gregg

tioned himself very slowly the last two years but started each campaign with a sore whip, just the same." Despite admonitions from new manager Joe Birmingham, Vean tried a different conditioning method — cutting loose from the start — and still got a sore arm. He also was stricken with malaria at the New Orleans training camp and lost 10 pounds, but went 20-13 for the year.

Gregg's arm ached from the beginning in 1914 and he didn't start a game until early May. He consulted famous baseball medic, Dr. John "Bonesetter" Reese, who diagnosed a misplaced tendon and torn ligament. After treatment, Gregg told friends he could wind up without pain for the first time in months, but he remained on the bench.

Convinced Gregg was unwilling to give his best, Cleveland tried to trade him the Red Sox for three young players. When one of the trio refused to report, Boston took Gregg for the waiver price. He went 12-7 for the season, 3-4 for Boston.

He was used sparingly over the next two seasons and was optioned to Buffalo briefly in 1916. After showing signs of recovery with 21 wins, 249 strikeouts in 267 innings and a 1.72 ERA at Providence in 1917, Gregg went to the Athletics in 1918 and slumped to 9-14.

His career appeared over when Gregg went home to Washington, where he pitched in the semi-pro Timber League for three years.

Gregg began a comeback with the Seattle Indians in 1922 at the age of 37. Vean did not appear to have arm

problems, although he relied on his curve far more often that his once fabled fast ball. Vean started slowly, losing four of his first five games and there was talk that he was finished. He rallied, threw 327 innings and went 19-20.

After a 17-15 year in 1923 — with 173 Ks in 281 innings and a 2.75 ERA — it was clear Gregg's career was far from over. Seattle had put all its pitchers on the spitball list developed by the PCL several years earlier, so Gregg experimented with a spitter the following year. He dominated the league with a 25-11 mark and 175 strikeouts in 326 frames as Seattle fans celebrated the first pennant in franchise history.

The Indians sold him to Washington for cash and players. Pitching mainly in relief, Gregg went 2-2 in 74 innings and finished the year with New Orleans.

Gregg attempted another come back two years later. He was dropped after spring workouts with the San Francisco Missions, pitched briefly and ineffectively with Sacramento and retired for good at age 42.

Vean won more than 200 games in his career. Not bad for a guy with a chronic sore arm.

HARRY HEILMANN

If Harry Heilmann hadn't forgotten his top coat that day in 1913, chances are he'd still have made it to the Hall of Fame as a line drive hitter who rivaled Rogers Hornsby among right-handers. But, he'd have missed a great pay day.

Harry left his bookkeeper's job at a San Francisco biscuit company one Saturday afternoon, but had to return for the coat. At the plant he met a former Sacred Heart High School teammate who was managing Hanford in the San Joaquin Valley League. Harry was promised $10 and expenses if he'd fill in for a sick player in a game at Bakersfield the next day.

Heilmann went and when he won the game with a hit in the 11th inning, Hanford fans showered him with coins and bills. "I counted $150," he said later, "more than I could have made in a month by keeping books."

A Portland scout was in the stands and later talked Harry into accepting a contract with a spaghetti dinner as his bonus. He was assigned to the Beavers' Northwestern League farm club, which also was in Portland.

Northwestern League president Fielder Jones scouted for Detroit and recommended the Tigers grab Harry, who had hit .305 in 122 games, along with teammates pitcher Carl Mays and shortstop Dave Bancroft. The Tigers took

HARRY EDWIN HEILMANN
Born: 8/3/94, San Francisco, CA, BR/TR, 6-foot-1, 195 pounds

		G	AB	R	H	2B	3B	HR	RBI	SB	AVG.
1915	SF	98	371	57	135	23	4	12	—	26	.364
PCL	1	98	371	57	135	23	4	12	—	26	.364
Majors	17	2146	7787	1291	2660	542	151	183	1538	112	.342

Heilmann and Mays, but passed over the future Hall of Fame shortstop.

The powerfully built Heilmann batted .225 in 67 games with the Tigers in 1915, but needed to improve his game. Detroit wanted to continue paying him $350-a-month, but San Francisco said they'd pay $800 if he could get the Tigers to release him. Detroit optioned him to the Seals.

Although Harry was slow and awkward, he played outfield about three-quarters of the time in his 17 years in the majors. Heilmann was exclusively a first baseman with the Seals. Still learning his craft, he led the league in errors, but more than made up for it with a .364 average and a dozen homers in 98 games.

One of his home runs was a prodigious blast off Lefty Williams that sailed over a cigarette sign in center field at Recreation Park. Harry once said it was a thrill, but not his most memorable four-bagger.

That one was in a game at Washington where Heilmann circled the bases on a home run and heard umpire Billy Evans shout, "you're out" as he crossed home plate. Harry thought Evans was kidding and responded, "sure, Billy, over the fence is out." Evans corrected him, pointing out that "over the fence is out when you bat out of turn."

Heilmann, who had suffered dizzy spells when stooping for grounders early in the season at San Francisco, fell ill in late July and missed the rest of the season. Manager Harry Wolverton said Harry had ptomaine poisoning and an ear infection that affected the nerves on one side of his head and body.

The Tigers called Harry up in 1917 and he hit between .276 and .320 in five seasons.

Called "Slug" by teammates, Heilmann was not a natural hitter and said his average didn't soar until the lively ball arrived and teammate Ty Cobb rebuilt his stance by placing his feet close together and moving his hands apart down at the end of the bat. That was in 1921 and Harry won his first batting title with a .394 average, five points better than runner-up Cobb.

For nine more years, Heilmann never hit lower than .328 and won three more American League titles, all in alternate seasons, in 1923 (.403), 1925 (.393) and 1927 (.398).

In the most exciting race in 1925, Heilmann battled Tris Speaker into the last days of the season. After getting three hits in the first game of a double-header, teammates told Harry to sit out the second to protect his lead. He refused and made two hits in three tries to take the title by four percentage points.

By the time he hung up his spikes, Harry had batted .342, which ties him with Babe Ruth and Dan Brouthers in ninth place all-time. Heilmann always seemed to get a

---

"No one ever picked up a club and marched to the plate more confident of getting a base hit."
— *Oscar Vitt about Harry Heilmann*

Harry Heilmann

piece of the ball when he swung and had nearly as many doubles (542) as strikeouts (550).

"No one ever picked up a club and marched to the plate more confident of getting a base hit," said former Tigers teammate Oscar Vitt. "Harry was uncanny with a bat, just uncanny."

Detroit sold Heilmann to Cincinnati for $40,000 after the 1929 season and he hit .333. Painful arthritis kept Harry out of baseball in 1931 and when he returned the following year he performed poorly in 15 games and retired.

In 1934, Harry moved into the radio booth at Briggs Stadium as a broadcaster. Good natured, humorous and popular with the fans, Harry sprinkled anecdotes and memories of his own experiences throughout his broadcasts and told listeners why the events he saw on the field were happening.

In a 1948 spring training game, Harry put on a mask and took his microphone behind home plate. When a young Detroit pitcher complained to manager Steve O'Neill that Heilmann's presence made him nervous, O'Neill told him to imagine how nervous he'd be if Harry was standing there, "with a big black bat in his hands instead of a microphone."

Heilmann was hospitalized during spring training in 1951. He came back to broadcast a few innings before leaving Briggs Stadium for good. Heilmann died of lung cancer on July 9, one day before the annual All-Star game was played on the field where he had thrilled Detroit fans for so long.

JIMMY JOHNSTON

If you attended a San Francisco game in 1913 the odds were pretty good that Jimmy Johnston would thrill you with a stolen base. Johnston shattered the Pacific Coast League record that year and set a minor league mark by pilfering 124 sacks in 201 games for the Seals.

The record-breaking performance came as no surprise, because Johnston had been one of the best at running the base paths since his career began in 1908. He already owned the Southern League record.

By the time he became a regular in the National League a few years later, the stolen base's popularity as an offensive weapon was on the decline. Jimmy never achieved the same prominence as a base thief in the majors and ranked as high as third among the leaders only once, when he stole 28 in 1921.

Johnston was built for speed. He swiped 33 bases in his debut with Kewanee in the Central League, but the Class D league was loaded with greyhounds and his total earned him 10th place. Johnston stole 45 and 46 bases in two more seasons in the league before moving to Seattle in the Northwest League near the end of 1910, where he stole eight bases in 25 games.

The speedster got into one game with the Chicago White Sox in 1911, but spent most of the year with Birmingham in the Southern League, where he stole 33 bases in 84 games. Returning to Birmingham, Johnston hit .296 and pilfered 81 bases to eclipse the league record of 77 that had stood since 1904.

The White Sox had an agreement to furnish players to San Francisco and as spring training at Boyes Hot Springs was coming to a close in 1913, the Seals bought Johnston and pitcher Phil Douglas.

"Manager Del Howard intends to shove Johnston right into the fray," said the *San Francisco Chronicle*. "His speed, hitting and fielding ability are needed badly."

"(Jimmy) Johnston will now endeavor to make a base hit and steal three bases."

— Judge Thomas Graham

Although the *Chronicle* said Johnston, "burnt up the paths in the Southern League and is undoubtedly a speed marvel on the bases," Jimmy started slowly. He failed to steal a base until April 11 and didn't break loose with a multi-theft performance until he took two in each game of a twin bill against Oakland on April 20. At the end of that week, Johnston was hitting .253 and his seven stolen bases were well behind the 15 racked up by leader Harl Maggert of Los Angeles.

Johnston's batting average and stolen base total began to rise in May. Aided by three thefts in a game against Oakland, he took over the base stealing lead near the end of May and never relinquished it.

The first week in July was his best as he picked up eight steals against Los Angeles to finish the series with 64 for the year and a .309 batting average — fourth best in the league. After stealing seven in a series near the end of the month, he slumped badly over the next two weeks by

Jimmy Johnston

adding only two steals.

Jimmy tied Rollie Zeider's 1908 league record of 93 steals on Aug. 26 and broke it the next day. He set his sights on Hap Myers' 1912 national mark of 116 in the Northwestern League. Hampered by a severe charley horse, Johnston still passed that figure in mid-October on his way to 124.

The fourth place Seals had seven others who stole at least 20 bases, including outfielder Howard Mundorff's 50 for seventh place in the base-stealing race. The Seals' 413 steals fell nine short of Sacramento's 1903 league record of 422.

Johnston was timed running the bases in 14.3 seconds during a San Francisco field day competition and his speed allowed him to score frequently from second base on short hits to the outfield. Once, he came home from second when a slow roller past the box eluded the glove of pitcher Spider Baum.

Jimmy was second in the league in runs with 111 and fifth in batting at .304. Two $100 checks from San Francisco and the visiting Venice team plus a gold watch purchased by fans were presented to the embarrassed speedster in his first trip to the plate on the season's final Saturday.

After the presentation, former PCL President Judge Thomas Graham announced, "Mister Johnston will now endeavor to make a base hit and steal three bases." Jimmy didn't live up to the prediction, but he did slam the first pitch for a single and steal second base before the first inning was over.

The Chicago Cubs bought Jimmy, but he lingered on the bench in 1914 with a .228 average and three steals in 50 games and was sold to Oakland. Johnston's second stay in the Coast League was productive. He was runner-up in the 1915 batting race at .348, hit 52 doubles and scored 140 runs. Johnston again led the league in stolen bases, but his production fell to 82.

Johnston jumped to the Federal League, but the circuit folded and his contract was assumed by Brooklyn. Jimmy spent 11 years in the Big Time, where his older brother, Wheeler "Doc" Johnston, had played since 1912. Jimmy hit between .252 and .291 the next five seasons while dividing his time between the outfield and infield.

The versatile Johnston played all the infield positions, but mainly third base. His best years were 1921 through 1923, when he batted .325, .319 and .325. A 1924 knee injury limited him to 86 games and a .298 average. After one more season, the Dodgers sent Jimmy to the Boston

Braves in 1926. Johnston lasted until July, when he went to the New York Giants on waivers. It was Johnston's last of 13 seasons at the top.

Except for 1928, when he hit .338 and stole 30 bases for Birmingham, and 1931, when he was a Brooklyn coach, Jimmy was a playing manager. His teams at Chattanooga, Atlanta and Montgomery finished in the first division only once between 1927 and 1932, but Johnston hit .309 or better almost every year and added 65 stolen bases to his career total of 686.

Bob Meusel

BOB MEUSEL

Bob Meusel spent 11 years in the big leagues and might have arrived sooner if World War I hadn't intervened.

Bob, who was three years younger than his brother, Emil — also a major league outfielder — made his Coast League debut with Vernon late in 1917. He had three hits in seven trips to the plate in a double-header against Salt Lake City.

Tigers manager George Stovall stationed the robust looking Meusel at first base to replace Gus Gleichman, who batted .210 for the year. Bob, whose nickname was "Dutch," responded with a .311 average and 11 doubles in 45 games.

Although he was near the bottom of the fielding table, the *Los Angeles Times* said Meusel, "is showing great promise for a youngster and is improving with experience and added confidence. He made a stop in the first inning . . . that no other first sacker in the league would have touched

JAMES HARLE JOHNSTON
Born: 12/10/89, Cleveland, TN, BR/TR, 5-foot-10, 160 pounds

		G	AB	R	H	2B	3B	HR	RBI	SB	AVG.
1913	SF	201	749	111	228	30	4	2	—	124	.304
1915	Oak	206	788	140	274	52	8	11	—	82	.348
PCL	2	407	1537	251	502	82	12	13	—	206	.327
Majors	13	1377	5070	754	1493	185	75	22	410	169	.294

(and) was good on low thrown balls."

Meusel didn't return to the Tigers in 1918, enlisting in the Navy instead under the "work or fight" order that decimated baseball team rosters across the country and caused the PCL to end its season in July.

While on leave, Bob played in Vernon's July 7 twin bill against Los Angeles, hitting three doubles in eight at bats in his only regular season appearance. Meusel was available for the entire post-season playoff series in late July and went 11 for 26 in champion Vernon's seven-game loss

---

"He's learning to say hello when it's time to say goodbye."
— *Frank Graham about Bob Meusel*

---

to the second place Angels.

Bob didn't trade his Navy uniform for Vernon flannels until the 1919 season was well underway. Meusel showed his versatility by playing 96 games at third base and 56 more in the outfield. Third base was thought to be Meusel's natural position, but his fielding remained poor wherever he played, partly because of his lack of hustle. Meusel wasn't lackadaisical at bat, pounding out 14 triples and a like number of four-baggers while compiling a .337 average and the Yankees acquired his contract.

Playing in a lineup that became known as Murderers Row, he batted .328 with 40 doubles. Bob played 45 games at third and two more at first, but still led the American League in outfield assists with 28. Meusel tailed off to .200 in the World Series loss to the Giants.

Bob had an even better year in 1921, hitting .318 with 40 doubles, 16 triples, 24 homers and 135 RBIs. Meusel showed off his legendary arm again with a league-topping 24 assists. Teammate Joe Sewell remarked that Meusel, "could hit a dime at 100 yards and flatten it against a wall."

After another World Series loss to the Giants, Bob joined Yankees pitcher Bill Piercy on Babe Ruth's barnstorming tour in violation of a rule that prohibited players who appeared in the World Series from performing in post-season exhibitions. The tour was unsuccessful financially and Yankees co-owner Col. T. L. Huston persuaded Ruth to end it after three games.

But, the damage had been done. All three players were

ordered by Baseball Commissioner Kenesaw Mountain Landis to forfeit their $3,510 World Series shares and were suspended until a month after the 1922 season began.

While other Yankees had quit the tour for fear of reprisals, Meusel's decision was in keeping with his laid-back personality and an indifferent attitude that won him the nickname "Languid Bob." Meusel's brusque and sometimes unfriendly demeanor mellowed late in his career, leading sportswriter Frank Graham Jr. to say, "He's learning to say hello when it's time to say goodbye."

Bob contributed eight more seasons to the Yankees, bettering .300 five times. He sent 103 or more runs across the plate annually from 1924 through 1928, except for 1926, when he broke an ankle and still produced 81 RBIs in 108 games. Meusel led the league with 33 homers and 138 RBIs in 1925.

Just before the 1924 spring training season opened, Meusel escaped serious injury in an automobile accident north of San Diego. The driver was Pittsburgh third baseman Tony Boeckel, who died in the crash.

After Meusel generated a lifetime low batting average of .261 in 1929, the Yankees sold Bob to Cincinnati, where he hit .289 in 113 games. He finished with a .309 big league average — one point below the .310 recorded by his brother. Their combined .309 average is third best among brothers.

Meusel played 59 games at Minneapolis in 1931 and wound up his career with 64 games at Hollywood the following season. He looked great at the start, batting .407 in his first 17 games and was at .329 when the Stars sent him packing him for economy reasons.

IRISH MEUSEL

Emil Meusel was an imposing batter who never hit less than .279 until he was well past his prime.

Playing for the two New York teams in the early 1920s, Emil and Bob Meusel became the only brothers ever to appear as opponents in three World Series. Emil, better known as "Irish" because he looked like a son of the Emerald Isle, played for the Giants and Bob, called "Dutch" to honor his Germanic background, was with the Yankees.

Irish followed a long and somewhat circuitous route on his journey to a decade of major league service. He stopped in Los Angeles three times.

Meusel broke into Organized Baseball in 1913 with Fresno of the California League, a Class D circuit that was backed by Pacific Coast League teams as an incubator for talent. Fresno finished second and at the close of the season, Irish — who had batted .306 — and five teammates were acquired by Los Angeles for prices up to $1,500. Meusel was the bargain of the bunch at $500.

Irish played 15 games with the Angels at the end of the season, hitting .283, but commiting six errors in the outfield. Nevertheless, Washington scouts saw something they liked in the swift outfielder and he was drafted by the

ROBERT WILLIAM MEUSEL
Born: 7/19/96, San Jose, CA, BR/TR, 6-foot-3, 190 pounds

		G	AB	R	H	2B	3B	HR	RBI	SB	AVG.
1917	Ver	45	164	16	51	11	3	0	—	3	.311
1918	Ver	2	8	2	3	3	0	0	—	0	.375
1919	Ver	163	655	113	221	39	14	14	—	31	.337
1932	Hwd	64	228	44	75	20	2	4	26	4	.329
PCL		4	274	1055	175	350	73	19	18	26*	38	.332
Majors		11	1407	5475	826	1693	368	95	156	1067	139	.309

* incomplete

Irish Meusel

Senators. Emil played most of 1914 on option at Elmira in the New York State League and hit .323.

Meusel began 1915 at Los Angeles, but after going 4 for 11 in a half dozen games, Washington transferred him back to Elmira. He batted .327 and won promotion to Birmingham in the Southern Association. The Chicago Cubs chose Irish in the 1916 draft, but sold him to Los Angeles and this time he stuck.

The second place Los Angeles outfield included the league's two best fielders, Red Killefer and Rube Ellis. Meusel couldn't match their range or fly-chasing abilities, but his powerful arm showed to advantage as he led the PCL with 44 assists. At the plate and on the bases he more than held his own, hitting .311 with 46 doubles, 121 runs

scored and winning the stolen base title with 69.

When the Philadelphia Phillies drafted Meusel at the end of 1917, Harry Williams of the *Los Angeles Times* thought they made a good choice and called Irish, "one of the most promising players" to come from the Coast League.

"Seldom has a player in this circuit shown such rapid development," Williams said. "From a rather overgrown, bungling player misjudging fly balls and running wild . . . on the bases, he has changed into a fielder who seems sure of himself and a base runner who knows something about using his speed to best advantage. There never has been any question about his ability to kill the ball."

Williams said that Meusel failed in previous major league trials because of poor spring training performances. "The fact that he is young and never had a full season facing class AA pitching gives him less consideration than a more experienced man," Williams said.

Meusel made the Phillies in 1918 and hit .279, .305 and .309 over the next three seasons. Irish was batting .353 in mid-1921, when Philadelphia sent him to the New York Giants for three players and $30,000 in a trade that drew the attention of Baseball Commissioner Kenesaw Mountain Landis. Phillies owner William F. Baker said he "no longer could stand the sight of Meusel" and accused him of indifference. Baker had sold a number of his stars previously and, although Landis disapproved, the judge took no action to stop the Meusel deal. Irish finished the

EMIL FREDERICK MEUSEL
Born: 6/9/93, Oakland, CA, BR/TR, 5-foot-11.5, 178 pounds

		G	AB	R	H	2B	3B	HR	RBI	SB	AVG.
1913	LA	15	53	8	15	3	0	1	—	4	.283
1915	LA	6	11	0	4	0	0	0	—	0	.364
1917	LA	210	811	121	252	46	9	7	—	69	.311
1928	Oak	108	374	52	100	25	5	11	65	4	.267
1929	Sac	44	153	22	50	6	3	2	21	2	.327
PCL	5	383	1402	203	421	80	17	21	86*	79	.300
Majors	11	1289	4900	701	1521	250	93	106	819	113	.310

* incomplete

year with a .343 average, the best of his big league career.

The Polo Grounds was the best kind of ballpark for a man with power and speed. Meusel batted .331 in 1922, popped 17 triples and 16 homers and batted in 132 runs, second only to Rogers Hornsby's 152. Giants teammate Casey Stengel called Irish the best right-handed hitter in baseball after Hornsby. Meusel led the league in RBIs with 125 the following year and was over 100 two more seasons while hitting .310 and .328.

The Giants played in the World Series the first four sea-

"There never has been any question about his ability to kill the ball."
— Frank Williams about
Irish Meusel in the Los
Angeles Times

---

sons Meusel was with them. Irish was one of the stars in the 1921 Subway Series win over the Yankees, hitting .345 with four extra base hits and seven runs batted in. Irish matched the RBI total the following year. Brother Bob's team turned the tables on the Giants when they met for the third straight year in 1924. Irish made it to post-season play for the last time as a part-time outfielder in the loss to Washington in 1924. Overall, he hit .277 and drove in 17 runs in 23 World Series games.

When his production fell to .292 and 65 RBIs in 1926, the Giants released Irish, who joined the Dodgers. He had only 74 plate appearances, mainly as a pinch hitter, and spent the rest of the year at Toledo.

Meusel drifted back to the Coast League in 1928 with Oakland, where manager Ivan Howard called him, "one of the most dangerous hitters in the game." Meusel's best days were over and the Oaks let him go with after 108 games with a .267 average. Sacramento picked up Irish, but dropped him after 44 games, although he was batting .327. Irish closed his career with seven games in Omaha in 1931.

ROGER PECKINPAUGH

The dead ball depressed Roger Peckinpaugh's batting statistics, but it couldn't disguise the fact that he was one of the best defensive players of his day.

The broad-shouldered and bow-legged Peckinpaugh was one of the widest ranging shortstops around. Roger had a good teacher as a youngster growing up in Cleveland, where he lived across the street from Cleveland star Nap Lajoie. The future Hall of Famer had quit as Cleveland's manager at mid-season in 1909, so he had little influence when Peckinpaugh arrived in training camp the following spring.

It was plain to see that Roger had a flair for fielding. Cleveland officials also noted his distinct inability to hit the curve ball. He played 15 games with Cleveland, but

spent most of 1910 hitting .255 in New Haven.

Peckinpaugh was optioned to Portland the following season. Although Roger only had one year in the professional game, Beavers manager Walter McCredie liked the youngster immediately.

McCredie said Peckinpaugh, "is one of the most natural fielders in the league" and compared him with San Francisco's Mickey McArdle, the paragon of PCL shortstops at the time.

"His hands follow the ball no matter how bad the bounce," McCredie said. "You will find he is one of the best shortstops in the league before the season is out."

Roger fielded well and Portland repeated as Coast League champion in a close race with Vernon. Peckinpaugh was hot at the plate in the early going, hovering near the .300 mark into the summer. His average plummeted below .240 as the season drew to a close until he raised it to a creditable .258 with 35 stolen bases at the end.

Still having difficulty handling the curve, Peckinpaugh hit .212 with Cleveland the next season and lost the shortstop job to Ray Chapman in 1913. Cleveland dealt him to the New York Yankees in May and he finished at .268.

In addition to his work in the field, Peckinpaugh showed leadership qualities that persuaded the Yankees to name him interim manager for the rest of the season in September, 1914, when Frank Chance quit. Roger was 23 years old, the youngest manager in major league history.

In the next seven seasons, Peckinpaugh became recognized as one of the American League's best shortstops, leading in assists three times and double plays twice. His batting improved and he averaged .305 (with a 29-game hitting streak), .270 and .288 in his last years as a Yankee.

Peckinpaugh was part of a trade among New York, Washington and the Boston Red Sox in 1921 and spent five seasons with the Senators, contributing at the bat and in the field.

He starred in the 1924 World Series, hitting .417 and fielding flawlessly as the Senators defeated the New York Giants in seven games. The Senators returned to the series in 1925 with Roger as the American League's most valuable player. He won in a close and surprising contest over Al Simmons, a member of the second place Athletics, whose .384 average exceeded Peckinpaugh's by 90 points.

After Washington lost to Pittsburgh in a nightmarish seven games for Peckinpaugh, who made a record eight errors, the writers decided never to vote on the MVP award until the series had concluded.

Peckinpaugh contended he was a victim of wet fields,

ROGER THORPE PECKINPAUGH
Born: 2/5/91, Wooster, OH, BR/TR, 5-foot-10.5, 165 pounds

		G	AB	R	H	2B	3B	HR	RBI	SB	AVG.
1911	Port	195	702	86	181	—	—	—	—	35	.258
PCL	1	195	702	86	181	—	—	—	—	35	.258
Majors	17	2011	7233	1006	1876	256	75	48	739	207	.259

Roger Peckinpaugh

Swede Risberg

soggy balls and Pittsburgh scorers who wanted to obliterate the record of six errors set by Honus Wagner in the 1903 Fall Classic. "It upset me then and it still does today," he said a half century later. "After my long career, the first thing people ask is, 'What about the 1925 World Series'?"

Roger played an additional season as a reserve and was traded to the Chicago White Sox. He retired at the end of 1927 and became Cleveland's manager. Peckinpaugh was skipper there until 1933 and returned in 1941 when Oscar Vitt was ousted after a player revolt.

Roger said his only rule was a midnight curfew for players. He was popular with the players and Earl Averill considered Roger his best manager. "He knew more baseball than the rest of them put together," Averill said. Peckinpaugh finished with a 500-491 twin-loss record.

Peckinpaugh continued in baseball as a member of the

> *"It upset me then and it still does today."*
> — *Roger Peckinpaugh about his poor performance in the 1925 World Series*

American League's promotion bureau, manager at New Orleans in 1939, Cleveland's general manager from 1942 to 1946 and Buffalo's general manager in 1947.

SWEDE RISBERG

Swede Risberg was another of the infamous Chicago Black Sox players who got his start in the Pacific Coast League.

Five of the eight men accused in the conspiracy to throw the 1919 World Series played in the league: Chick Gandil with Sacramento, Fred McMullin with Los Angeles, Buck Weaver with San Francisco, Lefty Williams with Sacramento and Salt Lake City and Risberg.

Swede was a month shy of his 27th birthday and had been in the American League only four seasons when the scandal broke late in the 1920 season. Although he had a consistently low fielding average, Risberg was regarded as a developing shortstop with decent range and a good arm.

In the beginning of his career, Risberg's arm strength put him on the mound. Swede honed his diamond skills playing in San Francisco's North Beach district and in 1912 — when he was 17 — Risberg earned a tryout as a pitcher with Vernon. Swede made it through spring training, but in his only appearance with the Tigers was unable to retire a single batter, giving up two runs on two hits and two walks before he was cut loose.

Swede began the next year with Spokane in the Northwestern League, where he pitched 42 innings and played infield. The rest of the season he played shortstop and hit .283 at Ogden in the Union Association. Risberg returned to the Utah team in 1914, averaged .366 and was among the base-stealing leaders with 26 when the league ended prematurely in August. Swede finished the year hitting .313 in 14 games with Venice.

The PCL club returned to Vernon and Swede was a regular in 1915 and 1916, but not at shortstop. He split the first season between first base, second base and the outfield. Vernon manager Doc White raved about his wonderful throwing arm and soft hands and called Swede, "one of the most remarkable youngsters I have seen" and "the best utility man in the U.S."

Risberg batted .274 the first year and contributed 31 doubles, 10 homers and 28 steals. In 1916, Swede blasted 51 doubles while his average dropped to .263. Risberg played the entire year at second base, which probably was his best position.

The Chicago White Sox took Swede in the draft, but not to play second base. That position was in the capable hands of future Hall of Famer Eddie Collins. The Sox put Risberg at shortstop and moved Buck Weaver to third base. The *Reach Guide* thought Swede was, "the missing link (who) made it possible for Chicago to win the American League pennant."

Risberg gained this accolade although he led the league in errors and hit a minuscule .203. In the World Series won by Chicago in six games over the New York Giants, Swede appeared as a pinch hitter, getting one hit in two at bats.

After hitting .256 in 82 games as a utility player in 1918's curtailed season, Risberg was the regular shortstop for two years, averaging .266 and .256.

Swede batted .080 and led both clubs with four errors in the tainted series against Cincinnati. His involvement in the fix ended Risberg's career in Organized Baseball, although he continued to play outlaw ball in Arizona and the upper Midwest.

CHARLES AUGUST RISBERG
Born: 10/13/94, San Francisco, CA, BR/TR, 6-foot, 175 pounds

		G	AB	R	H	2B	3B	HR	RBI	SB	AVG.
1912	Ver	1	0	0	0	0	0	0	0	0	.000
1914	Ven	14	32	3	10	2	0	0	7	2	.313
1915	Ver	175	602	94	165	31	6	10	—	28	.274
1916	Ver	185	691	101	182	51	5	6	—	25	.263
PCL		4	375	1325| 198	357| 84	11	16	7*	55	.269
Majors		4	476	1619	196	394	72	27	6	175	52	.243

		W	L	PCT	G	IP	H	ER	BB	SO	ERA
1912	Ver	0	0	.000	1	0	2	2	2	0	∞
PCL		1	0	.000	1	0	2	2	2	0	∞

Majors (did not pitch in the major leagues)
* incomplete

His lifetime expulsion was not Swede's last contact with Baseball Commissioner Kenesaw Mountain Landis. In the winter of 1926, Risberg told a Chicago newspaper that Detroit players "sloughed off" during a late season series in 1917, when the White Sox and Boston Red Sox were in a close fight for the pennant. Chicago took all four games. White Sox players purportedly repaid the Tigers in two games in 1920, when Detroit was trying to overtake New York for third place money.

Risberg and 35 players appeared before Landis at an open hearing. Risberg and Gandil said they collected $45 from each of the Chicago players and received permission from Chicago manager Clarence "Pants" Rowland to deliver the cash to the Detroit team in Philadelphia. Rowland and the other players denied the games were fixed.

Collins admitted contributing $45 to a fund for Detroit players, but not until after the 1917 World Series had started. It was common practice at the time for players on a contending team to contribute money to reward another club for bearing down against a pennant rival. Pitcher George Dauss of the Tigers acknowledged receiving $180 for beating Boston, but said any pitcher who downed the Red Sox could expect to be paid.

The judge never acted against anyone, but proposed rules later adopted by the owners which included a one-year ban against a player who offered or gave any reward to a player or official of another team or who bet on any game he was not involved in, and a lifetime ban for any player who bet on a game in which he played.

ALLEN SOTHORON

Spitballer Allen Sothoron was pitching well with the Portland Beavers in 1916, but he wasn't getting much support from a team headed for a seventh place finish.

It was Sothoron's first real opportunity against top-flight opposition over a long period of time. While he had appeared in 10 innings with the St. Louis Browns the previous two years, most of his experience was in the lower minors. Allen was a workhorse at Haverhill, pitching in 35 games in a 124-game schedule for a 15-18 record in 1914 and followed up with a 16-17 mark in 262 innings at Wichita.

Nevertheless, Sothoron thought he was worth some real money when he was transferred to Portland. He demanded $600-a-month, $100 more than the Browns paid for his services. Manager Walter McCredie said he could stay back East for that kind of payday.

Sothoron realized any possibility for advancement meant a trip to the West Coast, so he reported to the Beavers. Allen got off to a rocky start and was knocked out of the box in his first two outings. By August he showed a 15-15 record.

Then Allen began to win. He pitched a 6-0 victory over Los Angeles on Oct. 21 for his 15th consecutive win and his 30th victory. Sothoron was just one game shy of tying the Coast League record of 16 straight wins set by Frank

Allen Sothoron

Browning of San Francisco seven years earlier.

San Francisco protected the record in Sothoron's next start. Allen fooled almost no one and the Seals tagged him for 13 hits in a 10-4 loss. San Francisco knocked him out of the box in three innings in his final appearance and Sothoron finished the year with an excellent 30-17 record and a 2.65 earned run average. He led the PCL with six shutouts, 158 walks and 397 innings pitched and missed the strikeout title by one.

The Browns brought Allen back to the American League in 1917 and he gave the seventh place ball club a 14-19 record. He was 12-12 in the season that followed. Sothoron produced the best record of his 11-year big league stay in 1919, winning 20 and losing 13 with a 2.20 earned run average as the Browns finished fifth. Sothoron slumped to 8-15 in 1920.

The 1921 season produced mixed results. Sothoron started badly with the Browns, went to the Boston Red Sox and wound up the year with the Cleveland Indians, where he

pitched very well and had a 12-4 mark. Although he had been shuttled around the league and had a 13-8 record in 178 innings, Allen achieved the distinction of being the last big league pitcher to surrender no home runs while working in at least 154 innings.

Sothoron had attended Albion College and was regarded as one of the smartest pitchers in the league. He also had so much stuff that opponents thought he doctored the ball, although his spitball was legal under the agreement allowing 17 pitchers to continue throwing the outlawed pitch.

Allen was afflicted by a peculiar complex about throwing to first base. While he could throw accurately to the other bags, his tosses to first were likely to be wild, so he developed the habit of throwing to that base underhanded.

Allen dropped out of the majors after pitching briefly with Cleveland in 1923 and caught on with Louisville in the American Association. His 6-9 record with the Colonels wasn't out of the ordinary, but St. Louis Cardinals general manager Branch Rickey picked Sothoron off the discard pile in the draft.

Sothoron went 10-16 in 1924, but topped the sixth place Cardinals in wins and shutouts with four. After two more years with St. Louis, he became one of its coaches.

He moved to the minors and earned a reputation as a great teacher of young players while managing Louisville for three seasons. Allen's team finished fifth the first year and seventh the last, but in 1930 won the American Association championship and lost the Little World Series

ALLEN SUTTON SOTHORON
Born: 4/27/93, Bradford, OH, BB/TR, 5-foot-11, 182 pounds

		W	L	PCT	G	IP	H	ER	BB	SO	ERA
1916	Port	30	17	.638	57	397	341	117	158	202	2.65
PCL	1	30	17	.638	57	397	341	117	158	202	2.65
Majors	11	91	100	.476	264	1584	1583	582	596	576	3.31

to Rochester, the International League pennant winner.

After coaching with the St. Louis Browns for two seasons, Sothoron returned to the minors to manage Milwaukee from 1934 until 1938. His team finished in the first division four times and won the American Association title in 1936 when the *Sporting News* named him as its first Minor League Manager of the Year.

Sothoron left the team late in the 1938 season and died the following June in St. Louis at the age of 46.

DAZZY VANCE

If you saw Dazzy Vance pitching for the Sacramento Senators in 1919, you'd never have suspected he would begin a Hall of Fame career in the big leagues three years later.

The broad-shouldered, florid-faced Iowa country boy was 28 when he arrived in the PCL. Dazzy was rated not much more than the fourth best pitcher on the fourth place Senators. His 10-16 record in 294 innings didn't set off any bells. Official statistics place him midway in the ERA table at 3.32, but based on his innings pitched and earned runs the ERA should read 2.82.

It wasn't evident to Coast League fans in the first season after World War I that Vance was suffering from a nagging sore arm that had plagued him for years.

Dazzy — nicknamed as a youngster when he mimicked a cowboy who mispronounced the name of the flower, "daisy" — began his pro career at Red Cloud in the Nebraska State League. He worked three seasons in the Class D league, going 39-33, including a 17-4 mark and league-leading 194 strikeouts that won him promotion to the Western League late in 1914.

Vance was a big man, tall and solidly-built with long arms. His blazing fast ball sped toward the batter from a high kicking delivery and in 134 innings with St. Joseph he chalked up 108 Ks.

Unfortunately for Vance, his bosses looked at his physique the following season and decided there was no limit to Dazzy's durability as he posted a 17-15 record, 199 strikeouts in 264 innings and a 2.93 ERA. They sent him to the mound to pitch 45 innings in one week and the arm hung limply at his side as the season drew to a close. It wasn't just tired, it was painful.

He had brief trials with Pittsburgh and the New York Yankees and worked in the high minor leagues from 1916 through 1918, but his record was a disappointing 21-26 with only 175 strikeouts in 432 innings.

Dazzy Vance

Vance's arm was in bad shape when he arrived in Sacramento. He knew it, but Senators officials didn't and Dazzy worked in the starting rotation all year. His fast ball wasn't overpowering and only 86 opposing batters went down on strikes. At the end of the season, Vance was sent back to the Southern League.

The doctor who examined his right arm when it first became sore predicted that he could continue to throw without ill effects and that the arm would gradually strengthen in about five years. The diagnosis was born out by 1921 when Dazzy went 21-14 with New Orleans. By then, Vance was 30 and when Brooklyn expressed interest in catcher Hank DeBerry, the Pelicans said he was available, but only if Vance was part of the transaction.

With 10 years experience on 14 minor league clubs, Vance arrived in the National League in 1922 with his resurrected fast ball, a drop curve and catcher DeBerry, who worked behind the plate in many of his games over the next nine seasons.

Brooklyn protected his arm by pitching him with four days rest instead of the usual three. In the first seven years with the Robins, he established a National League record by leading in strikeouts annually and posted a 133-77 record with three 20-win seasons.

Batters were overwhelmed by his speed and teammate Johnny Frederick theorized Vance, "could throw a cream

CLARENCE ARTHUR VANCE
Born: 3/4/91, Orient, IA, BR/TR, 6-foot-2, 200 pounds

	W	L	PCT	G	IP	H	ER	BB	SO	ERA
1919 Sac	10	18	.357	48	294	264	92	81	86	2.82
PCL	1	10	18	.357	48	294	264	92	81	86	2.82
Majors	16	197	140	.585	442	2967	2809	1068	840	2045	3.24

Ossie Vitt (right) with Hal Trosky

puff through a battleship." Dazzy's delivery was helped by the tassels he cut in his sweatshirt's sleeves until the rule was changed to prohibit frayed sleeves that confused the batter.

Dazzy's best year was 1924, when he had 28 victories including a 15-game win streak and 262 strikeouts. He won the circuit's inaugural Most Valuable Player Award, taking the prize by eight votes over another great player, Rogers Hornsby, who had merely set a league record by batting .424.

Dazzy knew advancing age was working against him and the following spring he held out for more money, eventually signing a three-year contract for $50,000. He had other big paydays and when he left the Dodgers after 1932 with 187 wins, someone figured that he had been paid $187,000 — exactly $1,000-a-win.

Although Brooklyn had lost out to the Giants in a close race in 1924, the Dodgers slumped to sixth in 1925, but Vance again topped the league in wins with 22. The day after Labor Day, Vance faced only 27 batters in a 1-0 win over the Phillies. Chicken Hawks got a bloop single in the second, but was cut down trying to steal. In his next start, Dazzy threw a no-hitter against the Phillies, winning 10-1.

> *"(Dazzy Vance) could throw a cream puff through a battleship."*
> — *Johnny Fredericks*

Dazzy continued with the Dodgers through 1932, winning 22 games in 1928, the last year he topped the league in Ks. He had an amazing year in 1930, winning 17 and losing 15, but grabbing the earned run average crown for the last time with a 2.61 mark. His ERA was more than a full run better than runner-up Carl Hubbell's and more than two full runs below the ERA for all league pitchers.

When Vance left the Dodgers, he became a relief pitcher with the St. Louis Cardinals and Cincinnati and then drifted back to Brooklyn in 1935 for his final year. Cut loose at age 44 after 16 big league seasons and a 197-140 record, he pitched with the fast semi-pro Brooklyn Bushwicks before retiring to his 500-room hotel for hunters and fishermen in Florida. Dazzy was inducted into the Hall of Fame in 1955.

OSSIE VITT

Ossie Vitt is remembered as:
1) Manager of Cleveland's "Cry Baby Indians;"
2) Skipper of the 1937 Newark Bears — often called the best minor league team ever;
3) Pilot of numerous Coast League teams;
4) A golden glove fielder who hit modestly at sea level;
5) All of the above.
The answer, of course, is Number 5.

Vitt gained a greater reputation as a manager than as a player, but anyone who carries his glove onto the field for nearly two decades — including 10 seasons in the American League — must be recognized as a player of some skill. And his glove more than his bat was what kept Ossie in the game.

From the time he broke into pro baseball with Oakland in the outlaw California State League, Vitt's strong suit was fielding. His major league lifetime average of .238 marked him as a run-of-the-mill batter even in the last days of the Dead Ball Era. His PCL career mark of .301 was helped immeasurably by four seasons at high altitude Salt Lake City, where he never hit below .315.

Ossie was extraordinary around the third base bag. In seven full seasons in the Coast League, Vitt led in fielding five times and was second once and third once. His record with Detroit and the Boston Red Sox was nearly as good. He topped American League third sackers in fielding three times and almost always was no worse that third. Ossie set third base records for chances and assists with the Tigers in 1916.

Vitt developed as a player on San Francisco's sandlots. Following graduation from the Wilmerding School of Industrial Arts, Vitt became moderately wealthy by applying his talent as a bricklayer to the job of rebuilding a city that had been shattered by the great earthquake and fire in 1906.

But, Ossie wanted to play ball and his showing with the outlaws prompted the San Francisco Seals to hire him in 1910. He won the third base job, playing 174 of his 205 games at the hot corner. Ossie had no power, but showed speed on the bases and paced the Seals with 41 steals while hitting a modest .232.

Vitt was in and out of the lineup in 1911 when injuries and persistent stomach problems limited him to 124 games. He was hitting .233 in August, but came on with a rush in the last two months to close out the year at .269 with 44 steals. Detroit bought Vitt and he began a 10-year stay in the junior circuit in 1912. He was traded to the Red Sox in 1919 and was a regular the first season, but played less and less as his batting average declined to .220 in 1920 and .199 in 1921.

Ossie was back in the Coast League the following season with Salt Lake City. The effects high altitude and thin air had on batting statistics were never demonstrated more vividly.

He ripped the ball for averages ranging from .315 to .345 in four seasons with the Bees and his power production rose remarkably. Vitt had hit 106 doubles and four homers in a decade in the big leagues. He nearly duplicated the doubles total in two campaigns at Salt Lake City and hit four home runs his first season there, then followed with double digit totals twice.

Vitt's best season with the Bees was 1923, a year in which the team set the PCL record with a .327 team batting mark and averaged 6.5 runs a game. Ossie hit .337 — eighth best among Bees who played at least 100 games — with 60 two-baggers and 19 home runs. He batted in 112 runs and scored 179, which was second to teammate Paul Strand's 180.

Ossie played only 112 games in 1924. He held out during spring training and didn't report until a few days before the opener, then lost time to an injured wrist and more with an infected spike wound. Vitt still hit .333 with 106 runs scored.

Manager Duffy Lewis left the Bees in December to take over at Portland. Vitt, the team's field captain, succeeded Lewis and hit a personal best of .345 as the Bees finished just behind champion San Francisco. His biggest contribution was the development of shortstop Tony Lazzeri, who set Organized Baseball records with 60 home runs and 222 RBIs.

The Bees moved to Hollywood in 1926 and Vitt played less and less as he devoted more time to managing. Ossie was a disciplinarian who demanded his players work hard, pay attention and bear down all the time. He emphasized fundamentals and worked players hard in spring training to make sure they were in shape to play his daring, hustling style of ball.

Ossie had a knack for developing young talent, but veteran players were annoyed by his sarcasm and needling style. The press loved Vitt because he had a sharp wit and plenty to say about the game and its players. Sportswriters described him as "colorful."

Vitt was very successful in Movieland. The Stars finished sixth in his first two seasons, but from then on often finished first, second or third. Vitt's success didn't seem to help him get along with Hollywood owner Bill Lane. After the 1935 season, Vitt — now dubbed "Ol' Os" by sportswriters — quit to manage Oakland, where he had lived for years.

The Oaks were affiliated with the New York Yankees. After finishing third and fifth in the split seasons with Oakland, Vitt was moved by the Yankees to their farm club in Newark. His 1936 club finished second, but the 1937 team went 109-43 to walk away with the International League pennant by 25 1/2 games. Loaded with past and future major leaguers including Joe Gordon, Charlie Keller, George McQuinn, Babe Dahlgren and Buddy Rosar, the Bears swept the playoffs and won the Junior World Series over Columbus.

Success won Vitt promotion to the major leagues in

OSCAR JOSEPH VITT
Born: 1/4/90, San Francisco, CA, BR/TR, 5-foot-10, 150 pounds

		G	AB	R	H	2B	3B	HR	RBI	SB	AVG.
1910	SF	205	720	90	167	21	2	1	—	41	.232
1911	SF	124	401	51	108	13	4	1	—	44	.269
1922	SLC	163	642	104	202	39	6	4	52	8	.315
1923	SLC	188	811	179	273	60	7	19	112	18	.337
1924	SLC	112	435	106	145	33	5	15	90	4	.333
1925	SLC	152	579	109	200	42	3	6	73	8	.345
1926	Hwd	110	341	35	86	12	5	1	25	11	.252
1927	Hwd	32	24	7	9	2	0	0	5	0	.375
1928	Hwd	1	1	0	0	0	0	0	0	0	.000
PCL	9	1087	3954	681	1190	222	32	47	357*	134	.301
Majors	10	1062	3760	560	894	106	48	4	295	114	.238

* incomplete

Cleveland, where the Indians finished third in 1938 and 1939 and were among the favorites to take all the honors in 1940.

Vitt had replaced Steve O'Neill, who was popular with the fans and players. After two seasons of tongue lashings, Cleveland's players had enough and on June 13, 1940, pitcher Mel Harder asked owner Alva Bradley for a meeting. A dozen players including Bob Feller, Jeff Heath, Johnny Allen, Rollie Hemsley and Ken Keltner said they felt they could win the pennant, but not under Vitt's direction.

The players complained Vitt ridiculed them in front of sportswriters, fans and opposing teams; undermined their confidence with sarcastic criticism; was not sincere in his dealings and continually compared them unfavorably with his Newark champions.

The *Cleveland Plain-Dealer* had the details of the rift before Bradley heard from the players and ran the story on page one above another big event of the day — the German Army's occupation of Paris.

Some press wags thought so little of the complaints they dubbed the dissidents the "Cry-Baby Indians." Whatever their differences, the team played hard, took a lead into late August and lost the pennant to the Tigers by a game.

Vitt was fired in November and replaced by Roger Peckinpaugh. Ol' Os managed Portland to a fifth place finish in 1941, his last year as a skipper.

BUCK WEAVER

Of the eight players banned for life for involvement in the Black Sox scandal, only Buck Weaver qualifies as a tragic figure.

Chicago White Sox outfielder Joe Jackson receives most of the attention today because some fans feel he deserves a place in the Baseball Hall of Fame regardless of his part in throwing the 1919 World Series. They argue that Jackson did his best on the field, tricking the gamblers who paid him $5,000 to help fix the series between the Chicago White Sox and Cincinnati Reds. Support comes from the statistics of his outstanding performance in the eight-game series.

But, Jackson was a confessed conspirator while Weaver was an innocent victim who never participated in the fix. After nine big league seasons, Buck was banned from Organized Baseball by Baseball Commissioner Kenesaw Mountain Landis because he knew about the conspiracy, but failed to report it.

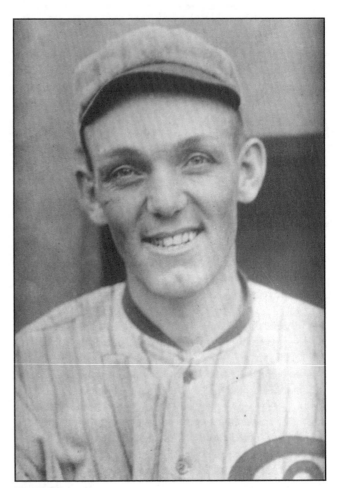

Buck Weaver

Weaver was 29 when he played his last game for the White Sox after the scandal came under investigation by a grand jury in Chicago as the 1920 season wound down. Although he led the American League in errors and was last in fielding among starting third basemen, Buck was regarded as one of the league's premiere infielders because of his range, strong arm and ability at the plate.

A slender switch-hitter, Buck batted .333 in his last season, the highest of his career. Before he was caught up in the scandal, Weaver seemed to be on the way to becoming a truly great ballplayer, if his steady development continued.

It took a decade for Weaver to reach the stage where his stardom was widely acknowledged. It had been a long trip from Pottstown, PA, where his father was a laborer in an iron works.

Buck was playing semi-pro ball in 1909 when he took the field against a team of barnstorming major leaguers managed by Philadelphia Phillies skipper Charlie Dooin. Scout Mike Kennedy watched the game and offered Weaver $125-a-month. When Kennedy switched over to Cleveland, Buck signed an Indians contract but never heard from the team. After the 1910 season opened, he wrote to the National Commission, which mailed him a check for $62.50. Buck was sent to Northampton in the Connecticut League, but had trouble seeing ground balls at

GEORGE DANIEL WEAVER
Born: 8/18/90, Pottstown, PA, BB/TR, 5-foot-11, 170 pounds

		G	AB	R	H	2B	3B	HR	RBI	SB	AVG.
1911	SF	182	674	90	190	—	—	—	—	30	.282
PCL		1	182	674	90	190	—	—	—	30	.282
Majors		9	1254	4810	625	1310	199	69	21	421	172	.272

shortstop and was released after batting .196 in 14 games.

Weaver went to Philadelphia where Dooin hired him for $175-a-month and shipped him to York in Tri-State League. After Buck hit .289 in 78 games he was passed over by Dooin, but Chicago White Sox scout Ted Sullivan bought his contract for $750. The Sox sent him to San Francisco in 1911.

When Buck came to the Seals, he was raw material with emphasis on the raw. But, manager Danny Long knew he had to find a place for Weaver in the lineup. The infield spots were held down by Kid Mohler, an outstanding left-handed second baseman; veteran shortstop Roy McArdle and smooth-fielding second year man Oscar Vitt at third.

San Francisco lost the opener to Vernon, but outfielder Weaver provided the only offensive punch with a two-run homer.

Weaver held his own playing in his new position and registered 11 assists in 50 games. Most of the time he moved to the infield when the others were hurt. Buck played 94 games at shortstop, where he covered a lot of ground but was erratic and showed a scatter arm, and 38 more at second base.

Weaver exhibited some promise in the batters box, hitting .282 — second among Seals regulars — with 30 steals and Long asked the White Sox to send him back in 1912. "The boy really needs another year (in the minors)," Long said.

Long might have gotten his wish, but a severe ankle injury to Chicago shortstop Lee Tannehill forced the White Sox to insert Weaver in the opening day lineup. Tannehill played only three games all season and the job was Buck's, despite hitting .224 and topping the league in errors.

Weaver was a natural right-handed batter, but he became a switch-hitter in an unusual way. Buck and Vitt were close friends at San Francisco and still saw each other in the American League because Ossie had been drafted by Detroit. Buck spent part of one off-season at Vitt's California cabin. While chopping wood, Buck noticed that he always hit the grove when he chopped left-handed, so Weaver tried swinging from that side of the plate. Buck hit well and became a superb drag bunter.

After batting .272 in his second year with the White Sox, Buck had three so-so years at the plate and in the field, but began to hit consistently in 1917 as the team won the pennant. He averaged .284, rose to .300 in 1918 and hit .296 the following season. His fielding improved and in 1919 he was shifted to third base, where he did his best work.

Weaver played with a lot of enthusiasm. He showed a ready smile and loved to kid his teammates, exhibiting a sunny disposition that made him a favorite with fans and players.

Buck performed in two World Series, hitting .333 in the 1917 win over the New York Giants and .324 in the loss to Cincinnati in 1919, a series in which he handled 27 chances flawlessly.

Buck continued to protest his innocence following his banishment. He tried several times to gain reinstatement, but Landis persisted in his view that Weaver's failure to reveal the fix made him as guilty as the players who had thrown the games. Weaver played semi-pro ball around Chicago, where he lived the rest of his life and worked in a drug store and as a parimutuel clerk at a race track.

In his last interview not long before he fell dead on a Chicago sidewalk in January, 1956, Weaver continued to proclaim his innocence.

"I never threw a ball game in my life," Buck told author James T. Farrell. "All I knew was win."

KEN WILLIAMS

When Cincinnati bought Ken Williams from Spokane for $4,000 in 1915, team officials may have thought they were acquiring a 22-year-old outfielder who combined that sought-after combination of speed and power.

The Reds were right about Ken's playing potential, but according to today's baseball encyclopedias the willowy Williams actually was 25. Early record books and the *Sporting News* obituary of his death in 1959 indicate his birth year as 1893. Apparently he was born three years earlier and simply lied about his age — a common practice as many players added or subtracted a year or two to suit their own purposes.

At any age, Williams showed he was a slugger from the day he took his first swings in professional baseball in 1913 with Regina in the Western Canada League. The Oregonian, who learned to play ball in logging camps around the Northwest, appeared in the outfield and at third base. Ken's 13 triples led the league and he averaged .292. Ken continued in the league another season, hitting .315 with 10 triples, 42 steals and a league-best 12 homers.

Spokane bought Williams and, although Ken's fielding left a lot to be desired, he was leading the Class B Northwestern League in hitting at .340 with 36 stolen bases when Cincinnati took him to the Big Time. Ken hit .242 with no homers and was returned to Spokane in 1915 after showing little in 10 more games with the Reds.

Cincinnati teammate Bill "Raw Meat" Rodgers said

KENNETH ROY WILLIAMS
Born: 6/28/90, Grants Pass, OR, BL/TR, 6-foot, 170 pounds

		G	AB	R	H	2B	3B	HR	RBI	SB	AVG.
1916	Port	53	183	21	52	11	1	4	—	14	.284
1917	Port	192	737	117	231	43	8	24	—	61	.313
1930	Port	148	546	93	191	32	4	14	110	23	.350
1931	Port	20	76	12	21	1	2	1	15	0	.276
PCL	4	413	1542	243	495	87	15	43	125*	98	.321
Majors	14	1397	4862	860	1552	285	77	196	913	154	.319

* incomplete

Williams failed with the Reds because manager Buck Herzog wouldn't let him swing a heavy bat, but insisted that he use a lighter club and shorten his swing.

Williams was hitting .295 midway through the 1916 season when he caught the eye of a Portland scout. The Beavers sent pitcher Oscar Harstad to Spokane in exchange for Ken, who batted .284 in 53 PCL games at the end of the year.

Williams really hit his stride — and the ball — in 1917. His fielding improved, but his batting was spectacular. On June 3, Williams rapped three home runs and a double in a 4-3 win over Vernon. The fans showered him with coins after his final solo shot won the game in the 14th inning.

The St. Louis Browns purchased Ken's contract soon afterward, but Portland officials said they'd have to wait until 1918 to see Williams in a Browns uniform because the Beavers needed him too much. Williams finished the season with Portland, where he hit .313 with 61 steals, third in the league behind speedsters Irish Meusel of Los Angeles (69) and Charlie Pick of San Francisco (62).

Only two other players hit at least 10 home runs in 1917, but Williams blasted 24 to take the title. It was a very impressive number. He accounted for 15 percent of all four-baggers produced in the league and his total was more than the number hit by four of the league's other five teams.

Ken played two games with the Browns in 1918, but spent most of the year in the Army at nearby Jefferson Barracks. A broken ankle cost Williams five weeks the next season, limiting him to 65 games as he averaged an even .300.

With the home field advantage he realized by playing in Sportsman's Park, Williams had productive years from 1920 through 1927. Most of his home runs (142 of 196) were hit in St. Louis. In this period, he took the home run title once, was second three times and fourth on three other occasions. Ken hit .280 in 1926, but his average ranged from .307 to .357 every other year.

Williams played in the shadow of St. Louis superstar George Sisler and in 1922 they combined to nearly win the team's first pennant, losing to the New York Yankees by a single game.

Sisler led the league with a .401 average that was built on the foundation of a record 41-game hitting streak. Williams had his best all-around year, batting .332 with 128 runs, 34 doubles, 11 triples and 37 steals. He wrested the home run title from Babe Ruth with 39 and topped the circuit with 155 runs batted in.

Ken Williams

Williams hit in 28 consecutive games on his way to becoming the first big leaguer to hit 30 home runs and steal 30 bases in the same season. He also tied a major league single game record with two home runs in the same inning.

Ken's downward spiral began in 1925 after he was hit on the head by a pitch in mid-August. When his power declined over the next two seasons, Williams was sold to Boston after 1927 for $10,000. He hit .303 and .345, but played in only 74 games in the second year.

Returning to Portland in 1930, Williams looked more like his former self, hitting .350 with 24 home runs, 110 RBIs and 23 stolen bases. But, the following year he retired after playing 20 games.

THE TURBULENT TWENTIES

VIC ALDRIDGE

Vic Aldridge had been Pittsburgh's hero during the 1925 regular season and in his first two starts in the World Series, but before the seventh and deciding game was two outs old, he was headed for the showers wearing the goat's horns.

The usually reliable Aldridge gave up two hits, three walks and two wild pitches before being lifted with one away in the first inning. Washington scored four times, but the potent Pirates banged out 15 hits to win, 9-7, and take Aldridge off the hook.

Aldridge had one of the best years of his nine-year National League career in that first season with the Bucs. He won eight straight games on the way to a 15-7 record and then took Games 2 and 5 before failing in the Fall Classic finale.

Vic had developed a reputation as a money pitcher so a post-season failure was out of character for the learned hurler they called "The Hoosier Schoolmaster."

The stocky Aldridge grew up in Indiana, attended Central Normal College and was a teacher when he decided to try his hand at pro baseball in 1915. He split the season between Erie in the Central League (19-9 with 154 strike outs and a 1.62 ERA), Denver (0-1) and Indianapolis (2-2).

He spent 1916 at Indianapolis and was purchased by the Chicago Cubs after going 16-14 with a 2.39 earned run average. Vic was given relief duty in 1917, posted a 6-6 record and was back in the bullpen in 1918 when he left the Cubs to enter military service.

With the war over in 1919, Aldridge trained with the Cubs on Santa Catalina island off the Southern California coast. Vic thought he had won a job, but was left behind

Vic Aldridge (right) with Glenn Wright

when the Cubs boarded the train to head home.

Upset that he received only 10 minutes notice about his assignment to Los Angeles, Aldridge refused to play on the coast. If the Cubs wouldn't send him to an eastern team, Vic said he would return to teaching. But, the prospect of receiving a $1,000 bonus from a local backer if the Angels won the pennant persuaded Vic to sign the contract.

Vernon swept past Los Angeles in the last week of the season to take the title. Vernon's victory later was tainted by charges that Tigers first sacker Babe Borton bribed

---

"If he expects to be a success in the majors . . . he will have to come through with more pepper."
— *Oscar Reichow about Vic Aldridge in the Sporting News*

---

three other players to throw games to insure his team's success. All four were expelled from the league.

Aldridge was one of three spitballers on the L. A. roster, but he relied mainly on his fast ball and curve to fool the opposition. Vic didn't overwhelm the batters so much as he finessed them.

"His work was sensational in the pinches," said *Los Angeles Times* sportswriter Harry William about Aldridge's first outing. "Twice he fanned two in-a-row with men on bases." Vic struck out 10 in nine innings, quite a performance considering he would KO only 87 batters all season on his way to a 15-10 record.

Aldridge worked 297 innings in 1920 — the most of his career — and brought home 18 wins and 15 losses for the third place Angels. The following season was Vic's PCL finale and the last of his 20 victories was the most important.

Aldridge, who led the league with a 2.16 ERA, pitched a 12-3 win over Portland on the season's last day to clinch the pennant over Sacramento. It was one of the league's closest finishes as six teams ended the year with win-loss percentages of .516 or better. Aldridge and outfielder Jigger Statz were acquired by the Cubs in a swap for outfielder Babe Twombly and catcher Tom Daly.

One of the criticisms about Aldridge was his attitude. After looking him over in Chicago's spring camp, *Sporting News* correspondent Oscar Reichow said Vic appeared unchanged after three years in L. A. "If he expects to be a success in the majors . . . he will have to come through with more pepper," wrote Reichow. "Manager (Bill) Killefer . . . does not like a man who is not willing to give his very best all the time he is in uniform."

Aldridge gave Chicago three good years, winning 47 and losing 36 before being sent to Pittsburgh. Following his fine 1925 season, Vic slipped to 10-13 in 1926. He rebounded to 15-10 the next year as the Pirates won the pennant again and lost the Fall Classic in four straight to the Yankees with Vic absorbing one of the defeats.

Aldridge went to the New York Giants in February in what must have been one of John McGraw's worst trades. In exchange, the Giants gave up Burleigh Grimes, the superb spitballer who had a 19-7 record in 1927. Both pitchers wanted more money and McGraw proposed to Pittsburgh owner Barney Dreyfuss that they swap the hold-outs even-up. Grimes won 25 and 17 games for Pittsburgh after the swap and Aldrich was out of the majors for good following a 4-7 season.

Vic pitched fewer than 100 innings over the next four years at Newark in the International League and then enrolled in law school. He passed the Indiana Bar in 1937 and served three terms as a state senator in the Indiana Legislature.

EARL AVERILL

Earl Averill came to professional baseball a little later than most, but made it to the majors in three years and to the Hall of Fame in 50 more.

A line drive hitter with power, the "Earl of Snohomish" — nicknamed for his home town — was the best center fielder of his day with Cleveland and hit .318 during 13 seasons between 1929 and 1941.

Earl's logger father died when he was 18 months old and he was raised by his mother on a Washington farm. Frequently truant, Earl still pitched for the school team until he hurt his arm at 15 and gave up the game. Averill quit school, worked in a lumber mill and a greenhouse run by his brother and forgot about baseball.

Townspeople built a ball diamond in 1922. Although he hadn't played in five years, Averill quickly won a position in the outfield. Earl was married and had an infant son two years later when his friends collected enough money to send him to the Seattle Indians training camp in California.

Averill was so ashamed when he failed to make the team that he didn't go home, but went to Bellingham, Washington, and played with a team in the independent Northwestern League. Manager Tealy Raymond recommended him to San Francisco manager Nick Williams, who got Earl a job with a Montana mining company that had a baseball team. Williams brought Earl to San Francisco after the 1925 season ended so he could play in the city's fast winter league and took him to camp the following spring.

Averill looked good, but had little confidence in his abil-

VICTOR EDDINGTON ALDRIDGE
Born: 10/25/93, Indian Springs, IN. BR/TR.
5-foot-9.5, 175 pounds

		W	L	PCT	G	IP	H	ER	BB	SO	ERA
1919	LA	15	10	.600	31	221	221	71	56	87	2.89
1920	LA	18	15	.545	39	297	291	95	80	123	2.88
1921	LA	20	10	.667	33	283	231	68	62	116	2.16
PCL	3	53	35	.602	103	801	743	234	198	326	2.63
Majors	9	97	80	.548	248	1599	1671	669	512	526	3.76

Earl Averill

June, he manufactured eight straight hits over a two-game span.

San Francisco's outfield was unsurpassed at the plate in 1928, pacing the team to the first half title, a second half tie with Sacramento and a playoff win over the Senators.

Jolley won his second straight batting crown with a .404 average and had 45 homers and 188 runs batted in. Johnson was next at .360 with 142 runs, 49 doubles and 16 triples. Averill brought up the rear with a .354 average, but more than held his own in other departments. He topped the league with 178 runs and had 53 two base hits, 36 homers and 173 RBIs.

Coast League players thought Earl was the best all-around performer of the three, but when Detroit officials bought a San Francisco outfielder it was Johnson who went for $45,000, not Averill.

Cleveland business manager Billy Evans arrived by train to look at Jolley and Johnson a short while later. He was disappointed that Johnson was no longer available, but paid $50,000 for Averill's contract.

Earl debuted with Cleveland on April 16, 1929 and became the first American League player to hit a home run in his initial time at bat. He smashed 17 more and finished with a .332 mark.

Earl anchored the Cleveland outfield for nine more years, hitting .301 or better seven times and scoring 100 or more runs every season but one plus batting in 100-plus runs five times. He was hitting .394 in late June, 1937, when his back went out and his average tumbled to .299. In retirement, Averill discovered his spine and tailbone were not properly joined and he underwent surgery to correct the problem.

Averill's extra base production was consistently high. Through the 1938 season, Earl averaged 37 doubles, 12 triples and 23 home runs.

In 1930, Earl hit four home runs and batted in 11 runs in a twin bill. He claimed the umpire deprived him of two more four-baggers by calling drives foul that hooked into foul territory after passing the screen.

From 1931 to late mid-1935 Averill played in 673 consecutive games. The streak ended when a firecracker blew up in his hand. Teammates called him "Rockhead" after the incident, but he preferred to shorten it to "Rock."

Averill is remembered as the man who hit a line drive off Dizzy Dean's toe in the 1937 All-Star game. The injury caused Dean to alter his pitching motion and ruin his arm. Earl was a member of the first six All-Star squads and was

ity and asked co-owner Charlie Graham if it was safe to rent an apartment for his family in San Francisco. Graham laughed and assured Earl he had made the team.

San Francisco had walked away with the 1925 title, but the Seals weren't much of a team in 1926. They finished a distant eighth, but if there had been a Rookie of the Year Award, Earl would have won it.

The muscular Averill beat out Lloyd Waner for the center field job and the Seals released the little outfielder. Earl led the Seals with a .348 average to edge outfielder Smead Jolley by two percentage points. He added 49 two baggers, 23 home runs and 119 RBIs.

Roy Johnson joined San Francisco the following year, adding the final ingredient to what would become known as the league's greatest hitting outfield. Johnson played left field while Jolley was stationed in right.

The emphasis was on their hitting, because none stood out as a particularly adroit outfielder. Averill was the best of the three, slower that the speedy Johnson, but much more mobile than the clumsy Jolley. Testament to Averill's powerful arm was his 45 assists in 1927 and 25 the following year.

San Francisco gave Oakland a run for the pennant in 1927, but finished second. Averill had a good year, leading the club with 47 doubles while contributing a .324 average with 134 runs, 20 four-baggers and 116 runs batted in. In

HOWARD EARL AVERILL
Born: 5/21/02, Snohomish, WA, BL/TR, 5-foot-9.5, 172 pounds

		G	AB	R	H	2B	3B	HR	RBI	SB	AVG.
1926	SF	188	679	131	236	49	6	23	119	9	.348
1927	SF	183	754	134	244	47	6	20	116	10	.324
1928	SF	189	763	178	270	53	11	36	173	13	.354
1941	Seat	78	223	24	55	9	0	1	17	2	.247
PCL	4	638	2419	467	805	158	23	80	425	34	.333
Majors	13	1668	6353	1224	2019	401	128	238	1164	69	.318

named to the *Sporting News* team four times.

Earl split 1939 between Cleveland and Detroit and made his only World Series appearance in three pinch hit appearances with the Tigers in 1940. After a few games the following season with the Boston Braves and half a season with Seattle, Averill retired to Snohomish, where he had lived during the off-season. He was inducted into the Hall of Fame in 1975.

LU BLUE

Lu Blue wasn't very big nor did he have notable speed, but managers liked to have him around because he had a knack for getting on base and scoring runs.

In his 13-year career in the Big Show, Blue scored 1,151 runs in 1,615 games. That puts him 63rd on the all-time list of runs per game.

Blue batted a modest .287 while playing through the lively-ball period from 1921 through 1933, but his greatest asset at the plate was his ability to work the pitcher for a base on balls. He drew 1,092 walks to rank 43rd among all the players who ever appeared in a big league game and is Number 38 with an on base percentage of .402. He was fifth or better in walks in the American League 10 times and second or third in six seasons.

When he arrived in the Detroit camp in the spring of 1921, the *Sporting News'* correspondent thought the left-handed Blue was, "one of the finest fielding specimens uncovered in a long while. (Detroit) could not get a better defensive first baseman than Blue and it is altogether likely that Harry Heilmann will be shifted to right field."

Lu did succeed Heilmann at first base, but it was Blue's switch-hitting talents more than his work with the glove that solidified his field position. While he covered a lot of ground around the bag, Blue was near the top of the league's first sackers in errors and near the bottom in fielding average annually.

Blue was pleased to be in the American League because it was the circuit he followed as a boy. Blue's father worked in the federal printing office in Washington, D.C. and Lu often cut school to go to the ballpark to watch the Washington Senators.

The family sent Lu to Maryland to attend military school where a former player convinced Blue that he had the ability to play ball for a living. Blue joined Martinsburg in the Blue Ridge League in 1916 and played there two seasons, hitting .320 with 78 runs in 99 games in 1917.

Lu Blue

Purchased by the Tigers, Blue was sent to St. Paul, where he hit .229 before enlisting in the Army. After being mustered out in 1919, Lu was optioned to Portland, which needed all the players it could get, even ones as inexperienced as Blue.

Portland had been dropped from the Pacific Coast League in 1918 and replaced by Sacramento because of costs associated with traveling to the Pacific Northwest. Gate receipts for a seven-game series frequently didn't meet the cost of sending a team to the Rose City. Once the war ended, league owners voted to bring Portland back into the fold along with Seattle, expanding the PCL to eight teams for the first time.

Most of the players Portland owned in 1917 had been sold to other teams or released, so manager Walt McCredie was building his new team from scratch. A working agreement with Detroit eased some of the burden by the assignment of Blue and seven other players. Even with all this help, the Beavers finished a distant seventh and fell to eighth in 1920.

McCredie penciled Blue into the third spot in the batting order at the start, but later employed him as lead-off man for the Beavers. Blue led Portland regulars at bat, stroking the ball for a .281 average with 35 doubles. Lu also stole 44 bases, the league's sixth best total. He struggled in the field, leading with 42 errors.

Back again in 1920, Blue batted .291 with 37 steals and led the loop in errors again. When Blue was recalled by

LUZERNE ATWELL BLUE
Born: 3/5/97, Washington, DC, BB/TL, 5-foot-10, 165 pounds

		G	AB	R	H	2B	3B	HR	RBI	SB	AVG.
1919	Port	174	679	91	191	35	7	9	—	44	.281
1920	Port	165	626	94	182	22	11	4	—	37	.291
PCL	2	339	1305	185	373	57	18	13	—	81	.286
Majors	13	1615	5904	1151	1696	319	109	44	692	150	.287

PCL PICTORIAL

Paul Waner

Babe Pinelli

Bill Cissell

Lyn Lary

Larry French

Detroit after the season, Billy Steep, the *Sporting News* correspondent in Portland, was skeptical.

Blue may be sent back to Portland, Steep said, "as he has several years of polishing left to make him a player capable of holding his own in the Ban Johnson circuit."

Steep's comments were way off the mark and Blue hit .308 as rookie, the second highest average of his major league career. Lu batted better than .300 three of the next six seasons and was traded to the St. Louis Browns, where he hit well before falling to .235 in 1930.

The hard-nosed Blue had poor relations with two Detroit managers, Ty Cobb and George Moriarty. Cobb thought Blue was dogging it on the field and criticized him in front of other players. Blue said he always hustled and felt Cobb should have talked to him in private.

Moriarty told Blue to go home to recover from an injury, but Moriarty refused to talk to Lu when he returned and used Johnny Neun at first base. Blue got the job back, but was replaced again by Neun.

The Browns installed Jack Burns at first base in 1931

and sold Blue for $15,000 to the ChiSox, who had struggled for years to find a reliable first sacker. After a .304 season with a club record 127 walks, Blue's average fell to .249 in 112 games in 1932 and he was released. Brooklyn signed Lu after the 1933 season started, but he was dropped after one game and finished his career with one more season at Toronto.

ED BRANDT

Ed Brandt was regarded as one of the National League's best southpaw pitchers in his prime. But, when he was a youngster trying to make his way in the Coast League, Brandt had so little confidence that he nearly gave up trying to earn a living on the mound.

Scouts and other baseball men always saw Brandt as a genuine prospect, but Ed's youth and lack of self esteem nearly cost him a baseball career that eventually included 11 years in the majors.

The youngest of six children, Brandt grew up in Spokane, where he pitched for Lewis and Clark High School and amateur teams. While doing a stint on the mound with the Willys-Overland team, Brandt was spotted by Joe Engle, president of the Chattanooga team in the Southern League. Engle told Seattle's Red Killefer about the 17-year-old with the powerful fast ball and big strike-out totals and Brandt was invited to spring training.

Brandt had never been away from home and the experience of living on his own with the Indians in San Jose, California, was too much for him and he left the camp.

"I knew I would win ball games in the semi-pro league," he said later, "but I also knew I would be a failure in Organized Baseball."

Club officials didn't agree and persuaded Ed to report to Aberdeen in the South Dakota League. When the Class D circuit collapsed in July, Ed went home and was suspended for failing to report to Seattle. He pitched semi-pro ball again and was asked to accept a $600 monthly contract by a Boston Braves scout who said he'd obtained Brandt's release from Seattle.

The contract was invalid, but when Seattle officials heard the Braves were interested in Ed, they signed him for $300-a-month. He jumped the team again and wound up pitching for $250-a-month in Baker, Oregon. Ed played in a game against Chick Gandil, one of the ringleaders of the

Ed Brandt

1919 Black Sox. Brandt, who had never heard of Gandil, was banned from baseball.

Killefer thought enough of Brandt's potential to get him reinstated and to keep him around as a batting practice pitcher. He won three and lost two for the Indians in 42 innings over the next two years.

Brandt was given an opportunity to show his stuff in 1927, starting and relieving on a Seattle team that finished third. He was wild — walking 107 and striking out 144 — but pitched 261 innings in 41 appearances. His 19-11 record produced the team's top winning percentage of .633.

Brandt — called "Dutch" by teammates — was a passable hitter throughout his career and contributed a .315 average with eight two-base hits and 19 runs batted in to Seattle's cause. The Braves were still interested in Ed and bought him at the end of the season.

To get an idea of how effective Brandt was in the majors, where his lifetime mark was 121-146, note that he played with only two teams that finished as high as fourth in his first eight years. Frequent losses in close games earned him a reputation as a hard luck pitcher.

Brandt was a starter for two seasons, going 9-21 with the club's only shutout victory and 8-13 while the Braves finished seventh and eighth. Brandt had control problems, walking more batters than he fanned. Ed had developed a fork ball by this time and spent most of 1930 in the bullpen and went 4-11.

Although Boston was seventh again the following sea-

EDWARD ARTHUR BRANDT
Born: 2/17/05, Spokane, WA, BL/TL, 6-foot-1, 190 pounds

		W	L	PCT	G	IP	H	ER	BB	SO	ERA
1924	Seat	0	0	.000	4	19	27	13	6	10	6.16
1925	Seat	1	2	.333	5	21	40	23	12	12	9.86
1926	Seat	2	0	1.000	4	21	26	10	4	13	4.29
1927	Seat	19	11	.633	41	261	274	115	107	144	3.97
1939	Hwd	2	3	.400	6	29	41	17	12	9	5.28
PCL	5	24	16	.600	60	351	408	178	141	188	4.56
Majors	11	121	146	.453	378	2268	2342	974	778	877	3.87

PCL PICTORIAL

Lu Blue

Willie Kamm

Sloppy Thurston

Mickey Cochrane

Earl Averill

son, Brandt's record soared to 18-11 with a 2.92 ERA, third best in the league. With better clubs over three more seasons, Ed posted a 50-44 record. Brandt had his best year at the plate in 1933, topping National League pitchers with a .309 average.

Brandt played with one of the most inept teams in National League history in his final year in Boston. The 1935 Braves won only one-quarter of their games, finishing 38-115 and 61 1/2 games behind Chicago. Brandt's record was even worse as he won 5 and lost 19. Teammate Ben Cantwell, who had won 20 games two years earlier, wound up with a 4-25 record.

Packaged with outfielder Randy Moore, Ed was sent to the Brooklyn Dodgers in a trade for four players. After an 11-13 season he went to Pittsburgh in a trade for pitcher Ralph Birkofer and infielder Cookie Lavagetto.

Ed was 16-14 in two seasons with the Bucs and finished his career with Hollywood, where he pitched in six games

> *"I knew I would win ball games in the semi-pro league, but I also knew I would be a failure in Organized Baseball."*
> — *Ed Brandt*

and retired.

Brandt operated a tavern after baseball. He was involved in a minor traffic accident in Spokane in 1944. While standing in the street discussing the mishap, another vehicle plowed into Brandt, inflicting fatal injuries.

BILL CISSELL

If you thought the stock market was on an upward roll in the 1920s, take a look at the Bill Cissell Index. Cissell was purchased for $82 in 1926, then $13,000 in 1927 and a finally $123,000 in 1928.

The Chicago White Sox paid the Portland Beavers that last amount for the infielder. The package included $75,000 in cash and two capable players, outfielder Ike Boone and pitcher Bert Cole.

Five years earlier, the ChiSox had dipped into the PCL for Willie Kamm, paying a record $100,000 plus players for the San Francisco third sacker. The soft-spoken Kamm settled into the big leagues without difficulty, but Cissell struggled under the pressure.

"The ballyhoo I got when Portland sold me for that sum was the greatest burden any player ever carried to the majors," he said bitterly.

Cissell had the kind of personality that wouldn't let him adjust easily to a new and more competitive environment. He was abrasive and a heavy drinker. But, despite these failings, Bill stayed in the majors for nine years before coming back to the Coast League.

Bill grew up 100 miles from St. Louis and played ball on the Cissell Family team composed of his dad, uncles and other relatives plus Jeff Tesreau, who later pitched with the New York Giants.

Cissell escaped notice by the scouts because he was serving a three-year hitch in the Army and was assigned to Fort Riley, Kansas. He was allowed to play weekends with a semi-pro team in 1925. Bill was seen by Des Moines team president Lee Keyser, who paid $82 to buy his discharge from the Army in 1926 and signed him to a Western League contract. Bill hit .345 in 78 games and looked good at shortstop.

Portland owner Tom Turner visited Des Moines to scout another player, but was liked Cissell's speed and range and bought him for $13,000. Bill played 22 games as the Beavers' shortstop, finishing among the fielding leaders and hitting .259.

Cissell came on strong from the opening bell in 1927. He showed great speed and during a field day circled the bases in 14.4 seconds and ran the 100-yard dash 10.2 seconds.

"He gets the ball away fast and should be a big (drawing) card around the circuit," said Owen Merrick in the *San Francisco Bulletin*. "The $13,000 beauty can certainly get around at shortstop." But, Merrick also cautioned that Cissell would, "make a lot of errors this season, as he tries for everything, but he will cut off a lot of hits."

Merrick was right. Cissell led the league in miscues with 76 in 182 games, finishing ahead of only Johnny Mitchell of the Angels among the league's regular shortstops. Some fans still thought he had better infield tools than former Portland shortstops Roger Peckinpaugh and Dave Bancroft — both major league stars — and many rated him superior to Oakland's Lyn Lary.

While not spectacular, Cissell's batting was a definite plus. He hit .323 with 32 doubles and scored 112 runs as the White Sox outbid other teams for his services.

Mainly a shortstop or second baseman, Cissell also played a few games at third base. He was average in the field and at the bat, although an injured knee in a 1931 collision with Jimmie Foxx and an appendix operation in 1934 contributed to his statistical standing. While he played during a period of inflated batting averages, he hit .267 in the big leagues.

Bill moved from Chicago to Cleveland to the Boston Red Sox, who sold him to Portland in May, 1935. He batted .316 and became manager when Buddy Ryan quit for health reasons. Shifted to Baltimore in the International League, Bill hit a career high .349 in 1936 and was drafted by the Philadelphia Athletics.

Cissell's alcoholism had become a major problem. Newspaper accounts described him as a "playboy" and "a drinker of epic proportions." He had been suspended by the Orioles for drinking and was arrested later the same month for disorderly conduct.

When he arrived with the Athletics, a reporter asked owner Connie Mack if service in the minors had taught Cissell any lessons. Mack replied with a straight face that, "I understand he's not drinking in the daytime now." Mack knew he couldn't change Bill's habits, but he made Cissell promise he wouldn't take any of the younger players along on his nighttime bar-hopping excursions.

Cissell went to the New York Giants in 1938, but played most of the year at Baltimore and joined Hollywood in 1939 for his last three seasons.

Before the season was half over, Cissell was in trouble over a tavern interview he gave to *Oakland Tribune* sportswriter Art Cohn. Cissell was quoted as saying PCL president W. C. Tuttle didn't know how to run a league. Bill also made disparaging remarks about baseball in general, said the Coast League was filled with too many rookies and was weaker than both the American Association and International League.

CHALMER WILLIAM CISSELL
Born: 1/3/04, Perryville, MO, BR/TR, 5-foot-11, 170 pounds

		G	AB	R	H	2B	3B	HR	RBI	SB	AVG.
1926	Port	22	85	10	22	5	0	0	12	1	.259
1927	Port	183	696	112	225	32	6	5	64	18	.323
1935	Port	165	646	106	204	43	4	8	84	14	.316
1939	Hwd	167	696	92	187	38	8	3	83	4	.269
1940	Hwd	162	629	89	182	32	3	4	76	7	.289
1941	Hd-SF	40	77	7	19	1	0	0	8	0	.247
PCL		6	739	2829| 416	839	151	21	20	327	44	.297
Majors		9	956	3707| 516	990	173	43	29	423	114	.267

Bill Cissell

Mickey Cochrane

Tuttle fined Bill $200, put him on probation for the rest of the season and warned that any further published remarks against him or baseball would result in a severe penalty. National Association president W. G. Bramham wanted to suspend Cissell for life, but Tuttle said the sentence was sufficient because he didn't want to penalize Hollywood.

Cissell played two years with the Stars, batting .269 and .289 before ending his career in 1941, when he split the season between Hollywood and San Francisco. Cissell went to the Seals when Ted Jennings broke his ankle, lasted two weeks and was cut loose.

In late January, 1949, the *Sporting News* reported Cissell was destitute and ailing with a circulatory disease in Chicago, where he had most recently worked as an electrician at Comiskey Park. One of his three children, a 13-year-old boy, was living with Cissell in an apartment where the landlord looked the other way when the rent came due. White Sox officials had Cissell moved to a hospital and arranged for the boy to be taken in by neighbors before Bill died on March 15.

> *"The ballyhoo I got when Portland*
> *sold me for that sum was the greatest*
> *burden any player ever carried to the*
> *majors."*
> — *Bill Cissell*

MICKEY COCHRANE

Mickey Cochrane was the greatest catcher to come out of the Coast League and the league's first graduate inducted into the Baseball Hall of Fame.

While he was a prospect of enormous potential when he joined the Portland Beavers in 1924, Cochrane was raw and untutored. Mickey developed during his only season in the league to such a degree that many major league officials, including Branch Rickey of the St. Louis Cardinals and John McGraw of the New York Giants, openly coveted his services.

The 21-year-old Cochrane batted above .300 from the beginning of the season, but was used sparingly. The majority of catching duties fell to the more experienced Tom Daly and Ray Query. The brawny Cochrane had little experience behind the plate and it showed as he made 14 errors, three more than his catching teammates combined.

Nevertheless, major league representatives liked what they saw and wanted to know why the "gingery young catcher" wasn't being used more often, since he was one of Portland's best attractions.

Seeing the potential for a sale, team officials ordered Cochrane into the lineup on a regular basis with the season nearly two-thirds over. Mickey played more than 50 of his 99 games in the last third of the season, hitting .333.

The Philadelphia Athletics bought Cochrane and launched a 13-year career that showed he was the greatest catcher of his time and possibly all time. Left-handed in

PCL PICTORIAL

Hal Rhyne

Vic Aldridge

Doug McWeeny

Sammy Hale

Ray Kremer

Jimmy O'Connell

the batters box, he hit .320 lifetime, had power and decent speed for a catcher. A good eye earned him many walks.

Cochrane grew up in Massachusetts and attended Boston University, where he starred on the football team as a triple-threat halfback. On the gridiron and in the boxing ring, Cochrane showed the tenacity, leadership qualities and fiery temperament that epitomized his diamond career.

Mickey played summer ball for a Saranac Lake semipro team to earn money for tuition and was told by a teammate about an opening at Dover in Eastern Shore League. He had never worked behind the plate, but Cochrane talked the manager into giving him job as catcher so he could get into the lineup.

Playing as "Frank King" to protect his amateur status, Cochrane led the league in errors and hit .327 in 65 games as Dover won the pennant. Portland scouts liked his batting ability and gave him a contract.

He remained at Boston University until February, 1924, and was so unsure of his abilities that he refused to report to Portland until owner Tom Turner agreed to send him round-trip train fare from Boston. When Turner asked what everyone called him, Cochrane said, "Kid." Turner replied he'd be called "Mickey" in Portland in keeping with his status as a Boston Irishman.

Mickey knew he was a rotten catcher and did not like the position. Cochrane told Portland manager Bill Kenworthy he wanted to play in the outfield, but he stayed behind the plate.

Connie Mack owned a controlling interest in the Portland franchise, so the $50,000 and four players he exchanged for Cochrane may have been pretty much a paper transaction.

"He was crude at receiving the ball, his stance and crouch were both wrong and on foul balls he was simply pathetic."
— *Connie Mack describing rookie Mickey Cochrane*

When Cochrane arrived in the Philadelphia camp in 1925, he looked so bad behind the plate that Mack tried him at third base, where he was worse. Mack told regular catcher Cy Perkins to teach Cochrane the finer points of catching, because, "he was crude at receiving the ball, his stance and crouch were both wrong and on foul balls he was simply pathetic."

Perkins taught Cochrane well, although he knew it would cost him the starting job. Mickey took over and batted .331 as a rookie. In the next eight seasons with Philadelphia, Mickey hit .322 or better five times as the Athletics grabbed three pennants and won the World Series in 1929 and 1930. In 1928, he hit .293 with 23 homers and 112 RBIs and was the league's most valuable player.

Mack said Cochrane was most responsible for Philadelphia's success, but financial setbacks in the Great Depression forced him to sell the catcher to Detroit for $100,000. Mickey became the Tigers' player-manager and pushed himself and the team to the pennant in 1934 and 1935. Near exhaustion, Cochrane fared poorly in the World Series loss to St. Louis, but promised to win the series the following year. True to his word, the Tigers downed the Cubs in what Mickey called "my greatest day in baseball."

Mickey hit .320 in 1934 to take the MVP award over teammate Charlie Gehringer by two votes and batted .319 the following season.

Cochrane drove himself to a nervous breakdown early in 1936, when he left the team to spend time at a Wyoming

ranch, then returned to guide his team to a second place finish. Cochrane seemed recovered in 1937 when he lost sight of a pitch by New York's Bump Hadley on May 26 and was struck on the right temple. Cochrane spent 10 days in a coma and never played again. Mickey returned as manager but was fired midway through the following season.

He later was general manager of the Athletics and a vice president of the Tigers. Cochrane was elected to the Hall of Fame in 1947.

LARRY FRENCH

When Larry French was reintroduced to an old friend — the knuckle ball — the meeting came too late in life to change his career, but just in time to give him the best season in 17 years.

The big Californian suffered through his worst season ever in 1941 after breaking the thumb on his pitching hand in a charity softball game during the winter. It was a terrible blow for a player who had never had a serious injury.

French's record was 5-14 in late August when the sixth place Chicago Cubs put him on waivers and Brooklyn took his contract. He pitched six games with the Dodgers and threw a shutout inning in two relief appearances in Brooklyn's loss to the New York Yankees in the World Series. He had compiled an 0-2 record in two previous Fall Classics with the Cubs.

At 34 years of age, French fate's seemed uncertain at the start of 1942. But, manager Leo Durocher put French on the mound and Larry gave the Ebbets Field faithful an unlikely new Bum to cheer on.

Brooklyn's veteran pitching staff — Kirby Higbe, Whitlow Wyatt, Hugh Casey and Curt Davis — was back and Durocher used Larry sparingly until late April.

When his troops lost four straight, including a doubleheader to the St. Louis Cardinals, Lippy Leo decided to give the veteran a chance to be the stopper. French drove in two runs the next day with timely hits and threw a four-hitter at St. Louis, beating the Cards in 11 innings, 2-1.

French won his next nine games as a spot starter before suffering a defeat. Larry said his success was a combination of factors and one of the most important was the help in developing a knuckle ball he'd received in spring training from teammate Fred Fitzsimmons, one of the game's best knuckle ball pitchers.

Larry's once awesome fast ball had faded, so the addition of the knuckler to his screwball and jug handle curve was the missing ingredient that put him back on the winning track. French threw a knuckler early in his career, but when he arrived at Portland in 1926, catcher Frank Tobin talked him out of using it on grounds that, "a knuckle ball fools nobody but the catcher."

French was a high school classmate of shortstop Lyn Lary in Visalia. While Lary was signed by Oakland, French's potential wasn't recognized immediately and he was playing semi-pro ball in Oregon's Willamette Valley

GORDON STANLEY COCHRANE
Born: 4/6/03, Bridgewater, MA, BL/TR, 5-foot-10.5, 180 pounds

		G	AB	R	H	2B	3B	HR	RBI	SB	AVG.
1924	Port	99	300	43	100	8	5	7	56	1	.333
PCL		1	99	300	43	100	8	5	7	56	1	.333
Majors		13	1482	5169	1041	1652	333	64	119	832	64	.320

Lefty Gomez

Earl McNeely

when Portland offered a contract.

Larry pitched in seven games for the Beavers in 1926, but spent most of the season at Ogden in the Utah-Idaho League where he compiled a 8-7 record in 134 innings.

The following season, French came out of the bullpen most of the time to win 11 and lose 12. French started with Portland the next year, working 251 innings in 43 games for an 11-17 mark. Two of the losses came on Sept. 28, when he pitched a double-header against San Francisco and lost both games by shutout.

Larry's biggest problem in his early years was lack of control. He improved, but in two-plus Coast League seasons, French walked 235 and struck out 183 in 452 innings.

While French's win-loss record of 23-29 with Portland wasn't overwhelming, Pittsburgh officials listened to scout Joe Devine, who liked Larry's durability and noted the Beavers' poor record. The Pirates acquired French for cash

and infielder Mack Hillis.

After pitching only 123 innings in 1929, French was a workhorse on the Pittsburgh and Chicago Cubs staffs for 11 more years. He averaged 276 innings annually for the Pirates with 18-16 and 18-13 seasons in 1932 and 1933, respectively. Traded to the Cubs after 1934 with infielder Fred Lindstrom for pitchers Guy Bush, Jumbo Jim Weaver

LAWRENCE HERBERT FRENCH
Born: 11/1/07, Visalia, CA, BB/TL, 6-foot-1, 195 pounds

		W	L	PCT	G	IP	H	ER	BB	SO	ERA
1926	Port	1	0	1.000	7	20	20	11	9	7	4.95
1927	Port	11	12	.478	44	181	191	96	98	71	4.77
1928	Port	11	17	.393	43	251	274	113	128	105	4.05
PCL	3	23	29	.451	94	452	485	220	235	183	4.38
Majors	14	197	171	.535	570	3152	3375	1206	819	1187	3.44

and outfielder Babe Herman, Larry continued carrying a heavy load. He had a winning record four of his first five years and threw between 194 and 252 innings annually.

Over his career in the majors, Larry completed 52 percent of his starts and tossed 40 shutouts.

His last game with Brooklyn was a brilliant finish to his career. He shut out Philadelphia, 6-0, allowing just one hit while facing only 28 batters.

French went to war in 1942 by enlisting in the Navy. After World War II ended, French announced his retirement from baseball. He returned to the Navy during the Korean War and chose to make it his career this time, retiring as a captain in 1969.

LEFTY GOMEZ

When Lefty Gomez arrived in the New York Yankees camp in 1930, general manager Ed Barrow was stunned by the sight of his $50,000 purchase from the San Francisco Seals.

The 20-year-old pitcher was tall at 6-foot-2, but terribly thin, weighing around 145 pounds. At his peak, Gomez tipped the scales at nearly 180. But, Lefty's success on the mound didn't prevent Barrow from constantly badgering him to put on weight.

Barrow continued his relentless campaign after the 1934 season, when Gomez was first in the American League with 26 wins, 282 innings pitched, 25 complete games, 158 strikeouts and a 2.33 ERA. He said Gomez would make the fans forget Jack Chesbro — the first pitcher to win 16 straight games — if he'd put on 20 pounds.

Gomez complied and lounged through the winter at a health spa where he gained 23 pounds. The following season, Lefty slumped to a 12-15 mark and reporters wondered why.

"Barrow told me if I'd put on 20 pounds I'd make the fans forget Chesbro," Lefty laughed. "I go him three better and almost make the fans forget Gomez." When Barrow wanted to cut his pay from $20,000 to $7,500, Gomez reportedly said, "You keep the salary, I'll take the cut."

These were typical Gomez stories. A Hall of Fame pitcher with a 189-102 record, Lefty was 6-0 in 50 1/3 innings on five World Series teams and went 3-1 in five All-Star game appearances. Lefty — also called "Goofy" — is remembered as much for his wit and personality as for his splendid mound career. Some examples:

√ He invented the phrase "gopher ball" to explain that he pitched, the batter swung and the ball "will go for three or four bases."

√ "The secret of my success was clean living and a fast-moving outfield."

√ "I talk 'em out of hits."

Gomez grew up on a dairy ranch in Rodeo across the bay from San Francisco and attended Richmond High School. The Seals were aware of the skinny pitcher during his undergraduate days and manager Nick Williams once saw Lefty toss a perfect game against San Francisco's

Larry French

Lefty Gomez

Commerce High School. Following a tryout, the Seals sent him home to add a few pounds to his slender frame.

After graduation, Gomez joined the Seals and was dispatched to Salt Lake City in the Utah-Idaho League. Lefty's record was only 12-14 with a 3.48 earned run average, but he struck out a league-high 172 batters in 194 innings. Gomez held his own in comparisons with two highly-regarded San Francisco right-handers on the same team, Val Glynn (16-8, 3.64 ERA) and Curt Davis (16-8, 4.51 ERA). The trio led Salt Lake City to the pennant.

"The secret of my success was clean living and a fast-moving outfield."
— Lefty Gomez

All three were ushered into training camp in the spring to compete with a pitching staff whose four veterans — Elmer Jacobs, Sloppy Thurston, Walter Mails and Johnny Couch — were expected to provide four-fifths of the 1929 starting rotation. Clearly, two of the three rookies might be disappointed.

It appeared early in the campaign that Gomez was the least likely to grab a spot in the rotation. While Glynn and Davis started, Lefty appeared infrequently and always as a relief pitcher until the season was nearly a month old.

Gomez defeated Hollywood in his first start on April 24. Lefty always had a lot of action on his fast ball and a lack of control was his big minus on the scouting charts. He showed a better sense of where the plate was located in 1929 than in his major league career, walking 3.6 batters per nine innings. His major league base on balls average was nearly four per game.

Lefty's early starts resulted in a few wins and losses, but in mid-year he reeled off 12 straight victories to equal the PCL's season high posted earlier by teammate Jacobs. Yankees scout Bill Essick followed him for two weeks near the end of the streak and recommended that New York grab him quickly before some other club took him. The Seals sold Gomez to the Yankees on Aug. 16 for delivery in 1930.

Gomez completed the season with an 18-11 record and a 3.44 earned run average, the highest league-leading ERA since the PCL started compiling the statistic in 1914. It was a record until 1974, when Tacoma's Juan Vientidos won the title with a 3.67 mark.

After beginning 1930 with the Yankees, Lefty was sent to St. Paul in the American Association for more experi-

ence. He made a funny story out of going back to the minors, saying he was the only player ever farmed out by the Bulova Watch Co.

Bulova gave timepieces to major leaguers who hit home runs, Gomez explained, "and (batters) hit so many off me that I found myself back in St. Paul." His 8-4 record with the Saints brought him back to the big leagues to stay.

Gomez won 21 or more games three of the next four seasons before he slipped and wrenched his pitching arm in 1934, an injury that cost him a chance to win 30 games. Gomez blamed his only losing year in 1935 on his quest to gain weight, but Lefty never was as fast as before the injury, although his curve improved.

Lefty's complete game numbers were down for two years, but he had 21 and 18 wins in 1937 and 1938, respectively. He won only 15 games in two more seasons, but climbed to 15-5 in 1941, his last good year.

Gomez joined Washington in 1943, but quit after one poor outing. Lefty returned to the Yankees organization in 1946 and 1947 as manager of their Binghamton farm team.

SAMMY HALE

Sammy Hale was a small, but powerfully-built third baseman who hit the ball consistently, but threw it away with nearly equal regularity.

Hale averaged .337 in four Coast League seasons, two before and two after his decade in the American League. Sammy's erratic fielding was overlooked in the PCL because he hit so well, but it reduced his opportunities to start regularly with the Philadelphia Athletics, where he spent most of his major league career. Hale still played in 883 games at the top and hit .302.

After three seasons with San Antonio in the Texas League, the Detroit Tigers picked up Hale's contract and he made 116 plate appearances in 76 games, hitting .293. Sammy pinch hit most of the time and set a rookie record with 17 hits off the bench in 52 at bats.

Sammy pinch hit in nine games in 1921 and was sent to Portland in late May as part of the deal to entice Beavers president Bill Klepper to sell pitchers Herm Pillette and Syl Johnson to the Tigers.

Hale immediately endeared himself to the Portland faithful, hitting near .400 over the first few weeks. The fans theorized Sammy might have stuck with the Tigers if manager Ty Cobb had let him play regularly.

While they liked his hitting, spectators soon saw that his fielding was not major league caliber. He batted .342 with 39 doubles in 136 games, but was seventh in fielding among third basemen, one spot better than the Beavers finished in the standings.

Sammy remained Detroit property in 1921, but was turned over to the Beavers after Klepper agreed in December to sell Pillette and Johnson for $75,000 and five players. Klepper hoped to rebuild his team through the transaction in 1922, but the Beavers moved up only one notch to seventh place.

VERNON LOUIS GOMEZ
Born: 11/26/08, Rodeo, CA, BL/TL, 6-foot-2, 173 pounds

		W	L	PCT	G	IP	H	ER	BB	SO	ERA
1929	SF	18	11	.621	41	267	277	102	108	159	3.44
PCL		1	18	11	.621	41	267	277	102	108	159	3.44
Majors		14	189	102	.649	368	2503	2290	930	1095	1468	3.34

Sammy Hale

Hale was the key to the transaction and showed he was up to the challenge by improving both on the field and at the plate. There was talk of moving Sammy to the outfield to make room at third base for Joe Sargent, another player provided in the Pillette-Johnson transaction. But, Hale stayed at the hit corner and was inserted into the lineup as the Beavers free-swinging clean-up batter.

"(Hale) is a different player than 1921, when he looked bad on the infield (and) was poor on ground balls and flies," the *San Francisco Bulletin's* Abe Kemp said early in the year. "He no longer takes his eye off the ball."

Hale contended for the batting title through the early part

SAMUEL DOUGLAS HALE
Born: 9/10/96, Glen Rose, TX, BR/TR, 5-foot-8.5, 160 pounds

		G	AB	R	H	2B	3B	HR	RBI	SB	AVG.
1921	Port	136	530	80	181	39	9	9	78	14	.342
1922	Port	152	525	91	188	39	6	10	93	18	.358
1930	Port	36	140	19	41	10	3	1	18	4	.293
1931	Port	133	555	95	179	35	5	2	80	7	.323
PCL	4	457	1750	285	589	123	23	22	269	43	.337
Majors	10	883	2915	422	880	157	54	30	392	41	.302

---

of the year. In August, *Sporting News* correspondent Lou Kennedy said Sammy had missed a few games through injury, but if he, "continues to hit and field as he has so far this year, he is certain to be in faster company next year."

Hale appeared as a pinch hitter even when he was hurt, getting four straight hits in one stretch and batting nearly .800 off the bench.

"He has shown the best base running on the club and his throwing has been accurate and deadly," Kennedy said in September. Kennedy thought Hale was the PCL's best player except for San Francisco's Willie Kamm. Klepper already had turned down a reported offer of $40,000 for Hale.

Sammy closed out the year at .358 — third best in the circuit — with 39 doubles and 93 RBIs. Connie Mack gave Portland $75,000 plus pitcher Charlie Eckert for him at the National Association's winter meeting. Mack would not confirm the price, but admitted that widespread interest by other teams made him pay twice what he intended for Hale's services.

Sammy played with Philadelphia through 1929 and was traded to the St. Louis Browns for catcher Wally Schang. Generally he was in the lower half of the third base fielding tables, but he averaged 105 games annually during seven years in Philadelphia. His batting average ranged from .277 to .345 and he hit better than .300 four times.

Hale played 62 games with the Browns in 1930, went to Portland after his release and hit .293 in 36 games. In 1931, Hale averaged .323 in his last season on the coast and played for Indianapolis, Tulsa and Oklahoma City after leaving the Beavers.

BABE HERMAN

How many Babe Herman stories are there? Dozens, and many of them are based on fact.

The most important fact is that, in spite of his imperfections as a fielder and base runner, Herman belted the ball at a .324 clip for 20 years in the Coast League and majors.

"Herman was not a good fielder or . . . thrower and there were several faster players in every game he played," said writer Ken Smith. "He was a hitter for a pure and simple fact."

Lean and blond with a world of power in his bat, the tall slugger achieved a kind of baseball immortality as a flake because of a continual flow of funny failings on the diamond and goofy comments off the field.

His most famous faux pas occurred in 1926 when Babe doubled into a double play with Brooklyn. With the bases loaded and one out, Herman lined the ball off the right field wall. Pitcher Dazzy Vance was the runner at second and thought the ball would be caught so he was late leaving the bag. By the time he saw the ball was not caught, it was too late for Vance to score and he stopped at third base while Chick Fewster from first and Herman kept running. All three wound up at third base, where Fewster and Herman were tagged out.

Babe Herman

Roy Johnson

Many of Babe's base running and outfielding gaffes were based on his tendency to daydream instead of concentrating on the game. Once, with one out and two runners on base, he caught a fly ball, stuck it in his pocket and ran to the clubhouse while the winning runs scored. Many thought he was simply a lousy fielder. "He wore a glove for one reason," said Fresco Thompson. "It was a league custom."

Babe denied the story that he had been hit on the head by a fly ball, contending it was his shoulder that took the blow. He explained away one of his perpetual spring hold-outs by saying, "I don't do it for the money. The longer I stay away from training camp, the less chance I have of

being hit by a fly ball."

Herman's career began in 1921 when he was declared ineligible for prep ball after taking money to play in an Elks picnic game on Santa Catalina island. He left Glendale High School and joined Edmonton in the Western Canada League. Coach Dan Howley once knew a boxer named Babe Herman and started calling his new player by that nickname and it stuck. After hitting .330 and leading the league in hits and triples he was bought by Detroit and spent three more seasons bouncing around the minors, playing first base and hitting an aggregate .353 along the way.

The big first sacker arrived in Seattle in 1925 with a huge plug of tobacco in his cheek and a load of heavy bats on his shoulder. The writers described Babe as a "behemoth of a man" with a reputation for hitting the ball hard and often. He started slowly and was batting only .275 at mid-season, but came on strong to finish at .316.

The PCL was a hitter's league, so Herman's average did not even make the top 20. His 131 runs batted in was third with the Indians and he contributed 115 runs, 52 doubles and 15 home runs as Seattle finished third.

Brooklyn bought Herman, who opened his 13-year stay at the top by batting .319. Converted to the outfield in 1927, Babe's average fell to .272, his lowest as a major league starter.

He posted solid totals annually after that. Herman's most

FLOYD CAVES HERMAN
Born: 6/26/03, Buffalo, NY, BL/TL, 6-foot-4, 190 pounds

		G	AB	R	H	2B	3B	HR	RBI	SB	AVG.
1925	Seat	167	651	115	206	52	13	15	131	22	.316
1939	Hwd	90	350	69	111	36	5	13	71	2	.317
1940	Hwd	148	469	62	144	45	7	9	80	0	.307
1941	Hwd	110	272	41	94	16	1	11	63	2	.346
1942	Hwd	85	149	18	48	5	0	5	42	0	.322
1943	Hwd	81	147	15	52	8	1	4	22	1	.354
1944	Hwd	78	107	8	37	8	1	0	23	0	.346
PCL	7	759	2145	328	692	170	28	57	432	27	.323
Majors	13	1552	5603	882	1818	399	110	181	997	94	.324

productive seasons were 1929 (.381, 21 HR, 113 RBI), and 1930 (.393, 143 Runs, 35 HR, 130 RBI). His .393 average is the Dodgers' single season record and the highest for a National League runner-up in a batting race this century. Babe hit 11 or more triples six times and led the league with 19 in 1932, his first year in Cincinnati after the Dodgers traded him away.

Herman continued to hit well as he traveled from Cincinnati to Chicago to Pittsburgh, back to the Reds and finally to Detroit. He spent the next two seasons in the high

---

"He wore a glove for one reason. It was a league custom."
— *Fresco Thompson about Babe Herman*

---

minors.

Hollywood acquired Herman during the 1938 winter meetings and, as usual, Babe held out for more money. Herman, who had averaged $14,000-plus a season with a top of $19,000, finally accepted $10,000, big money in the minors.

Herman was worth every penny. After missing spring training, Babe pinch hit on opening day and ripped the first pitch for a home run. He missed some time after breaking his wrist in July, but still hit .317 with 13 homers and 71 RBIs in 90 games.

Herman's power began to fade as he moved into his late 30s, but his batting eye remained undimmed. Over five more seasons with the Stars, he blasted 29 homers with 230 RBIs in 502 games and posted batting marks between .307 and .354.

When he wasn't hired to replace manager Charlie Root after the 1944 season, Herman refused an offer to join Hollywood's front office staff and retired to his 18-acre turkey ranch near Glendale.

Brooklyn general manager Branch Rickey telephoned in 1945 and asked Babe if he could still hit. "I guess so," Babe replied and signed a contract. "I don't have to run, he tells me, just meet the ball once in awhile," said Babe, who averaged .265 off the bench in 37 games.

Herman later was a scout for the Pirates, Yankees, Mets, Phillies and Giants and coached with Seattle in 1952.

ROY JOHNSON

Roy Johnson was a swift and hard-hitting player from the Pacific Northwest who was dropped by Seattle only to land in San Francisco with one of the most potent outfields in Coast League history.

Roy was the brother of Indian Bob Johnson, another PCL player who went on to a long and successful major league career. Both were born in Oklahoma and came to Washington with their family in 1913.

Roy was shorter than his brother by three inches. But, he

generated decent power and supplemented it with blazing speed that put him among the leaders in triples in the PCL and the American League and made him dangerous threat on the base paths.

Johnson began playing baseball seriously for Everett in the Southwest Washington League that featured future teammate Earl Averill on another ball club. A New York Yankees scout expressed interest in him in 1924, but Roy spurned the offer because he wanted to stay closer to home.

Seattle gave him a chance late in the year and Johnson sat on the bench as manager Red Killefer tried to convert him from pitcher to the outfield. Roy got one hit in two tries in September and was supposed to report to the Indians the following spring, but Seattle lost interest when he went to California to play winter ball.

Johnson, who threw right-handed and batted left, pitched briefly for Tulsa (0-3) in the Western League, but spent much of 1925 playing semi-pro ball in San Francisco. The Seals signed Roy and sent him to their farm club in Idaho Falls, where he hit .369, led the league with 133 runs and had 31 doubles, 19 triples and 19 homers. He also hit .260 in 25 games with San Francisco.

San Francisco manager Nick Williams intended to send Johnson out again, but when training camp ended Roy was on the outfield roster with a trio of southpaw batters — Earl Averill, Smead Jolley and Lefty O'Doul. Williams inserted Johnson into the lineup against left-handers and he hit .306 in 109 games. Johnson showed his inexperience in the outfield as he made 21 errors and was near the bottom of the fielding list.

Johnson and the Seals both had outstanding years in 1927. Featuring an outfield that batted a combined .373, Johnson (.360), Jolley (a league-leading .404) and Averill (.354) made the sportswriters' Coast League all-star team. The Seals took the first half title and won the pennant in a playoff with second half winner Sacramento.

Detroit liked Johnson's stat sheet, which showed 142 runs, 49 doubles, 16 triples (tops in the league), 22 home runs and 29 steals. Although Roy still struggled in the outfield, where he was next to last in fielding, he showed a strong arm and the ability to cover lots of ground.

The Bengals bought Roy for $45,000 and players and he responded with a fabulous rookie year in 1929. Johnson paced the league in at bats (640) and doubles (45) and

ROY CLEVELAND JOHNSON
Born: 2/23/03, Pryor, OK, BL/TR, 5-foot-9, 175 pounds

		G	AB	R	H	2B	3B	HR	RBI	SB	AVG.
1924	Seat	2	2	0	1	0	0	0	0	0	.500
1926	SF	25	77	15	20	7	1	1	11	2	.260
1927	SF	109	327	57	100	17	7	4	24	6	.306
1928	SF	170	650	142	234	49	16	22	76	29	.360
1944	Seat	115	369	38	96	14	5	2	35	12	.260
1945	Seat	69	214	29	58	15	0	1	29	11	.271
PCL	6	490	1639	281	509	102	29	30	175	60	.311
Majors	10	1155	4359	717	1292	275	83	58	556	135	.296

tacked on 128 runs, 201 hits, 14 triples and a .314 average.

Six good seasons followed with Detroit and the Boston Red Sox. He batted .275 in 1930 and .279 with 19 triples and 33 stolen bases the following year before moving to Bean Town in a trade in mid-1932. After hitting below .300 again in the trade year, Roy delivered .313, .320 and .315 marks for the Red Sox.

Johnson was traded to Washington late in 1935 and sent on to the New York Yankees in a second swap before the 1936 season opened. Joe DiMaggio arrived at the same time for his rookie season and Roy was relegated to a utility outfield role along with Myril Hoag and Ben Chapman. He batted .265 in 63 games and appeared in two World Series games as a pinch hitter.

After 12 games the following year, Johnson went to the Boston Braves on waivers. He hit .277 and was given his release early in 1938. Roy spent four more seasons in the American Association and International League and then retired, or so he thought.

Johnson was out of Organized Baseball for two years when the Seattle Rainiers, desperate for warm bodies during the war, hired Roy as an outfielder in 1944. At age 41, he batted .260 in 115 contests and .271 in 69 more the following season before hanging up his spikes for good.

WILLIE KAMM

Willie Kamm couldn't believe his ears. It was May 30, 1922, and the young San Francisco third baseman was walking along San Francisco's Market Street when he heard newsboys shouting his name.

What was that they were saying about me, wondered Kamm, who had been left at home with a severe charley horse while the Seals were on a two-week road trip. "Willie Kamm sold to White Sox for $100,000," called out one of the boys. The news scared him to death, he admitted later.

One hundred thousand dollars was a remarkable amount of money in 1922.

"Do you realize you can purchase a franchise in the Pacific Coast League for (that) sum?" asked *San Francisco Bulletin* baseball writer Abe Kemp.

The figure also was a record price for a minor league player. If you combined it with the former record of $75,000 paid a year earlier by the New York Giants for Jimmy O'Connell, along with recent sales of infielder Jimmy Caveney ($65,000) and pitchers Lefty O'Doul ($10,000) and Johnny Couch ($20,000), it left San Francisco's owners sitting pretty financially, Kemp added.

Salt Lake City's Oscar Vitt, a former Seal often held up as a model for smooth-fielding third basemen, said White Sox owner Charles Comiskey got Kamm "dirt cheap" and predicted Willie would become an American League star.

Vitt's opinion was right on the money. Kamm had a brilliant 13-year career in the majors, leading third basemen in fielding eight times while hitting a steady .281. He set many fielding records, including 75 straight errorless

Willie Kamm

games in 1928.

Only two years before his sale, no one would have bet a plugged nickel that Kamm would be purchased by a big league club at any price.

Kamm was a 5-foot-10, 170-pounder during his major league career, but he was shorter and much lighter in weight as a teenager. Willie was playing sandlot baseball in San Francisco in 1918 when Sacramento trainer Spike Hennessy saw him and persuaded the Senators to employ the 18-year-old. Kamm got two hits in nine trips to the plate before the Senators released Willie and Hennessy got

WILLIAM EDWARD KAMM
Born: 2/2/00, San Francisco, CA, BR/TR,
5-foot-10.5, 170 pounds

		G	AB	R	H	2B	3B	HR	RBI	SB	AVG.
1918	Sac	4	9	0	2	0	0	0	0	0	.222
1919	SF	136	485	58	114	21	2	3	—	13	.235
1920	SF	182	596	63	141	39	3	7	—	24	.237
1921	SF	168	598	101	172	38	9	13	105	21	.288
1922	SF	170	650	137	222	56	9	20	124	35	.342
1936	Miss	9	19	2	6	1	0	0	0	0	.316
PCL	6	669	2357	361	657	155	23	43	229*	93	.279
Majors	13	1693	5851	802	1643	348	85	29	826	126	.281

* incomplete

him a job in a Portland shipyard that had a baseball team.

Willie came home to San Francisco to play ball for the Union Iron Works in 1919 and Seals co-owner Doc Strub signed Kamm after seeing him in a game at Recreation Park. The shy and soft-spoken infielder told manager Charlie Graham that he should be farmed out to get some experience. Instead, Graham stationed him at third base in 136 games, where he led the league with 42 errors and hit .235 with little power. The following season Kamm hit .237 and again topped the PCL with 53 miscues in 182

"Willie Kamm sold to White Sox for $100,000."
— *San Francisco newsboy calling out 1922 newspaper headline*

---

games at the hot corner.

After the 1920 season, Willie had his tonsils removed and gained about 25 pounds to weigh 165. The added weight and another year's maturity helped immeasurably. He led the league in fielding and boosted his batting average to .288 with 13 home runs and 105 runs batted it.

During the off-season, Kamm played for the San Francisco Mission team in a four-team California Winter League that included a number of major league players. Ty Cobb managed the rival San Francisco Seals team and spent time during the 10-week season working on Kamm's batting stroke.

Improvement was evident in 1922. Kamm got off to a great start and when he set a record by blasting two home runs over Oakland's left field fence in mid-April, the *Bulletin's* Kemp enthused, "the once despised weakling at the plate is tearing the cover off the ball."

Kamm's hitting feats continued all year. Although his average fell to the low .300s in late June, Kamm was an integral cog in the San Francisco offensive machine as the Seals grabbed their first pennant in five seasons. Three pitchers sent by the White Sox as part of the Kamm deal — Doug McWeeny (15-7), Shovel Hodge (2-2) and Harry Courtney (5-2) — also helped the cause. Kamm hit .342, was second in the league in runs (137) and had 56 doubles, 20 home runs and a club-leading 124 RBIs.

He was brilliant again in the field, losing the golden glove title by a percentage point to Los Angeles third sacker Charlie Deal. Willie had great range and an uncanny feel for the ball and could throw accurately with a rifle arm. He was not fast on his feet, but studied hitters and knew where to position himself before each pitch.

After the Seals sold Kamm, they tore up his contract and gave him a new one with a $2,500 raise. He later asked for more money, but took management's rejection in typical style without a whimper.

Nothing changed when he arrived in Chicago. Kamm hit .292 the first year and continued at a steady pace over the rest of his career, topping .300 only once with a .308 aver-

age in 1928.

Kamm was traded to Cleveland early in 1931 for another San Franciscan, Lew Fonseca. White Sox owner Comiskey forgot to tell Kamm about the trade, so Willie read about it in the newspapers. The owner later wrote Kamm a letter commending Willie for his deportment on and off the field and wishing him good luck.

Willie had poor luck with the Indians when he disagreed with manager Walter Johnson in 1935 and The Big Train sent him home to Cleveland, "for the good of the club." Johnson called Kamm a "disturber" and said younger players objected to his efforts to improve their play. Kamm was made a scout and then handed his release in June. Johnson was fired at the end of the season.

As a Coast League manager in 1936, Kamm led the San Francisco Mission team to a fifth place tie with Los Angeles on an 88-88 mark. The Missions finished eighth (73-105) the following season and Willie's long career in baseball was over.

RAY KREMER

An inflated price tag kept Ray Kremer toiling for Coast League pay far too long. But when he made it to the majors as a 31-year-old rookie, Kremer showed his stuff with a 143-85 record over the next decade.

Fortune didn't smile on Kremer in the PCL, where he worked for second division Oakland clubs for seven years. Kremer had better luck in the big leagues. He played with Pittsburgh during a period when the Pirates won two titles and finished as low as fifth only twice.

The powerful pitcher was given the nickname "Wiz" for the sound made by a potent fast ball that once struck out 52 sandlot batters in three games. Later, reporters said it was short for "Wizard" in recognition of his mastery over batters. Ray got his start in pro ball with Sacramento in 1914 and didn't show much, going 2-8 with an inflated 5.19 ERA while walking more batters than he fanned. He had a 7-5 record at Vancouver in the Northwestern League in 1915.

Kremer had a 1916 spring trial with the New York

REMY PETER KREMER
Born: 3/23/93, Oakland, CA, BR/TR, 6-foot-1, 190 pounds

		W	L	PCT	G	IP	H	ER	BB	SO	ERA
1914	Sac-Ms	2	8	.200	29	137	158	79	42	34	5.19
1917	Oak	9	15	.375	40	224	227	82	76	55	3.29
1918	Oak	5	14	.263	22	158	166	58	35	69	3.31
1919	Oak	15	23	.395	49	298	233	127	88	94	3.84
1920	Oak	13	22	.371	49	321	336	108	66	90	3.02
1921	Oak	16	14	.533	48	294	331	118	66	123	3.61
1922	Oak	20	18	.526	48	356	368	110	74	154	2.78
1923	Oak	25	16	.610	45	357	374	122	77	127	3.08
1933	Oak	1	5	.167	7	31	30	—	10	10	—
1934	Oak	0	1	.000	4	10	18	—	3	6	—
PCL	10	106	136	.438	341	2186	2241	804	537	762	3.37
Majors	10	143	85	.627	308	1955	2108	818	483	516	3.76

Ray Kremer

Lyn Lary

Giants, but spent two months on crutches when he contracted inflammatory rheumatism. After pitching in the Northwestern League, Ray hooked up with Oakland in 1917.

Kremer was a mature and durable pitcher who had relatively little experience when he joined the Acorns. His control still was spotty and he walked 76 and struck out 55 in 224 innings while compiling a 9-15 record. In the war-shortened 1918 season, Ray won five of 19 decisions, but KO'd batters nearly twice as often as he walked them.

> *"(Ray) Kremer is no kid, but he has several years left."*
> — San Francisco Bulletin

Although his earned run average was 3.84 in 1919 — the highest of his PCL years as a regular — Ray's fast ball became more effective and was joined by a respectable curve and improved control. He won 15 and lost 23 and gave up only 233 hits in 298 frames. Pitching as a starter and coming out of the bullpen, he won 13 and lost 22 the following season in 321 innings.

Ray posted his first winning season in 1921 and began drawing attention. Major league scouts inquired about buying Kremer, but Oakland's management was only willing to sell him for big money, so he continued to be a prisoner of the minor leagues as his 30th birthday approached.

Kremer was one of the PCL's top pitchers in 1922 and 1923. He went 20-18 with 154 strikeouts in 356 innings and his best ERA (2.78) the first season. The following year, the majors no longer could ignore Kremer at almost any price as he compiled a 25-16 record and led the PCL in wins, complete games (35) and innings (357) with 127 Ks and a 3.08 ERA. His 25th win brought him a $500 bonus specified in his Oakland contract.

During the 1923 season there were reports the Oaks tried to trade Wiz to a major league team for three players who would be subject to a future draft, but league president William McCarthy nixed the arrangement.

Pittsburgh owner Barney Dreyfuss had a choice to make between Kremer and Seattle's Elmer Jacobs (24-10 with a 3.14 ERA). He made the right selection, picking Kremer and paying the Oaks $25,000 plus three players. There was one more stumbling block, however, because Ray insisted the Pirates pay him a $3,500 bonus.

Dreyfuss balked, but relented after the Pirates matched Ray against his former Oakland teammates during spring training. When he allowed only one hit and struck out nine in the six inning exhibition, Ray got his money.

"Kremer is no kid," said the *San Francisco Bulletin*, "but he has several years left."

Several turned into 10 years for the Bucs. Kremer's rookie season gave only a hint of how good he was. The Pirates finished third with Ray pitching a league-leading 41 games for an 18-10 record. Pittsburgh harvested a great rookie crop that year, including outfielder KiKi Cuyler

(.354), shortstop Glenn Wright (.287 with 111 RBIs) and pitcher Emil Yde (16-3, 2.83 ERA).

Pittsburgh took it all in 1925, annexing the pennant with five pitchers winning 15 to 19 games, including Ray's 17-8. He won two and lost one in the World Series as the Bucs downed Washington in seven games.

Kremer kept the Bucs in the 1926 race until September, but they finished third as he tied for the league lead with 20 wins. Over the next four seasons, including the 1927 pennant-winning year when the Pirates lost the World Series in four straight to the Yankees, Kremer was one of the league's leaders, winning 19, 15, 18 and 20 games.

He fell to 11-15 in 1931 and was 5-3 over the next season-and-a-half before Pittsburgh released Ray on July 7, 1933. He rejoined the Oaks two weeks later. Kremer's skills had eroded and Oakland needed to give its pitching starts to prospects they could sell. Kremer had a 1-5 mark in 1933 and was 0-1 when he was cut early the following season.

Kremer continued to go the route after baseball as a mailman in Berkeley for many years.

LYN LARY

Shortstop Lyn Lary and his second base sidekick Jimmie Reese were insured for $100,000 by Oakland, presumably to cover the amount paid by the New York Yankees for the much heralded keystone combination.

Sadly, they weren't worth anywhere near amount to the Yankees. Lary played only two seasons as a regular with the Bronx Bombers near the start of his 12-year career and Reese was out of the majors after three seasons as a part-timer.

When Lary came into the Coast League as a 19-year-old fresh off the University of California campus, Oakland's management knew it had a shortstop with extraordinary potential. Tall and skinny, the kid from Visalia proved to be everything they hoped for.

The young Irishman — the family's name originally was O'Leary — broke into the lineup in June and shared the shortstop's chores with Jake Flowers, one of Oakland's leading offensive players. Lyn appeared in 70 games and couldn't match Flowers with the bat, averaging .257. But, he was third in fielding average right behind San Francisco's Hal Rhyne, acknowledged as one of the

LYNFORD HOBART LARY
Born: 1/28/06, Armona, CA, BR/TR, 6-foot, 165 pounds

		G	AB	R	H	2B	3B	HR	RBI	SB	AVG.
1925	Oak	70	241	30	62	9	1	0	21	6	.257
1926	Oak	170	566	55	143	19	5	7	44	6	.253
1927	Oak	195	765	124	224	40	12	12	102	12	.293
1928	Oak	167	614	79	193	34	10	7	94	19	.314
PCL		4 602	2186	288	622	102	28	26	261	43	.285
Majors	12	1302	4603	805	1239	247	56	38	526	162	.269

league's most skillful defenders.

Flowers graduated to the St. Louis Cardinals in 1926 and Lary was paired with Reese on a full-time basis. Lyn finished a disappointing last among the regular shortstops in fielding and didn't show well at the plate with a .253 average.

Lary showed in 1927 that a year's maturity and experience can make a world of difference for a young player. The Oaks took the pennant for the first time since 1912 largely on the strength of strong pitching and the best fielding in the league. Lary, Reese and first baseman John Fenton each led the league with their gloves as the *San Francisco Bulletin* pronounced the trio and veteran third sacker Ike Caveney, "the best infield in the Pacific Coast League in years."

Lary's offense improved appreciably. Lyn batted .293, scored 124 runs, knocked in 102 and banged out 40 doubles, 12 triples and 12 homers.

"If Willie Kamm was worth the hundred grand," said the *Bulletin's* Owen Merrick, "then Lary must be worth a grand or two more."

The Yankees agreed and took Lary and Reese in the package, but left both with Oakland because they already had a rock solid keystone combination with Tony Lazzeri at second base and Mark Koenig at shortstop.

Injuries caused Lary to play almost 30 fewer games in 1928 than the previous year. Lyn's average rose to a career high .314, but his other numbers fell off slightly.

The Yankees called him up in 1929 and Lyn hit .309 in a utility role while Leo Durocher held forth at shortstop. When Durocher was waived out of the league the following season, Lary took over and hit .289. Lyn had his best year in the majors the following season. Playing in all 155 games he was one of the top fielders and hit .280 with 100 runs scored and a team shortstop record of 107 RBIs.

Nicknamed "Broadway" by close friend Babe Ruth, Lary fit the bill with his flashy clothes and marriage to musical comedy star Mary Laylor. Lary was at the top of his game until Frank Crosetti arrived from the PCL. Crosetti shared the shortstop job with Lary in 1932 and took it away from him the following season.

After Lyn hit .220 as a reserve in 1933, the Yankees sold him to the Boston Red Sox, who sent Lary and $150,000 to Washington the following year for shortstop Joe Cronin.

Before 1935 was half over, Lary was passed along to the St. Louis Browns in a swap and was sent off to Cleveland in yet another trade in 1937. It's hard to understand why Lary moved so often. During this period he hit the ball adequately — averaging between .241 and .290 — and led the league in fielding once, in put outs twice and assists once.

After one more year as a regular with Cleveland, Lyn was a reserve again as his big league career wound to a close in 1940. He played two more seasons in the minors and retired.

TONY LAZZERI

Tony Lazzeri got his unusual nickname, "Poosh 'Em Up," during his stay in Salt Lake City, where he followed that instruction from the fans to push the ball over the fence a record 60 times.

The stories differ, but it seems clear that Tony was urged to "poosh 'em up" — hit the ball — either by an Italian fan, fans or restaurateur Tony Raffetti, who fed Tony spaghetti as an inducement to do well.

The lithe San Francisco let his bat do all his talking. One reporter complained that interviewing the shy and silent Lazzeri was, "like trying to mine coal with a nail file and a pair of scissors."

There's a story about Tony and his San Francisco teammates with the New York Yankees, Joe DiMaggio and Frank Crosetti. It's usually set either in the lobby of a hotel or in a car as the trio motored across country to the Florida training camp.

After sitting silent for an hour or more, DiMaggio cleared his throat. "What did he say?" Crosetti asked. "He didn't say nothing," replied Lazzeri. "Shut up."

If Lazzeri was uncommunicative, he was also a hard worker from San Francisco's tough Cow Hollow neighborhood. Tony was expelled from school in 1918 and his dad got him a job as a helper in a boiler factory. When he wasn't building his muscles as a boilermaker, Tony spent his leisure hours playing baseball. Lazzeri wanted to be a boxer, but his father stopped his first bout.

Somehow the San Francisco Seals ignored Lazzeri. A friend induced Salt Lake City manager Duffy Lewis to give Tony a tryout and Lazzeri accepted a $250-a-month contract in 1922, hitting .192 in 78 times at bat. After spending most of the next season at Peoria, Lazzeri played 39 games with the Bees and hit .354 with seven homers.

A robust swinger, Lazzeri blasted 28 home runs at Lincoln in the Western League and returned to hit 16 more in Salt Lake City's thin desert air in the second half of 1924.

Lazzeri and Lewis did not get along particularly well, but third sacker Ossie Vitt was named manager in 1925 when Lewis went to Portland. Although Tony had played everywhere in the infield and showed he could cover ground and had a strong arm, Lazzeri preferred to play second base. The Bees had Johnny Kerr there, however, so Lazzeri spent most of 1925 — his only full season in the PCL — playing shortstop.

Vitt smoothed off some of Lazzeri's rough edges as a fielder, although he led the league in errors. Vitt didn't have to do anything to improve Tony's hitting. Lazzeri was averaging in the mid-.400s at the end of April, although his home run total wasn't out of the ordinary.

By early June, Tony's batting average had dropped from the stratosphere to a more mundane .346. His home run total stood at 11 when the Bees started a long home stand. Lazzeri — who hit 39 of his 60 homers at Salt Lake City — produced 12 in the next 18 days before the Bees went on the road again and was never headed in the race for the home run title.

Lazzeri came into the season's final double-header at Sacramento in October needing one to reach 60 homers and break Babe Ruth's "world's record" of 59. He already had shattered the PCL mark of 43, set in 1923 by the Bees' Paul Strand.

In the last game of the year, Sacramento pitcher Frank

Tony Lazzeri

ANTHONY MICHAEL LAZZERI
Born: 12/6/03, San Francisco, CA, BR/TR,
5-foot-11.5, 170 pounds

		G	AB	R	H	2B	3B	HR	RBI	SB	AVG.
1922	SLC	45	78	9	15	4	2	1	8	0	.192
1923	SLC	39	130	25	46	7	1	7	21	4	.354
1924	SLC	85	293	51	83	15	3	16	61	8	.283
1925	SLC	197	710	202	252	52	14	60	222	39	.355
1941	SF	102	315	40	78	22	3	3	39	5	.248
PCL	5	468	1526	327	474	100	23	87	351	56	.311
Majors	14	1740	6297	986	1840	334	115	178	1191	148	.292

Shellenback grooved the ball on purpose and when Lazzeri hit a liner, outfielder Bill Cunningham trotted after the ball so his San Francisco pal could circle the bases with ease. In addition to his homer record, Lazzeri also set an Organized Baseball mark with 222 RBIs while batting .355 with 202 runs and 52 doubles.

Scouts wondered about the effects Salt Lake City's high altitude had on Tony's batting statistics. While they hesitated, New York Yankees scout Bill Essick became more enthusiastic and the Yanks bought him for $55,000 cash

---

"Like trying to mine coal with a nail file and a pair of scissors."
— *Reporter describing an interview with Tony Lazzeri*

---

and players.

It was a great deal. Lazzeri gave New York 12 good seasons as their second baseman. The Yankees won six titles during the period and Tony contributed heavily to their success.

Lazzeri batted .292 for New York with five years above .300 and seven 100-plus RBI seasons. In his best year in 1929, Tony batted .354 with 106 runs batted in and finished second to Al Simmons in the most valuable player balloting. In his best single day performance in 1936, Lazzeri hit two grand slams and drove in a record 11 runs against Philadelphia.

Lazzeri is remembered for being struck out with the bases loaded by Grover Cleveland Alexander of the St. Louis Cardinals in the pivotal play of the 1926 World Series. Like Alexander, Lazzeri was afflicted with epilepsy that he struggled to keep under control.

Tony lost the second base job to Joe Gordon in 1938 and played out the string as a reserve with Chicago, Brooklyn and New York in the National League.

He managed Toronto in parts of 1939 and 1940 and joined San Francisco in 1941, hitting .248 in 102 games before his release. Lazzeri managed in the lower minors for two more seasons and retired to run a bar in San Francisco. He died when he was 42.

RED LUCAS

In the early days of his career, it seemed that everyone wanted to take the ball away from pitcher Red Lucas and replace it with a bat. That made sense, since Lucas was a decent hitter at any of the four positions he played occasionally and one of the best pinch hitters in baseball history.

Before his 16 seasons in the majors were completed, the little southpaw had set a career mark of 114 pinch hits that stood until Smoky Burgess broke it almost 30 years later.

The red-headed and jut-jawed Lucas, whose given name

Red Lucas

was Frederick, began traveling along the professional baseball trail in 1920. He was pitching on weekends in the Nashville municipal league when he joined the local Southern Association team and was shipped to the Georgia State League. He had a trial with Nashville the next year, but spent most of the season in the Mississippi State League, where he was 14-8 record in 24 appearances, played elsewhere in 23 games and hit .210.

Seventh place Nashville won only 56 games in 1922, but the New York Giants bought Lucas after he produced 20 wins and 18 losses with a .307 batting average.

Lucas didn't have much of a fast ball, but his soft curves and baffling change of pace were combined with extraordinary control. Red was considered too small to hold up under the rigors of major league pitching and manager John McGraw sent him to San Antonio with instructions to convert him to the outfield.

San Antonio had no place for him in the outfield on a team that hit .307 and was led by batting champ Ike Boone's .402, so Red pitched (18-9) and batted .285.

The Boston Braves bought him, but after pitching without distinction in relief in 1924, Red was included in a swap with Seattle. Boston acquired outfielder Jimmy Welsh from the Indians during the winter in a $50,000 trade for Lucas, two pitchers and cash.

The following spring, Braves manager Dave Bancroft

decided to take advantage of Red's strong batting capabilities by making him a second baseman. "The Braves think that Fred Lucas . . . at second base is the best looking young man they have had for that berth since (Johnny) Evers, raved *Sporting News* correspondent Burt Whitman. "He can hit, is fast, throws from any angle and, for a pitcher, he has an alert, quick pair of hands."

Lucas played six games at the keystone in the first month of the 1925 season before Seattle executives insisted that the Braves send Red to complete the Welsh deal.

The Indians didn't need Lucas at second, where the PCL's best fielder, C. F. Brady, resided and three of Seattle's best players were outfielders Brick Eldred, Bill Lane and Ernie McCabe.

Manager Red Killefer used all of Red's talents judiciously. Although he missed a month with a leg injury, Lucas appeared in 55 games for the Indians. He batted .386 in 70 trips to the plate as a pitcher, outfielder and pinch hitter. Used mostly as a closer out of the bullpen, Red compiled a 9-5 record in 121 innings and his ERA of 2.83 was third among pitchers who appeared in at least 100 frames.

One July series in San Francisco showcased all of Red's talents. Lucas appeared in five of the eight games. On Wednesday, he gave up only one run and a hit in 4 1/3 innings to collect a save. Two days later, Red ripped a three-run pinch hit homer in the eighth to win the game. On Saturday, he registered a save with two shutout innings.

Lucas appeared in both games of the Sunday twin bill. He got the win in a 20-12 victory with three innings of relief in the opener and pinch hit a two-run homer in the second game, lost by the Indians, 13-11.

"I've never seen a player deliver like Lucas," said Killefer after the series. "It sounds and reads like a chapter from Frank Merriwell."

Cincinnati liked the looks of this versatile player and brought him to spring camp in 1926. He was a reliever (8-5) as the Reds finished second. Cincinnati lived in the second division for seven more seasons and were seventh or eighth the last five. Red's record was 101-94 during the period.

He went to Pittsburgh in a trade in 1934. The Pirates were a much better team, first division caliber most of the time, and he compiled a 47-32 record in his last five seasons.

Red showed remarkable durability and control as a pitcher. He completed two thirds of his starts and led the league in complete games four times. Between August, 1931, and July, 1932, he completed 27 straight games and in the latter year finished 28 of 31. His career record of 1.6 walks per game is best in the last 75 years.

Lucas compiled a .281 lifetime batting average in 907 games. As the premiere big league pinch hitter he never led in percentage, but was tops in hits four years, times at bat three times and hit .261. His 114 pinch hits was nearly double the number compiled by the second best pinch hitting pitcher, Red Ruffing.

Leaving the majors after 1938, Lucas continued to play, coach and manage in the minors, primarily with teams in the South, until 1949. His last year as a pinch hitter was 1945 at Nashville, where he had 16 hits in 38 official appearances plus 11 walks for a .421 average. He might have done better, but the 43-year-old Lucas was removed from the roster to make way for younger players. He later was a truck inspector for the State of Tennessee and a deputy sheriff.

EARL McNEELY

To keep his ball club operating in the Coast League's smallest market, Sacramento owner Lew Moreing had to discover and develop inexpensive local talent that could be sold to major league teams.

During the 14 years he controlled the Senators, Moreing made a profit selling many Sacramento-area players, including Earl Kunz, Myril Hoag, Stan Hack, Frank Demaree and Hank Steinbacher.

One of the first of his recruits to rise to the top was outfielder Earl McNeely. Moreing had sold pitcher Kunz to Pittsburgh in 1922 for $7,500 and four players, but the McNeely sale, consummated two years later with the Washington Senators, was the first really big payday for Sacramento. It brought $35,000 cash and three players valued at $5,000 each. Washington also loaned outfielder Wid Matthews to Sacramento for the remainder of the 1924 season.

McNeely, a fleet-footed and sure-handed fly chaser, was a key player in Washington's drive for its first American League pennant. Earl was not up to par when he arrived in the nation's capital in August, suffering from a shoulder injury he'd received during his last week in the PCL.

Washington owner Clark Griffith was upset and demanded that Moreing take McNeely back. Griffith tried to void the deal through an appeal to Baseball Commissioner Kenesaw Mountain Landis, but the commissioner ruled that McNeely deserved some time to recover.

Earl started slowly, performing as a pinch hitter in the

CHARLES FREDERICK LUCAS
Born: 4/28/02, Columbia, TN, BL/TR, 5-foot-9.5, 170 pounds

		W	L	PCT	G	IP	H	ER	BB	SO	ERA
1925	Seat	9	5	.643	26	121	119	38	33	47	2.83
PCL		1 9	5	.643	26	121	119	38	33	47	2.83
Majors 16#		157	135	.538	396	2543	2736	1053	455	602	3.72

Lucas pitched 15 seasons and in 1925 appeared only at second base.

Earl McNeely

beginning. Success coming off the bench led manager Bucky Harris to put McNeely in the outfield and he batted .330 in 43 games.

The Senators won the pennant in a close race against New York and Detroit and took on the New York Giants in the World Series. McNeely played in all seven games and started six as Washington's lead-off batter. He batted .222 on six hits in 27 at bats, but his last blow was the most important of the Fall Classic.

It came in the 12th inning of the seventh and deciding game. McNeely stepped to the plate with the score tied at three with one out, Muddy Ruel on second and Walter Johnson on first. McNeely bounced a routine grounder toward third baseman Fred Lindstrom. As Lindstrom bent down, the ball hit a pebble and bounded over his head for the game-winning hit.

McNeely was an unlikely hero in some respects. Although he was 26, Earl was playing only his third year of professional ball. He had been regarded as too small to make the team in high school. After serving with an Army engineering unit in World War II, McNeely came home to Sacramento and got a job as a surveyor with the state highway department.

Winter was a slow time for the department, so Earl played with a clothing store team in the Sacramento Winter League for three seasons before winning a tryout with the Senators in 1922.

The Senators finished a distant eighth, 51 1/2 games behind champion San Francisco. Sacramento was last in team batting, helped to that unenviable position by McNeely's .213 average in 106 games.

Sacramento improved greatly in 1923 and rose to second place. McNeely was injured part of the year, but appeared in 75 games, batting .333 with 20 steals. Earl led outfield-

---

> *"(Earl) McNeely plays the game for all he is worth. He is out there hustling every minute of the game and is not afraid to take chances."*
> — *Abe Kemp in the San Francisco Bulletin*

---

ers with only one error and was a regular in the outer garden the following season.

"McNeely plays the game for all he is worth," said Abe Kemp in the *San Francisco Bulletin*. "He is out there hustling every minute of the game and is not afraid to take chances."

Earl fielded well again the following season and duplicated his .333 batting average with 33 doubles in 112 games when Washington bought his contract. He stayed in the American League for eight seasons, the last four with St. Louis.

McNeely was a regular in Washington in 1925 and 1926, batting .303 the latter season. After hitting .276 as a part-timer in 1927, the Senators traded him to the Browns. He hit only .236 as a full-time player his first season and played a back-up role the rest of the time.

Earl returned to the Sacramento outfield in 1932, batting .281 in 100 contests. Long-time manager Buddy Ryan quit on Aug. 4 with the team in sixth place and Moreing named Earl as his replacement. McNeely directed the Senators to a third place finish. Sacramento was fourth the following year as McNeely appeared as a reserve, batting .308 in 94 games.

Three banks took over the ball club in 1934 when Moreing could not make loan payments and McNeely was

---

GEORGE EARL MC NEELY
Born: 5/12/98, Sacramento, CA, BR/TR, 5-foot-9, 155 pounds

		G	AB	R	H	2B	3B	HR	RBI	SB	AVG.
1922	Sac	106	315	29	67	8	1	0	15	10	.213
1923	Sac	75	213	35	71	11	0	1	27	20	.333
1924	Sac	112	460	93	153	33	4	8	41	14	.333
1932	Sac	100	377	55	106	25	1	1	28	6	.281
1933	Sac	94	279	79	86	18	2	5	20	15	.308
1934	Sac	26	38	4	11	2	0	0	6	0	.289
PCL	6	513	1682	295	494	97	8	15	137	65	.294
Majors	8	683	2254	369	614	107	33	4	213	68	.272

named team president. PCL president Hy Baggerly praised McNeely's selection: "(He) is popular, knows baseball and showed a quality of leadership after he took hold of the club as manager. I confidently expect a revival of interest in baseball in Sacramento."

McNeely had little time to play, hitting .289 in just 26 games and in 1935 turned the managerial reins over to veteran catcher Kettle Wirts. After the team lost nine straight to fall to last place on June 1, McNeely fired Wirts in an economy move and became manager. The Senators were last in both halves of the season and were on the verge of being moved out of the city late in the year when the St. Louis Cardinals bought the franchise.

McNeely returned to Washington as a coach in 1936 and 1937.

DOUG McWEENY

The bad news for Doug McWeeny in 1922 was that he was being sent back down to the minor leagues, in this case halfway across America to the Pacific Coast League.

The good news was that the slender pitcher was going to San Francisco, where he would work three of the next four seasons and produce a 55-24 win-loss record for a stunning .696 percentage.

In addition to generating the best three seasons of his dozen years playing for pay, McWeeny also exceeded the odds in the pennant department as the Seals raced to a trio of championships during his time with the team.

McWeeny tried out with Marshalltown in the Central Association in 1917, but inked his first contract two seasons later.

Doug began his professional career with Evansville in the Three I League and showed an excellent overhand fast ball and curve by striking out 187 batters in 263 innings. His 18-15 record and 3.05 earned run average moved him up to Milwaukee in the American Association late in the year.

A 15-14 record at Milwaukee in a full season in 1920 led to his purchase by the Chicago White Sox. The Sox used him as a reliever for a 3-6 mark the following year and were employing him in the same role at the beginning of 1922.

Doug and two other White Sox pitchers were shipped to San Francisco at the end of May as part of a $100,000 transaction for third baseman Willie Kamm. The other hurlers, Shovel Hodge and Harry Courtney, became San Francisco property and never returned to the majors, but the White Sox thought McWeeny might still make it and sent him out west on option.

The lanky Scotsman, who sometimes was called "Buzz," started and relieved with San Francisco as the Seals took the title by four games over Vernon. McWeeny had 15 wins and seven losses with a 2.78 ERA.

The Seals repeated in 1923 and McWeeny was one of three 20-game winners on their staff with a 20-12 record. His 160 strikeouts led the team and was the league's third

Doug McWeeny

highest total.

Chicago recalled Doug in 1924, but after producing a disappointing 1-3 record in 13 games he was sent to Milwaukee in a trade and fashioned an indifferent 6-9 record.

The Seals had finished a close third in 1924 and were pleased to buy McWeeny from the Brewers the following season. His acquisition helped San Francisco become one of the best teams in Coast League history. The Seals won by 12 1/2 games over Salt Lake City. Seven of their pitchers won a dozen or more games and four — including McWeeny with a career best 20-5 — hung up at least 20 wins. McWeeny and teammate Marty Griffin (16-4) tied as the league's percentage leaders at .800 and Doug took the ERA title at 2.70.

DOUGLAS LAWRENCE MC WEENY
Born: 8/17/96, Chicago, IL, BR/TR, 6-foot-2, 190 pounds

		W	L	PCT	G	IP	H	ER	BB	SO	ERA
1922	SF	15	7	.682	31	175	161	54	59	130	2.78
1923	SF	20	12	.625	48	253	272	110	73	160	3.91
1925	SF	20	5	.800	49	263	239	79	78	175	2.70
PCL	3	55	24	.696	128	691	672	243	210	465	3.16
Majors	8	37	57	.394	206	948	980	439	450	386	4.17

Doug might have won more games and pitched more than 263 innings, but he damaged his shoulder and, when he recovered, suffered an ankle injury. Doug worked out of the bullpen for a month after his return before regaining his starting assignment.

Brooklyn drafted McWeeny and put him in the starting rotation for four seasons. The Dodgers finished sixth each year and Doug's 33-45 record reflected that. His best season of 14-14 was in 1928, but his control faltered as he walked 114 and struck out only 79.

In 1930, Doug was sent to Cincinnati, who moved him to Columbus with an 0-2 record. His career ended when he refused to report.

JIMMY O'CONNELL

Jimmy O'Connell was happy-go-lucky, popular, honest and an accomplished hitter. But, most of all, O'Connell was incredibly naive. And, naivete cost Jimmy his baseball career.

O'Connell polished his game on Sacramento's playgrounds as a youngster. By 1919, he was playing center field for the Santa Clara University baseball team in a program that had turned out many outstanding Coast League and major league players, including Hal Chase, Justin Fitzgerald, Bobby Keefe, Tillie Schaffer and Harry Wolter.

San Francisco co-owner Alfie Putnam spotted O'Connell in a Sacramento semi-pro game late in the summer and persuaded Jimmy's father to let him join the Seals. Jimmy made the last road trip of the year with San Francisco, pumping out 10 hits in eight games for a .313 average.

Jimmy rode the bench early in 1920. He had a brief outfield trial, but showed little mastery of the position and demonstrated only a fair throwing arm so manager Charlie Graham sent him back to the pine.

First baseman Phil Koerner quit the Seals halfway through the season, complaining he could no longer stand abuse from the fans. O'Connell went to first base, but was near the bottom of the fielding table after 16 games when the Seals acquired Bob Hasbrook from Des Moines to man the initial sack and Jimmy moved back to the outfield.

At the end of the season, Hasbrook said he wanted to retire from baseball and Graham decided to start 1921 with O'Connell — who had hit a modest .262 with little power in 102 contests — at first base.

O'Connell was an unfinished product at the infield's gateway post. He played ground balls fairly well and handled accurate throws nicely. But, he showed a marked uncertainty at fielding any toss that was off the mark and sometimes seemed bewildered about where to position himself. Jimmy led the league in errors with 40 in 170 games.

O'Connell never was much to rave about with his glove at any position. In 1921, he showed why his bat kept him in the lineup. Jimmy led the regulars with a .337 mark and 101 runs batted in. O'Connell had a good eye at the plate, drew many walks and showed signs of developing some

power with 32 doubles and 17 home runs.

John McGraw wanted O'Connell and shelled out the unheard of sum of $75,000. There were reports the Giants were willing to pay the record amount for a minor league player because it was better to spend the money on a prospect with potential than turn it over to Uncle Sam in taxes.

What they got for their money was the most attractive young batter in the Coast League, a dangerous two-strike hitter who grew stronger each season and was fast on his feet.

But, Jimmy was a project with many rough edges. O'Connell's main flaw was a lack of hustle that put his intensity into question. Putnam told McGraw that Jimmy, "was not the most aggressive player," but the Giants manager replied, "if he's got the ability . . . I'll supply the pepper."

In 1922, Jimmy once again showed he had the potential to become a big league star. He was batting better than .400 near the middle of the Coast League season, but slumped to .335 with 39 two-base hits, 10 triples, 13 homers and 39 stolen bases.

Jimmy was a reserve with the Giants in 1923, playing in 87 games, primarily in the outfield where his work improved. But, he batted only .250 and the newspapers dubbed him "the $75,000 bust." O'Connell seemed to regain his batting stroke in 1924 when he hit .317 in 52 games up to the final weekend of the year as the Giants fought off Brooklyn in their quest for a fourth straight National League title.

Before the Giants-Phillies game on Sept. 27, O'Connell walked up to Philadelphia infielder Heinie Sand and offered $500, "if you don't bear down too hard against us today." Sand, a former Salt Lake City player who knew Jimmy from their days in the Coast League, angrily rejected the bribe and reported the offer to manager Art Fletcher.

The Giants clinched the pennant by beating the Phillies, but within days Commissioner Kenesaw Mountain Landis

JAMES JOSEPH O'CONNELL
Born: 2/11/01, Sacramento, CA, BL/TR, 5-foot-10.5, 175 pounds

		G	AB	R	H	2B	3B	HR	RBI	SB	AVG.
1919	SF	8	32	3	10	1	0	0	—	0	.313
1920	SF	102	305	28	80	6	6	0	—	5	.262
1921	SF	170	600	113	202	32	9	17	101	23	.337
1922	SF	187	671	133	225	39	10	13	92	39	.335
PCL	4	467	1608	277	517	78	25	30	193*	67	.322
Majors	2	139	356	66	96	13	4	8	57	9	.270

* incomplete

67

was investigating the incident. When Landis questioned O'Connell, Jimmy readily admitted the bribe attempt, but said he was acting on orders from New York coach Cozy Dolan and that teammates Frank Frisch, Ross Youngs and George Kelly all knew about the offer. O'Connell was puzzled by the furor since Sand had turned down the proposal and the game was played on the square.

Dolan told Landis he could not remember anything about his conversation with O'Connell and the three stars denied any knowledge of the fix, although Frisch remarked there "always was a lot of kidding going on on every bench." Landis rejected requests to cancel the World Series or substitute runner-up Brooklyn for the Giants and banned O'Connell and Dolan for life.

Everyone who knew Jimmy was shocked by the story. Putnam said he "could hardy believe that O'Connell would do something like that." San Francisco manager Bert Ellison spoke for many when he described Jimmy as, "a swell kid, a likable chap, a conscientious ball player admired by every one of his teammates."

When O'Connell came home to San Francisco two weeks later, he stepped off the ferry boat from Oakland and spoke at an impromptu press conference: "I know now that I did wrong. Yet I didn't think it was wrong when I did it. I thought Dolan was representing the New York club and I was obeying orders."

After Sand rejected the fix, O'Connell said Dolan didn't seem upset and remarked, "We'll beat them anyway."

"The affair passed out of my mind," Jimmy added. "I was surprised when Landis sent for me . . . (and) I didn't think of denying what had happened for I didn't realize there was any harm done. I'm the goat, that's all."

In a postscript to the scandal a few weeks later, Kelly of the Giants and fellow San Franciscan Sammy Bohne of the Cincinnati Reds agreed to play with a San Francisco professional basketball team that had O'Connell on its roster. Complaints were made and Jimmy was dismissed from the team. He organized Jimmy O'Connell's All-Stars and played against Northern California semi-pro baseball teams and later appeared in the outlaw Copper League in the Southwest with such notable fixers as Chick Gandil and Hal Chase.

O'Connell lived his last 34 years in Bakersfield where he worked for the Atlantic-Richfield oil company.

BABE PINELLI

A leopard may not be able to change its spots, but Babe Pinelli's remarkable attitude adjustment led to a 25-year career as one of baseball's best umpires after 16 seasons as a player.

Pinelli was well known for a belligerent and feisty demeanor when he was a third baseman in the Coast League and the majors. The pugnacious Pinelli fought foes on the field and off.

Babe even took on his manager early in his career. Pinelli and Sacramento skipper Bill "Raw Meat" Rodgers

Jimmy O'Connell

Ralph Pinelli
INFIELDER CINCINNATI N.L.

Babe Pinelli

differed over a $50 fine in 1919 and moved their argument into the clubhouse. Pinelli beat Rodgers badly. But the skipper, who had managed Pinelli as a PCL rookie at Portland the year before, downplayed the disagreement and they seemed to get along well after the fight.

Pinelli engaged in another locked door brawl with manager Jack Hendricks eight years later with the Cincinnati Reds. And in only his second game in the big leagues with the White Sox, Pinelli was thumbed out of the game for complaining about a strike call.

Pinelli's aggressiveness can be traced to his childhood in San Francisco. Born Rinaldo Angelo Paolinelli, Babe's prosperous merchant father was killed when a telephone pole fell on him during the 1906 San Francisco earthquake.

The death left Pinelli's mother nearly destitute with three young children, so 10-year-old Rinaldo — later called Ralph — and his brother, Orlando, quit school and went to work. Babe was an errand boy, a newsboy, an iron worker and a sign painter.

Pinelli hung around with group of older boys who tagged him with the nickname "Babe." It was a tough crowd and Pinelli's aggressive behavior often got him in trouble with the law and he was taken to the police station in a paddy wagon several times. He boxed as an amateur, accepting money under the table because professional fights were banned in San Francisco at the time.

His life changed in December, 1916, when he married Mabel McKee. She persuaded Ralph to quit both his job and boxing and try for a professional baseball career. Pinelli had gained a reputation as a good hit, mediocre field infielder playing on local playgrounds and in semi-pro games. Sportswriter Tommy Laird persuaded Portland to take a look at Pinelli. Babe was cut, but returned to training camp in 1917 where he competed with Paddy Siglin, an everyday player and a superior fielder. Pinelli got into 79 games, but batted only .199.

Fearful that the long distance between the Rose City and other communities would bankrupt them, Coast League magnates moved the Portland franchise to Sacramento in 1918. Babe and six other former Portland players went to California's capital with the ball club. He hit .267 and was sold to the Chicago White Sox, where he batted .231 and made 11 errors in 24 games at the hot corner.

Returned to Sacramento in 1919, Babe improved at bat and in the field and pilfered a personal best 51 bases on a club that stole 230. He moved up to Detroit in 1920, but failed at the plate with a .229 average in 102 games and was sent to Oakland.

One of Pinelli's new teammates was Denny Wiley. Although they had fought on the field years before, Babe became friends with the outfielder, who said he'd teach Pinelli how to hit. Wiley made Babe use a golf club to understand the idea of following through with his swing and a 40 ounce bat to learn timing and bat control. Babe had his best year, stroking the ball at a .339 clip and scoring 127 runs.

All his hitting didn't come with a bat and on May 21 Babe smashed the Coast League's famous singing umpire,

William "Lord" Byron, in the eye and knocked him down. Pinelli was fined and suspended for five days.

Cincinnati needed a replacement for Heinie Groh, who had been traded to the New York Giants, and bought Pinelli for $35,000 and three players. He hit .287 over five years playing with San Francisco infield pals Ike Caveney and Sammy Bohne. Pinelli had calmed down by the time he reached the majors this time and he was ejected only once for arguing with an umpire, although he was thrown out for fighting with players.

After playing 30 games in the sixth season, the Reds sold him to San Francisco for $17,500. Babe played everywhere in the infield except first base when he returned. For three more seasons he was a fixture at third base, batting .310, .311 and .313. He was dealt to Oakland part way through 1931 and finished there in 1932, posting a .307 average.

While he batted .295 in a decade in the Coast League, Babe was never a power hitter. He had only 13 home runs in 1,289 games in the league, but three came in the second game of a 1929 Independence Day twin bill. Pinelli ignited his personal fireworks in a 22-10 romp over Seattle. He went six for six with the three boundary belts — which included two grand slams — and a dozen RBIs. Later, Pinelli explained that Seattle rookie catcher Charlie Borreani tipped off pitches by the way he held the glove, straight up for a fast ball and down in a scoop position for a curve. "I knew what was coming every time," said the observant Babe.

Pinelli thought about life after his playing career ended and became interested in the umpire's work when he was at Cincinnati, frequently talking to arbiters about their duties and experiences. He worked as a volunteer umpire during spring training games.

Nearly 37 at the end of the 1932 season, Pinelli asked PCL President Hy Baggerly to hire him as an umpire. It was an unlikely request given Babe's hot head reputation. Although he was a genial, likable fellow away from the game, many thought his temperament made him unsuitable to be an arbiter. He had even been tossed out of his last game in the PCL. Baggerly told Babe to get some experi-

RALPH ARTHUR PINELLI
Born: 10/18/95, San Francisco, CA, BR/TR, 5-foot-9, 165 pounds

		G	AB	R	H	2B	3B	HR	RBI	SB	AVG.
1917	Port	79	211	21	42	5	2	0	—	8	.199
1918	Sac	94	348	40	93	9	6	0	—	15	.267
1919	Sac	150	548	76	138	20	3	1	—	51	.252
1921	Oak	181	720	127	244	38	5	2	57	47	.339
1927	SF	49	142	20	46	5	2	0	14	2	.324
1928	SF	114	422	62	131	26	0	2	31	3	.310
1929	SF	167	679	109	211	34	4	5	65	12	.311
1930	SF	140	579	95	181	22	1	3	55	16	.313
1931	SF-Ok	155	553	71	148	29	6	0	63	11	.268
1932	Oak	160	554	57	170	26	2	0	57	16	.307
PCL		10	1289	4756	678	1404	214	31	13	342*	181	.295
Majors		8	774	2617	327	723	101	33	5	298	80	.276

* incomplete

ence and hired him in 1933 after watching his progress in the San Francisco Winter League and spring training games.

Babe was assigned to an umpiring crew with veteran Perle Casey, an arbiter Pinelli described as, "the best at handling players I've ever seen." Casey had some simple advice for the belligerent Babe: "I don't want to see you get mad, Babe, until I do." The next season he learned some more working with colorful ex-big league ump Bill Guthrie. After two years, Pinelli had gained a reputation as a capable umpire who was respected by the players. The National League bought his contract in 1935 and he started a 23-year career behind the mask in the majors.

Pinelli was proud of his durability. Babe never missed an assignment in more than 3,400 major league games, although he came close at least twice.

One was on opening day in Brooklyn in 1945. Pinelli lifted the telephone in his hotel room to tell the league he was too ill to work when a driving rainstorm washed away the game. Earlier, Pinelli and his umpiring crew traveled from New York to Boston on a boat and were fogged in at sea. Pinelli wired Braves manager Casey Stengel that they would be late and the umpires arrived in the second inning to take over from players who filled in for the tardy crew. "You're still fog bound," Stengel shouted at Pinelli in later years whenever he thought Babe had missed a call.

These taunts did not deter Pinelli from becoming a great umpire and one who never showed his former ill temper. He rarely tossed out protesting players, perhaps because he knew how they felt. "The players thought a lot of him," said National League President Warren Giles.

Babe worked four All-Star games and six World Series. He closed his career as plate umpire in one of the most exciting games in World Series history, calling Don Larsen's 1956 perfect game for the Yankees over Brooklyn.

Giles told Pinelli that he could continue working, but Babe declined. "If I went on, I might become a bad umpire," he said. "I wouldn't want to finish that way."

HAL RHYNE

Hal Rhyne was a magician who transfixed Coast League fans with his outstanding glove work for nine seasons, but who couldn't hit big league pitching well enough to make a name for himself at the top.

Rhyne batted .288 lifetime with the San Francisco Seals, 38 points higher than his career mark in the majors. When he was with the Boston Red Sox in 1930 — a year when the entire American League averaged .288 at the plate — Rhyne hit only .203, the lowest mark for anyone appearing in at least 100 games.

His value as a fielder allowed him to bring home a major league paycheck for seven seasons, but for a long time it looked like Hal might never get a shot at playing in The Show.

Hal graduated from San Jose High School and sharpened

Hal Rhyne

his game with Santa Clara Valley semi-pro teams. San Francisco paid the San Jose Merchants team $350 for Rhyne and teammate Gene Valla in 1921 and sent Hal to Des Moines in the Class A Western League, where he hit .311.

Back with the Seals in 1922, Hal looked good at short-stop from the very start. "He goes to either side and he throws from all positions and with force," wrote Abe Kemp in the *San Francisco Bulletin*. "Another point you don't want to overlook is the boy will get better." Kemp noted that Rhyne had one bad habit at the plate. "He runs up on all pitches rather than taking a firm position at bat. Good hitters of this type are rare."

Rhyne batted .285, the lowest of any every day player on the Seals, who hit .298 as a team and took the pennant from Vernon by four games.

Hal's batting average and his value to the Seals rose annually to .315 over the next three seasons. A line drive hitter with average power, fans began comparing Rhyne to Jimmy Caveney, the best shortstop in San Francisco history, who had been sold to Cincinnati in 1921. The wide-ranging Rhyne's glove work improved and he led the PCL in put outs, assists and fielding average in 1924 and 1925.

At the beginning of 1925, Rhyne predicted, "this is going to be my last year in the minors." The scouts knew he could field with the best, but had grave doubts about his hitting. The real decision came down to money.

"If you pay big money for a ball player, you expect him to help you in every department of the game," said

Yankees scout Eddie Holly. "My interest in Rhyne will center largely on what they ask for him."

Hal and outfielder Paul Waner were sold to Pittsburgh at the end of the season for a reported $100,000. Given the fact that Waner had led the league with a .401 average and a remarkable 75 doubles, Rhyne's share of the price tag was regarded as minimal.

The Pirates already had one of the best shortstops in the business, Glenn Wright, so they tried to make a second baseman out of Rhyne. He played in 109 games, including

---

"My interest in (Hal) Rhyne will center largely on what they ask for him."

— Scout Eddie Holly

---

66 at second, hitting .251 for the second place Bucs. His average improved to .274 in 1927. But, Hal was a utility player and appeared in only 62 regular season games and one in the World Series, where Pittsburgh was swept in four games by a great New York Yankees team.

Hal was sold to the Seals at the end of the year and it looked like his days in the major leagues were over. Rhyne batted .312 with 106 runs batted in as the Seals won the championship with a victory over second half champion Sacramento.

The Philadelphia Athletics drafted Rhyne, but sold him to the Boston Red Sox, where he started at shortstop for three years. Hal fielded well, set the pace in fielding average and assists in 1931, but his batting remained suspect at .251, .203 and .273.

Shortstop Rabbit Warstler hit only .211 with the BoSox in 1932, but still got the call over Rhyne, who was tops at fielding the position and sported a .227 batting average.

Rhyne went to the Chicago White Sox in 1933 as part of a six-player trade. He played 38 games and returned to the Coast League in 1934 for his last four seasons. Hal was among the fielding leaders annually and hit .294 and .255 twice.

Bob Ray of the *Los Angeles Times* paid him a compli-

HAROLD J. RHYNE
Born: 3/30/99, Paso Robles, CA, BR/TR, 5-foot-8.5, 163 pounds

		G	AB	R	H	2B	3B	HR	RBI	SB	AVG.
1922	SF	189	699	80	199	39	8	0	93	19	.285
1923	SF	168	611	94	181	26	4	5	77	21	.296
1924	SF	196	751	110	224	34	2	2	80	26	.298
1925	SF	188	724	109	228	48	3	3	97	17	.315
1928	SF	185	692	82	216	37	0	6	106	17	.312
1934	SF	184	675	78	174	34	7	0	65	15	.258
1935	SF	150	523	78	154	34	2	1	81	12	.294
1936	SF	137	518	75	132	22	2	1	53	11	.255
1937	SF	121	416	53	106	22	1	0	46	3	.255
1938	SF	5	1	0	0	0	0	0	0	0	.000
PCL	10	1523	5610	759	1614	296	29	18	698	141	.288
Majors	7	655	2031	252	508	98	22	2	192	13	.250

---

ment, calling Rhyne, "The Jigger Statz of Coast League shortstops (who) goes along playing great ball year after year."

Rhyne retired early in 1938 and spent two years managing Tacoma in the Western International League. For the next 25 years until his retirement in 1965, Rhyne was a guard at Folsom Prison.

CHARLIE ROOT

If Babe Ruth pointed to the Wrigley Field bleachers before hitting his "called shot" homer in the World Series, Charlie Root never saw it, because if he had, Charlie would have knocked the Bambino down with the next pitch.

"I'd have loosened him up," said the tobacco-chewing Root. "Nobody facing me would have gotten away with that."

The compactly-built Root contended Ruth was saying, "there's one more strike" and gesturing at Charlie to emphasize the point in the famous 1929 incident between the Yankees and the Cubs.

It makes sense, because Root had a reputation as a strong willed fireballer and a notorious headhunter. Cubs manager Charlie Grimm was so taken by Root's jaw-thrusting belligerence that he called him "Chinski."

Root was tough because he had to grow up early in life. He quit school at 13 and drove a grocery wagon in Middletown, Ohio. When he got a job as a pattern maker, Root began to play baseball for the shop team. He graduated to the town team at $5-a-game and won a $35-a-week job throwing for a company nine.

Former St. Louis Browns pitcher Carl Weilman saw him perform and the Browns sent Charlie to Terre Haute in the Three I League in 1921. He broke a leg sliding into third base late in the year, but returned to Terre Haute the following season. Root's team took the title with Charlie contributing a 16-14 record and the second best ERA in the loop (2.28). Promoted in 1923, Root pitched 60 innings in relief for an 0-4 record with the Browns.

St. Louis first baseman George Sisler sat out the 1923 season in Los Angeles trying to recover from a sinus problem that impaired his vision. After watching pitcher George Lyons (18-16) and catcher Tony Rego (.281) perform for the Angels, Sisler persuaded St. Louis owner Phil Ball that acquisition of the battery would insure a pennant in 1924, when Sisler would return to the Browns as manager.

The Browns traded Root and four reserves to get the pair. Lyons went 3-2 and Rego played 44 games in the majors and both were back in the bushes in two years. With Root as their best pitcher, the Angels rose to second place in 1925 and fell back to fourth a year later.

When he arrived at the Los Angeles training camp in Long Beach in 1924, the trademarks of Root's game were a blazing fast ball, a nice change of pace and good control. Veteran pitcher Doc Crandall went to work to help Charlie

Charlie Root

perfect his curve.

Root won 12 of his last 14 as the Angels just missed catching Seattle for first place. He posted a 21-16 record and finished in the top ten with a 3.69 ERA. Root showed he was always ready to work, pitching 322 innings as a starter and reliever. He set down 199 batters on strikes, second best in the league.

The Cubs bought Root's contract, but when Rabbit Maranville broke an ankle during spring training, Chicago sent Charlie and infielder Pinky Pittenger back to L.A. in exchange for shortstop Jimmy McAuley. Root took the PCL strikeout crown with 211 in a career high 324 innings. He won 25, lost 13 and cut his earned run average to 2.86.

The Cubs brought Charlie up again in 1926. He became the bulwark of the Windy City club's pitching staff for 16

CHARLES HENRY ROOT
Born: 3/17/99, Middletown, OH, BR/TR, 5-foot-10.5, 190 pounds

		W	L	PCT	G	IP	H	ER	BB	SO	ERA
1924	LA	21	16	.568	55	322	316	132	102	199	3.69
1925	LA	25	13	.658	52	324	268	103	91	211	2.86
1942	Hwd	11	14	.440	30	215	205	76	39	103	3.18
1943	Hwd	15	5	.750	25	166	170	57	28	70	3.09
1944	Hwd	3	5	.375	21	87	91	31	28	58	3.22
PCL		5	75	53	.586| 183	1114	1050	399	288	641	3.22
Majors		17	201	160	.557| 632	3197	3252	1274| 889	1459	3.59

years, winning a team record 201 and losing 156 to go along with his four American League losses.

Charlie was a starter during the first eight seasons, a period in which the Cubs were always in the first division and won pennants in 1929 and 1932. He never won fewer than 14 games and had two fine years, 26-15 and a league-leading 309 innings pitched in 1927 and a 19-6 mark in 1929, when he lead the league with a .760 percentage.

Coming out of the bullpen in later years cut down Charlie's work load, but he still averaged 140 innings-a-year the rest of his career. The Cubs were among the leaders and won championships in 1935 and 1938. Charlie pitched in six games in four World Series and lost all three of his decisions.

At 42, Root was the big leagues' oldest player when the Cubs dropped him at the close of the 1941 season. The *Sporting News* predicted he would become a coach at the Cubs' affiliate in Los Angeles, but Charlie wasn't ready to quit the mound.

He signed with the Angels' cross-town rival in Hollywood, started fast with seven wins in eight starts and closed the season 11-14 in 215 innings.

The Stars took a chance on Charlie in 1943. Although he had no experience as a manager, they fired skipper Oscar Vitt and gave Root the job. Hollywood moved up to fifth place under his direction, but his biggest contribution was a 15-5 record, produced by pitching one game a week. The Stars slipped to sixth the following season as Charlie won only three games coming out of the bullpen.

Fired by Twinks owner Bob Cobb after the Stars folded near the end of the season, Root moved to Columbus in the International League, where he was deposed after two eighth place finishes. He managed three seasons in the lower minors and was a coach in Hollywood in 1949 and with the Chicago Cubs and Milwaukee Braves for five more seasons. Charlie retired after that to his Diamond R Ranch in Hollister, California.

SLOPPY THURSTON

When sportswriters picked their annual Pacific Coast League All-Star team in 1928, they deviated from custom by selecting a tenth man, naming Sloppy Thurston as their favorite utility player.

Thurston joined four other members of the champion San Francisco Seals on the All-Star squad, sharing the glory with pitcher Dutch Ruether and outfielders Earl Averill, Roy Johnson and Smead Jolley.

Hollis Thurston — nicknamed "Sloppy" as a child when he spilled milk on himself — had pitched in spots for a 9-7 record, pinch hit and played a few games in the outfield. But his major contribution to San Francisco's first half title and post-season playoff win over second half champion Sacramento came in 85 games at first base.

Thurston batted a lofty .347 in 129 games, the highest average of his 18 years in baseball. It was the fourth best average on the powerhouse Seals, who hit .308 as a team

Charlie Root with movie serial stars Red Ryder (left) and Little Beaver (played by Robert Blake).

behind PCL batting champ Jolley (.404) and his outfield cohorts, Johnson (.360) and Averill (.354).

Thurston had never played first base before, but he took over in June from light-hitting Solly Mishkin and racked up 26 doubles and 24 homers while knocking in 98 runs.

Sloppy played in more games off the mound (307) than he did as a pitcher (291) in a decade in the Coast League, because of the potency of his bat. Thurston carried a .276 average in the PCL with 74 doubles, 18 triples and 49 homers and was an effective hurler who won 106 games and lost 96.

His major league pitching figures over nine seasons were similar (89-86) and he also was an outstanding batter, hitting above .300 four times and compiling a .270 lifetime mark with a .383 slugging average.

Thurston played outlaw ball in Arizona in 1919 and broke into Organized Baseball with Salt Lake City in 1920 when he was 19. The Bees were an strong offensive aggregation playing at high altitude and in a relatively small ball park.

Sloppy went 9-13 and 7-13 in his first two years with the team with earned run averages that reflected both his inexperience and being forced to work in that pitcher's nightmare called Bonneville Park. He struck out more batters than he walked and his ERAs of 4.38 and 5.58 were among the league's highest.

By 1922, Sloppy appeared to be gaining command of his fast ball and curve. His change of pace and control improved and Thurston won 15 and lost 16 with a 4.31 ERA — misreported as 3.91 by the league — that was well down on the PCL list again. Thurston's batting average was below his career mark all three years, but the Bees called on him to pinch hit and play in the outfield.

Thurston started 1923 with the St. Louis Browns, but was sold to the Chicago White Sox after he'd worked two games and finished at 7-8. The White Sox were last for the first time the next year, but Sloppy was one of only four American league pitchers to reach the 20-win mark with a 20-14 record and 3.80 earned run average. His control was suspect and he walked 60 and struck only 37 to show a pattern that continued most of his career.

Thurston's ERA ballooned to 5.95 the next season as he

Sloppy Thurston

went 10-14 and stayed above 5.00 in a 6-8 year that followed. The Sox traded him early in 1927 with pitcher Leo Mangum to Washington for shortstop Roger Peckinpaugh. A 13-13 season with the Senators led to Thurston's release and he went with San Francisco, thinking his major league career had ended.

After his all-star utility season in 1928, Sloppy won 22 games for the Seals the next year and hit .302 in 182 at bats — which included appearances off the bench and in the outfield — and he was drafted by Brooklyn.

The Dodgers used him in relief to begin with, but Thurston broke into the rotation when they ran out of starters and went 6-4. After winning 27 and losing 25 in three more seasons, the Dodgers sent him to St. Paul. The San Francisco Mission team bought Sloppy after he expressed a desire to return to the West Coast, if he had to play in the minors.

Thurston won 15, 15 and 13 games in three seasons. He went 1-5 in 10 games with Seattle in 1937 and lost his final decision with Oakland early in 1938.

The next season was his last in baseball. As playing manager of the champion Tacoma team, Thurston was

HOLLIS JOHN THURSTON
Born: 6/2/99, Fremont, NE, BR/TR, 5-foot-11, 165 pounds

		W	L	PCT	G	IP	H	ER	BB	SO	ERA
1920	SLC	9	13	.409	39	220	260	107	50	76	4.38
1921	SLC	7	13	.350	35	158	224	98	40	64	5.58
1922	SLC	15	16	.484	49	255	301	122	44	69	4.31
1928	SF	9	7	.563	26	137	184	70	22	37	4.59
1929	SF	22	11	.667	37	282	338	138	45	78	4.40
1934	Miss	15	10	.600	31	233	260	83	65	66	3.20
1935	Miss	15	10	.600	29	201	244	107	49	46	4.80
1936	Miss	13	10	.565	34	197	247	99	55	68	4.52
1937	Seat	1	5	.167	10	41	47	30	13	8	6.59
1938	Oak	0	1	.000	1	2	4	4	0	1	18.00
PCL		10	106| 96	.525	291	1726	2109| 858	383	513	4.47
Majors|	9	89	86	.509	288	1542	1859| 726	369	306	4.24

accorded honorable mention status on the Western International League's all-star squad after hitting .295 at first base.

Thurston scouted for Pittsburgh, Cleveland and the Chicago White Sox for more than a quarter century.

PAUL WANER

Paul Waner was a little guy, but he hit so well that the Flatbush baseball cognoscente nicknamed him "Big Poison."

In Brooklynese, Big Poison translated into big person, but it had a double meaning that also acknowledged Waner's prowess on the ball field. Paul's younger and smaller brother, Lloyd, was called "Little Poison."

The Waners achieved major league stardom as the best hitting brother combination in big league annuls. They are enshrined at Cooperstown and both got their start with the San Francisco Seals. Lloyd was only up at bat 64 times in two years with San Francisco before he was cut loose after rookie outfielder Earl Averill arrived on the scene.

But, Paul fulfilled his promise in the PCL by setting a league doubles record (75) that still stands and becoming the first man to lead the league with a .400-plus average.

Paul Waner

Waner was an unknown quantity when he arrived on the San Francisco scene in 1923 and for a time in training camp he was tried as a pitcher because of his diminutive size and strong arm. Since he swung a powerful bat, the mound experiment was abandoned quickly.

Paul grew up just outside Oklahoma City and was attending a state teacher's college when San Francisco scout Nick Williams used him as an excuse to explain away a 10-day drunk. Williams had been in Muskogee looking over Ray Flashkamper, who was taken by the Seals on his recommendation.

The scout was heading home on a train, wondering how to explain his long disappearance, when a conductor whose daughter went with Waner spoke glowingly of the little outfielder. Williams told Seals officials he was late arriving back in town because he had been scouting this 19-year-old phenom. He corresponded with Waner and sent him a contract the following spring.

Catcher Sam Agnew told the *San Francisco Bulletin* that Waner would never succeed at pitching, but could develop into "as good a hitter as there is in the league." This high praise did not stop manager Dots Miller from relegating Paul to pinch hitting chores and filling in at first base when regular Bert Ellison broke his hand early in 1923.

Waner made seven errors in 21 games at the bag and spent most of his time in the outfield, hitting .369 — second highest in the PCL — with 30 doubles in 112 contests.

Waner missed some early season games because of leg problems in 1924, but was in the outfield to stay by May. He fielded well and his 28 assists tied for second place. Paul's batting average rose to .372 in early September, but he slowed down to finish sixth among PCL regulars at .356 with 46 doubles and 113 runs scored in 160 games.

Pittsburgh scout Joe Devine was interested in Waner, but the Seals — in keeping with their policy — set a high price tag on their budding star. San Francisco wanted $100,000 for the tiny prospect and Devine kidded Paul that the Pirates wouldn't buy him unless he hit .400.

Pitchers hated to hear such rhetoric. Speed Martin said he'd been told for two years that Waner, "hasn't any weakness and I believe them." Bill Piercy said he'd throw pitches the average hitter would not be able to handle "nine out of 10 times, but he hit them right on the nose."

A line drive hitter and great bunter, the little southpaw stood well back in batter's box with his feet close together. Paul took a full stride and raised his right foot slightly when he hit.

Waner batted above .400 most of the 1925 season, then slipped to .392 in late September before winning the batting crown with a .401 mark. Along with his record-setting two bagger total, Paul knocked in 130 runs and scored 167 with 280 hits for the champion Seals. The Bucs bought Waner and shortstop Hal Rhyne for a reported $100,000.

Arriving at Pittsburgh, Paul gave his younger brother a new life in baseball as the Pirates listened to his recommendation, signed Lloyd and sent him to Columbia in the Sally League. Lloyd hit .345 and joined Paul in the Pittsburgh outfield a year later as they started careers that made them the only brothers in the Hall of Fame.

Paul had a great rookie season with Pittsburgh and his .336 average in 536 at bats would have won the league batting title under today's rules. But, Cincinnati's Pinky Hargrave took the crown with a .353 mark in 326 trips to the plate. Waner received 15 votes for the National League Most Valuable Player Award, but was second among the Pirates on the ballot as the league's best pitcher, Ray Kremer, tallied 32.

Waner was crowned batting champ and MVP the following season with a .380 mark and league-leading totals in hits (237), triples (17) and runs batted in (131). He never hit lower than .309 in the next decade and won titles in 1934 (.362) and 1936 (.373).

The Waner brother combination was broken up in December, 1940. The Bucs released Paul and he joined Brooklyn, who cut him in May. Waner went to the Boston Braves at age 38 as a utility outfielder and began wearing glasses when the ball started looking fuzzy coming up to the plate. Manager Casey Stengel — who called Waner the greatest National League right fielder — said Paul, "probably (had) been hitting from memory the past couple of years." In four seasons with the Braves and back with the Dodgers, Paul never approached his previous production.

Waner had 2,999 hits on June 19, 1942, when the Braves played Pittsburgh at Boston. Waner lined a drive at shortstop Eddie Miller, who knocked it down, but threw late to get Paul at first base. When the umpire tried to hand Waner the ball, Paul signaled he did not want a tainted hit for Number 3,000 and scorer ruled it an error. Paul hit a liner off the right field wall his next time up.

At the close of his career, Paul had 3,152 hits and a batting average of .333 and struck out rarely. He hit 603 doubles (ninth all-time) and 190 triples (10th). A heavy drinker who often took his cuts while nursing a hangover, Waner believed alcohol actually made him a better hitter because he was relaxed.

After retirement, he was a batting coach. Waner's distaste for enforcing discipline cost him any chance to become a manager in the majors. Paul ran the Miami club in the Florida International League for a time in 1946, but only because he was a stockholder.

PAUL GLEE WANER
Born: 4/16/03, Harrah, OK, BL/TL, 5-foot-8.5, 153 pounds

		G	AB	R	H	2B	3B	HR	RBI	SB	AVG.
1923	SF	112	325	54	120	30	4	3	39	4	.369
1924	SF	160	587	113	209	46	5	8	97	12	.356
1925	SF	174	699	167	280	75	7	11	130	8	.401
PCL	3	446	1611	334	609	151	16	22	266	24	.378
Majors	20	2549	9459	1626	3152	603	190	113	1309	104	.333

TAKE ME OUT TO THE ...

The Pacific Coast League was dotted with interesting ballparks. By the time the league was about to be done in by the National League's invasion, most of its baseball emporiums were at least 25 years old and some had taken on a threadbare look.

The fans didn't seem to care much, since just about any ballpark is a good place to be on a summer afternoon or evening.

The weather was pretty good up and down the coast. San Diego was mild and sunny after the morning fog cleared away. Los Angeles and Hollywood were blessed with warm temperatures, although the automobile added smog to the mix.

Sacramento was blistering hot in the summertime, but almost all its games were played at night after 1930, so the fans didn't bake in the sun.

Oakland had a moderate climate while across the bay, San Francisco fans sometimes bundled up to keep out the chill.

Seattle and Portland fans were used to dodging an occasional shower, but the weather in both locales was conducive to watching baseball.

While today's spectators clamor for comfort and major league teams expect local government to give them new stadiums with ample parking and luxury boxes, fans of the old Coast League recall the joys of sitting on a splintered bench or a wooden chair back seat and watching their favorites perform.

Recreation Park in San Francisco attracted Seals and Missions rooters for several decades.

Sick's Stadium served the Seattle Rainiers into the late 1960s, when it became home to the American League's Pilots.

This was the center fielder's view of Seals Stadium with the Rainier Beer sign visible over the rim of the stadium.

The wooden grandstand at Freeman's Park was filled with Oakland fans in the early days of the Coast League.

Sacramento's 1922 ballpark — last known as Edmonds Field — burned down in 1948.

Washington Park was the home of the Los Angeles, Vernon and Venice teams between 1911 and 1925.

The right field bleachers presented an attractive target for home run hitters at Oaks Park in Emeryville.

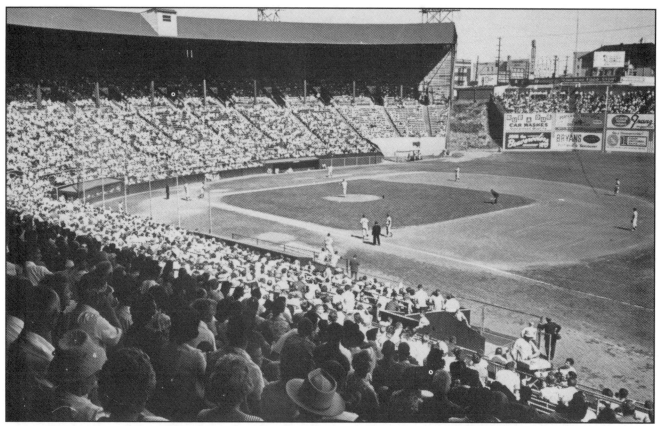

The Portland Beavers moved their Coast League games into multi-purpose Multnomah Stadium in 1956.

More than 23,500 fans packed Lucky Beavers Stadium in Portland for a split pair of openers in 1951.

Ball Grounds, Majestic Park, Salt Lake City, Utah.

A 1917 postcard shows Majestic Park, later called Bonneville Park, where the Bees played in Salt Lake City.

Venerable Vaughn Street Park in Portland was dedicated in 1901 and looked like this in 1953.

GOOD PLAYERS IN BAD TIMES

WALLY BERGER

Wally Berger was a free-swinging slugger who set home run records from one coast to the other.

Before leaving Los Angeles for the big leagues after the 1929 season, the big, blond powerhouse had racked up a new home run standard for the Los Angeles Angels, smashing 40 to eclipse Slug Tolson's old mark of 28.

Berger belted 38 four-baggers the following season with the Boston Braves. It was a club record and the most ever hit by a National League rookie. The former league standard was 25 by Brooklyn's Del Bissonette two years earlier.

Wally's game was fortified by home runs and a batting average that never fell below .285 until he was near the end of his 15-year baseball career. His lifetime major league average was an even .300 and he belted 242 four baggers in 11 National League campaigns.

Post-season play was a problem for Wally. A four-time major league All-Star, Berger was hitless in eight tries and also wore the collar in 18 trips to the plate in seven World Series games in 1937 and 1939.

Berger's childhood was spent in San Francisco's Cow Hollow district. He left Mission High School in his senior year to drive a laundry truck. San Francisco manager Nick Williams picked Berger off the sandlots, but let him go after he was injured during training camp in 1926.

Berger journeyed to Montana a year later to work in the copper mines and play for a company team. Wally left after a few months and was on his way home when his train stopped in Pocatello, Idaho. Two friends who were playing for the local team in the Utah-Idaho League urged him to try out.

Signed by the Pocatello team, Berger was switched from shortstop to the outfield by manager Ivan Olson and played in 92 games, heading the circuit in batting (.385) and home runs (24). Sold to Los Angeles, Berger and teammate Forrest "Woody" Jensen reported to the eighth place Angels late in the PCL season. In 14 games, Wally hit three homers and batted .365.

Berger and an equally powerful, but inexperienced rookie, Wes Schulmerich, were thrown into the Seraphs' lineup in 1928, when Los Angeles finished low in the standings in both halves of the split season.

Berger opened the season with a towering home run over the center field wall at Wrigley Field, a blow reportedly matched only by Lou Gehrig during an earlier barnstorming tour. Most of the Angels' home run power was generated by first baseman Tolson (28), Berger (20), Wally Hood (20) and Schulmerich (19). Hampered by injuries, Wally still hit .327 and batted in 94 runs.

In addition to his record-setting 40 homers in 1929, Berger was among the Coast League leaders in runs scored (170) and RBIs (166).

Chicago Cubs scouts and manager Joe McCarthy decided he wasn't a major league prospect because he swung stiff-armed, but his performance was good enough for the Braves, who bought Wally for $50,000 and two players. Oddly, the money to buy Berger came from an arrangement that had sent third baseman Les Bell from Boston to the Cubs.

Adding 119 runs batted in and a .310 average to his rookie home run total for the Braves, Berger became an established Bean Town star for seven seasons. He led outfielders in fielding average in 1932. The following year, Wally came into the season finale as a pinch hitter after riding the bench for three weeks with the flu and belted a grand slam to give the Braves fourth place and a first division finish for the first time in 12 seasons.

A clutch player, Wally averaged 103 runs batted in annually over his first seven seasons in the majors. He led the senior circuit in home runs (34) and RBIs (130) in 1935. A shoulder injury limited his performance after the 1936 season and Braves president Bob Quinn — never a big fan of Berger's talents — traded him to the New York Giants in 1937 for $35,000 and pitcher Frank Gabler. After hitting .285 with 17 homers for the season, he was sent to Cincinnati.

As his production slipped, Wally moved on to the

WALTER ANTONE BERGER
Born: 10/10/05, Chicago, IL, BR/TR, 6-foot-2, 198 pounds

		G	AB	R	H	2B	3B	HR	RBI	SB	AVG.
1927	LA	14	63	7	23	2	0	3	15	0	.365
1928	LA	138	535	94	175	34	7	20	94	5	.327
1929	LA	199	744	170	249	41	5	40	166	19	.335
1941	LA	59	141	19	34	7	0	8	18	0	.241
PCL	4	410	1483	290	481	84	12	71	293	24	.324
Majors	11	1350	5163	809	1550	299	59	242	898	36	.300

Wally Berger

Frenchy Bordagaray

Philadelphia Phillies in 1940, then played with Indianapolis in the American Association before coming back to the Coast League in 1941. The Angels let him go after he hit .241 with eight home runs in 141 times at bat.

He managed in the New England, Northern and Pioneer leagues in 1949 and 1950. Wally's younger brother, Fred, also played in the PCL.

FRENCHY BORDAGARAY

Some of the men who went to the big leagues from the PCL were better players that Frenchy Bordagaray, although the little Basque outfielder had a productive nine-year stay at the top.

But, Bordagaray is remembered as much for zany antics and funny lines as production.

Frenchy arrived at his first training camp with the Chicago White Sox in 1934. A reporter asked whether he was going to play that day and Bordagaray — not yet christened "The Bouncing Basque" by the scribes — replied matter-of-factly:

"Sure, (manager Lew) Fonseca is using all the regulars today."

Unfortunately for Bordagaray, he carried a guaranteed price tag of $12,500 if the Sox didn't return him to

Sacramento by early June.

Frenchy hung around long enough to hit .322 in 29 games, but White Sox official Harry Grabiner's feeling was that, while he "looks like a good hitter, has plenty of color and is fast," his fielding was terrible. Although he led the league in pinch hitting (8 for 12), Frenchy was shipped back to Sacramento before the payoff deadline to become a Coast League regular again.

Born and raised in Coalinga, Bordagaray was mascot for the town team and got into his first game at the age of 14 when a regular failed to show up. He batted ninth, but did so well the manager moved him to the clean-up spot.

The little pepper pot was a star prep athlete and moved on to Fresno State College, where he starred on the football and baseball teams, played basketball, ran the sprints and broad jumped for the Bulldogs' track team for two years.

Frenchy was ready to turn pro at age 20 and was offered a contract after a trial with the Senators during the spring of 1931. Bordagaray was agreeable to $500-a-month when school was out in June, but his father refused to sign the contract, a necessity since Frenchy was still a minor.

Frenchy began playing with Sacramento as an amateur on June 5, getting a single and double in three trips. His dad came around and Bordagaray became a pro a few days later. The youngster showed great promise in 70 games, batting .373 with 19 doubles.

Bordagaray was a standout on the 1932 Senators, a team loaded with young talent from the Sacramento area. In addition to Bordagaray, who scored 131 runs and counted 33 doubles and 10 triples among his 223 hits for a .322 average, infielders Alex Kampouris (.281) and Lenny Backer (.313) and outfielders Frank Demaree (.364) and Hank Steinbacher (.322) all were local products. All but Backer moved on to the big leagues.

Frenchy took time out from his ball playing chores to run a 100-yard match race against a horse at mid-season. He lost when the promoter substituted a thoroughbred for the nag Bordagaray had agreed to race.

Bordagaray had good years at the plate in 1933 and 1934, hitting .351 and .321 in 117 games each year, but his fielding was spotty and his mind tended to wander. On Aug. 30, 1934, he failed to show up in the outfield at the start of an inning, a fact that didn't escape Portland's Nino Bongiovanni, who lined a double into the vacant spot. Retrieved from the locker room, Frenchy nonchalantly said he had been adjusting his sliding pads.

His bizarre fielding habits carried over to the Brooklyn Dodgers, where he was sent in 1935 for $10,000 and the rights to outfielder Johnny Frederick and pitcher Art Herring.

On one occasion, Frenchy's cap flew off as he raced for a fly ball. He stopped, retreated to retrieve the headpiece and then continued chasing the ball. Another time, he muffed two fly balls in the early innings to ruin George Earnshaw's shutout bid, but later saved the game with a pair of spectacular catches. When the pitcher questioned him, Frenchy claimed the early miscues were merely "decoys" to set up the opponents for his later catches.

He hit .282 and stole 18 bases in 1935 and came into the Dodgers camp in Florida the following spring sporting a mustache, an unheard of facial adornment in baseball at the time. It caused quite a stir and one newspaperman wanted to run a contest so the fans could name the decoration on Frenchy's upper lip.

"I'd have kept the mustache if I hadn't come up with a batting slump while I was wearing it," Bordagaray told *Sporting News* editor J. G. Taylor Spink. The other story is that manager Casey Stengel told him to shave it off, because, "if there is going to be a clown on this ball club, I'm going to be it."

Frenchy gave Casey lots of gray hairs. Once, Bordagaray was picked off second base when Billy Jurges asked him to remove his foot from the bag so he could knock off the

dirt. Casey was furious and questioned how Frenchy could be out when he was standing on the bag. "He got me between taps," replied Frenchy.

Bordagaray became the Dodgers' utility man supreme, playing second base, third base and all three outfield positions in 1936. Although he batted .315, Frenchy was traded to the St. Louis Cardinals for Tom Winsett. It was a puzzling switch since Winsett could neither hit nor field as well as Frenchy. Still, Bordagaray fit in with the fun-loving Cardinals just as he had with the Daffy Dodgers, even playing washboard in the Cards' famous "Mudcat Band."

He wasn't all fun and games, however, and in 1938 led the league in pinch hitting with a .465 average (20 for 43). It was an out-of-character performance, since he was 1 for 16 as a pinch hitter the year before, and 0 for 11 in 1939. But, he had a lifetime average of .312 as a substitute batter.

Over six of the next seven seasons with the Cardinals, Cincinnati, New York Yankees and Brooklyn for a second time, Bordagaray never played in as many as 100 games. He appeared as a pinch runner in the 1939 World Series with the Reds and in 1941 with the Yanks.

Frenchy had the best year of his career in 1940 when he was sent down to Kansas City and set an American Association record with 13 straight hits while batting .358. This won him promotion to the New York Yankees, where he played a reserve role in 1942. New York sent him back to Kansas City, who sold him to Dodgers, where he played more or less regularly through the war years.

The volatile Bordagaray had several notable run-ins with umpires. After being fined and suspended for spitting on a major league ump, Frenchy told reporters, "maybe I did wrong, but the penalty was more than I expectorated."

Bordagaray managed in the minors after the war, first at Three Rivers in the Canadian-American League — where he led the league with a .358 average and his team won the pennant and playoffs — and then at Greenville in the Sally League, where he was fined $50 and suspended for 60 days for slugging an umpire.

Frenchy retired to run a successful chain of cemeteries in the Midwest and later was a municipal groundskeeper in Ventura.

JOE BOWMAN

Joe Bowman was a successful knuckle ball pitcher in the Pacific Coast League who might have done better in the majors if he hadn't been talked out of using his best pitch.

Near the end of his big league career in 1945, Joe thought he might have been able to win 17 or 18 games annually, "if I had started using my knuckler as regularly as I do now." Bowman said the pitch was a key part of his repertoire in three seasons at Portland in the early 1930s. But, when Joe arrived in the majors he was told by managers and catchers to abandon the pitch because it would damage his arm.

"Of course, I didn't have to listen," he said. "but, if a young fellow doesn't listen, they mark him down as a

STANLEY GEORGE BORDAGARAY
Born: 1/3/10, Coalinga, CA, BR/TR, 5-foot-7.5, 175 pounds

		G	AB	R	H	2B	3B	HR	RBI	SB	AVG.
1931	Sac	70	252	35	94	19	4	5	32	4	.373
1932	Sac	173	692	131	223	33	10	5	77	20	.322
1933	Sac	117	416	67	146	26	3	7	65	10	.351
1934	Sac	117	483	84	155	34	1	6	46	23	.321
PCL	4	477	1843	317	618	112	18	23	220	57	.335
Majors	11	930	2632	410	745	120	28	14	270	65	.283

Joe Bowman

Pete Coscarart

hardhead and he doesn't get anyplace anyway."

As an 18-year-old, Bowman pitched for a semi-pro team that won 30 straight and was invited to play the Kansas City Blues, managed by Spencer Abbott. Joe beat the American Association team, 1-0, and Abbott signed him for Pueblo of the Western League in 1929. He played in the outfield, hit .267 in 44 games and pitched 23 innings.

Portland owner Tom Turner was in Pueblo scouting outfielder Bob Johnson — who had hit 16 homers in just 66 games — and saw Bowman. Taylor paid $12,000 for Johnson, who later became a big league star, and got Bowman for next to nothing.

JOSEPH EMIL BOWMAN
Born: 6/17/10, Argentine, KS, BL/TR, 6-foot-2, 190 pounds

		W	L	PCT	G	IP	H	ER	BB	SO	ERA
1930	Port	(played three games, but did not pitch)									
1931	Port	18	11	.621	39	246	265	104	62	126	3.80
1932	Port	10	7	.588	23	133	145	62	47	66	4.19
1933	Port	23	11	.676	38	283	330	131	65	155	4.17
1946	SD	1	2	.333	15	40	40	—	22	16	—
PCL		5	52	31	.627	115	702	780	297*	196	363	4.04 *
Majors	11	77	96	.445	298	1466	1656	717	484	502	4.40
* incomplete											

The following season, Joe played three games at third base for Portland, but spent most of the year at Omaha, where he combined infield and outfield assignments with pitching. He batted .255 and compiled a 6-4 record.

His manager was Abbott, who gave him a dozen balls and a bat and told Bowman to stand the bat up against the bleachers and throw at it until he could hit it anywhere he wanted every time. The drill improved Joe's control enormously.

Abbott was promoted to Portland in 1931 and took Bowman along. Abbott felt that Joe was strictly a pitcher and put him into the Portland rotation, where he threw 246 innings and went 18-11 for a team that won 100 games.

Philadelphia took a look at Bowman early in the year in 11 innings on the mound, but Connie Mack didn't like his sidewinding style, although it created a natural screwball. Mack sent Joe back to the Beavers with instructions to convert his delivery to straight overhand.

Abbott ignored the order and told Bowman to continue throwing the way he always had and to keep using the knuckler. Joe finished at 10-7 for the champion Beavers. He pitched the entire 1933 season in Portland, where his record was 23-11 with 155 Ks in 283 innings, both career highs.

The New York Giants bought Bowman during the winter, took away his knuckler and made him a relief pitcher. After a 5-4 season in 107 innings, he was part of a four player trade with the Philadelphia Phillies for shortstop Dick Bartell. When the swap was proposed, the Phillies demanded one of New York's young pitchers and the Giants elected to send Bowman.

Phillies manager Jimmy Wilson changed Joe's motion and used him as a starter and reliever in 1935 and Bowman fashioned a 7-10 mark. He was in the rotation the following season, starting 28 games with a 9-20 record. The Phils

---

"If a young fellow doesn't listen, they mark him down as a hardhead and he doesn't get anyplace anyway."
— Joe Bowman

---

finished seventh and eighth.

Bowman escaped the Phillies in a 1937 trade with Pittsburgh, where he worked for five years. After an 8-8 mark the first season, bullpen duty and a sore arm limited him to 60 innings. He went 22-28 over three more seasons and was sent to the American Association in 1942, where he pitched at St. Paul and Louisville.

Joe returned to the Big Time with Boston in 1944, resurrected his knuckle ball and had his best season in years, winning 12 and losing eight. Boston sent him to Cincinnati shortly after the 1946 season began and he had an 11-13 record with the Reds in his last appearance in the majors. Bowman was 77-96 lifetime in the majors and never duplicated his PCL pitching numbers as his walks nearly matched his strikeouts.

Bowman registered a 1-2 mark in 40 innings of relief with the San Diego Padres in 1946 and later managed in the minor leagues.

PETE COSCARART

The Pacific Coast League had scores of players who never made it in the major leagues because they could hit a ton, but couldn't field a lick. Pete Coscarart was the opposite, a mediocre hitter whose glove allowed him to stay at the top levels of baseball for 17 years.

Pete might not have had baseball a career if it hadn't been for Steve Coscarart, one of his two ball-playing brothers. Pete, Steve and Joe Coscarart grew up on a farm near Escondido in San Diego County. Their dad was a Basque, who frowned on baseball, but couldn't ignore the fact that all three boys were very good at sports.

When Pete graduated from Escondido High School, he and high school football teammate Ed Goddard enrolled at Washington State College. Goddard became a three-time All-American quarterback for the Cougars, but Pete had little opportunity to show his gridiron skills on the freshman team and left school at the end of the year.

Brother Joe was an infielder with the Seattle Indians in

1934 when Portland manager Walt McCredie received a tip from former Beavers shortstop Dave Bancroft about a prospect named Steve Coscarart, who had played for Banny in an independent league.

After taking a look at the young man, Portland owner Tom Turner offered Steve a contract. Steve said he'd agree to join the team if Turner would take his kid brother at the same time. Turner had little interest in Pete, but wanted Steve under contract so he took them both.

Pete turned out to be the best of the trio. Joe had a long career in the Coast League and played two years in the American League. Steve never rose above the PCL.

Steve hit .311 in 150 games at Portland in 1934 while Pete rode the bench, getting into 58 games and batting .253.

Portland officials thought neither was ready for the PCL and sent them to St. Joseph in the Western League in 1935. Steve was hurt early in the year and by the time he was returned to action, Pete had nailed down the shortstop assignment, so manager Earle Brucker switched Steve to the outfield.

Back with Portland the following season, manager Max Bishop made Pete his second baseman. Pete batted only .233 and led the league in errors, but showed enough promise that he was in the lineup in all but five games as the Beavers won the pennant and swept to victory in the post-season playoffs.

Coscarart was paired with shortstop Dudley Lee, one of the PCL's smoothest fielders, who helped Pete learn the intricacies of playing the keystone position. The slender, broad-shouldered Coscarart had big hands and long, powerful arms. Coupled with outstanding speed, Pete covered so much ground that he was referred to as a fourth outfielder.

"Don't be surprised if this steady, even-tempered lad becomes the toast of the circuit by next fall," wrote *The Oregonian's* Stub Nelson as the 1937 season approached. "Toward the end of (1936), Coscarart started hitting (and) was getting away from the old fault of being continually behind the pitcher. Then, to climax the season, he drove out the hit that clinched the pennant and the $2,500 first place bonus."

Coscarart came into his own as the Beavers' second

PETER JOSEPH COSCARART
Born: 6/16/13, Escondido, CA, BR/TR, 5-foot-11.5, 175 pounds

		G	AB	R	H	2B	3B	HR	RBI	SB	AVG.
1934	Port	58	198	24	50	8	0	1	20	2	.253
1936	Port	170	602	71	140	32	1	3	58	7	.233
1937	Port	123	434	52	110	22	1	2	41	8	.253
1946	SD	76	251	23	54	10	1	4	24	2	.215
1947	SD	142	545	72	139	29	2	6	55	21	.255
1948	SD	114	309	34	64	14	0	3	25	6	.207
1949	SD-Sc	148	481	55	131	27	2	5	65	6	.272
1950	Sac	18	43	5	7	0	0	0	1	1	.163
PCL	8	849	2863	336	695	142	7	24	289	53	.243
Majors	9	864	2992	399	728	129	22	28	269	34	.243

Frank Crosetti

Pete Coscarart

Wally Berger

Curt Davis

Monte Pearson

baseman and was batting .333 when Sacramento's Dick Newsome broke Pete's wrist with a fast ball. When Coscarart returned to the lineup after missing 50 games, he could not grip the bat properly and pulled a muscle in his back with an awkward swing. He was hitting .220 with three weeks to go, but elevated it to .253 at the end.

Coscarart's ticket to the big leagues wasn't in his bat anyway, but the Brooklyn Dodgers acquired him after Pete led the PCL's second sackers with a .970 fielding average. Pete split 1938 between Nashville, where he hit .315 in 66

games, and Brooklyn, where he only managed a .152 average.

Following two seasons as a starter, Pete lost his job to Billy Herman in 1941 and generated a .129 average in 62 at bats. He went hitless in seven trips to the plate in his only World Series. In December, Pete was packaged with catcher Babe Phelps, pitcher Luke Hamlin and first sacker Jimmy Wasdell and dealt to Pittsburgh for future Hall of Fame third baseman Arky Vaughan.

He was the Pirates shortstop in 1943 and played second

base for three more seasons. Coscarart's fielding improved and he was among the leaders at second base, his best position.

Released by the Bucs a few games into the 1946 season, Pete went home and signed with San Diego, averaging .215 in 76 games. He stuck with the Padres for two more season, hitting .255 with 21 steals in 1947 and dropping off to .207 the next year.

Pete was a late addition to the Sacramento lineup in 1949 when the Solons traded catcher Dee Moore for him. It was his best year as Pete batted .272 with 27 doubles. He was cut after 18 games with the Solons in 1950 and finished with a .243 lifetime PCL batting average — exactly the same as his major league mark.

FRANK CROSETTI

Baseball records are made to be broken, but one that may stand forever is held by Frank Crosetti, who collected 23 World Series checks in 37 years as a player and coach with the New York Yankees.

Crosetti was one of many Californians who played for the Bronx Bombers in their heyday and one of three San Francisco Italian-Americans who came to the team from the Pacific Coast League between 1926 and 1936. The others were Hall of Famers Joe DiMaggio and Tony Lazzeri.

Frank spent the early part of his childhood on a farm in Los Gatos, where he and his brother created a substitute baseball from a corn cob and shaved a piece of lumber into a bat.

The family returned to San Francisco and Frank attended Lowell High School until he dropped out at age 16. He lied about his age to play semi-pro ball in Montana and returned to San Francisco to perform for the Young Men's Institute team, which played its games at Recreation Park.

Hired by the Seals for the 1928 season, Crosetti found himself sharing third base with veteran Babe Pinelli. He appeared in 96 games and hit .248.

Shortstop was where Frank belonged and he took over that spot in the San Francisco infield in 1929 after Hal Rhyne was drafted by the Philadelphia Athletics. Rhyne was an brilliant fielder and Crosetti was frequently compared in unfavorable terms with the departed star.

"He may come along," said the *San Francisco Bulletin*, "but he is not a Hal Rhyne yet." Crosetti had trouble charging slow hit balls — one of Rhyne's strengths — "but he is

Frank Crosetti

learning rapidly and has a world of promise" the *Bulletin* said later. The *Chronicle's* Ed Hughes predicted Crosetti, "is sure to graduate to the majors before he is of voting age."

Crosetti's 72 errors led the PCL shortstops, but his .314 batting average from the lead-off spot equaled the team average of the potent Seals, who featured nine .300 hitters. Frank contributed 151 runs — second on the team to Gus Suhr's 196 — and smacked 54 doubles with a dozen homers.

There were rave reviews for Crosetti from the start in 1930. "The flashy shortstop . . . is playing with the dash, speed and confidence of a veteran," said Hughes. "He is a corking player now." Hughes pointed out that Frank was "not yet 20 years old, but already he is one of the most powerful and dangerous hitters in the league."

After Crosetti went eight for 10 with two doubles and three home runs in a twin-bill against the Missions, Hughes compared him with former San Francisco greats Harry Heilmann, Paul Waner, Willie Kamm, Roy Johnson and Earl Averill.

San Francisco co-owner Charles Strub raised eyebrows in the spring by hanging a $150,000 price tag on Frank. By August, the Yankees had come calling with an undisclosed amount of cash — estimated at $50,000 — plus pitchers Sam Gibson and Bill Henderson. The Yanks agreed to

FRANK PETER JOSEPH CROSETTI
Born: 10/4/10, San Francisco, CA, BR/TR, 5-foot-10, 165 pounds

		G	AB	R	H	2B	3B	HR	RBI	SB	AVG.
1928	SF	96	326	79	81	18	1	4	22	4	.248
1929	SF	184	784	151	246	54	5	12	81	5	.314
1930	SF	189	782	171	261	66	8	27	113	21	.334
1931	SF	183	734	141	252	48	13	5	143	23	.343
PCL	4	652	2626	542	840	186	27	48	359	53	.320
Majors	17	1683	6277	1006	1541	260	65	98	649	113	.245

leave Frank in San Francisco for one more year.

Crosetti finished 1930 with a .334 average, topped the league with 171 runs and produced 66 doubles, 27 homers, 113 RBIs and 21 steals. His work at shortstop improved and he had the league's fourth best fielding average among regulars.

Frank moved down in the batting order in his final PCL season and responded with a .343 average, 141 runs scored and 143 runs batted in as San Francisco grabbed the second half title and beat Hollywood in four straight playoff games.

When Frank arrived at spring training as a New York rookie, the Yankees were loaded with shortstop candidates, including Bill Werber, Red Rolfe and incumbent Lyn Lary.

The Red Sox inquired about obtaining some of this talent and were told they could have Crosetti for $75,000 or Werber for $35,000. They chose Werber. Rolfe was sent to Newark and Crosetti and Lary shared the shortstop job in 1932. Frank became the regular in 1933 and in another year Lary went to Boston for $20,000 and Freddie Muller.

Crosetti was hardly a slugger in the American League, batting .245 in 17 seasons and standing atop the league in strikeouts in 1937 (105) and 1938 (97). But, he gave the Yankees a decade at shortstop and become a set-up man for the Bronx Bombers' power hitters who followed him in the lineup. Rogers Hornsby called him the "sparkplug" of the Yanks.

Crosetti was an every day player except for 1935 when injuries limited him to 87 games. From 1941 to the end of his career, he filled a utility role, although he played 130 games in 1945.

In seven World Series, Frank played in 29 games and batted .174. He became a player-coach in 1947 and was removed from the active player list in 1949, continuing as a full-time coach through 1968. He took a coaching position with the Seattle Pilots in 1969 and when the team disbanded Frank joined the Minnesota Twins staff for two seasons and retired to his home in Stockton, California.

BABE DAHLGREN

When it's trivia time, one of the frequently asked questions is to name the player Lou Gehrig replaced at first base when he began his run of 2,130 consecutive games. The answer is Wally Pipp.

Asked less often is who replaced the Iron Horse when Gehrig's skein ended in 1939? That would be Ellsworth Tenney Dahlgren, better known as "Babe."

The San Francisco native almost didn't get the call. New York Yankees manager Joe McCarthy thought about converting Tommy Henrich to first base, but Joe DiMaggio was hurt and Henrich had to stay in the outfield. Babe, who had filled in for Gehrig at first base in late innings and played some third base in 1938, was given the job and hit a home run in his first game.

Babe was a lot flashier around the bag than Gehrig, but couldn't carry his bat — an attribute he shared with many

Babe Dahlgren

of his contemporaries. Dahlgren didn't miss a game in two seasons, hit only .235 in 1939, but knocked in 89 runs as the Yankees won their fourth straight pennant and the World Series. Babe batted .264 in 1940 and then began a trip that would take him to seven teams before he left the majors after 1946.

Early in his career, it appeared Dahlgren might spend his whole life playing in San Francisco.

Babe lived in San Francisco's Mission District, where his stepfather made baseballs out of socks and rags and played with him every day in the yard of the family home or at a nearby park. The stepfather also made Babe — so named because he was the youngest of five children — mascot of a sugar refinery team, which he eventually joined as a player.

After graduating from Mission High School in 1931, Dahlgren hooked up with the neighborhood Coast League team. The Missions' roster included several other local prep phenoms who would spend considerable time as Coast Leaguers, including infielders Al Wright from Lowell High School and Dick Gyselman from Polytechnic. Like the unassuming Babe, each was shy of his 21st birthday.

Dahlgren definitely wasn't ready for the Coast League and was sent to Tucson in the Arizona-Texas League. After batting .347, Babe rejoined the Missions to hit .244 in 58 contests.

As his career progressed and he gained experience, Dahlgren's one-handed scoop style and agility around the bag led observers to regard him as a fielding artist, or as

Will Connolly of the *San Francisco Chronicle* put it, "perhaps the niftiest right-handed first baseman of our time." John Lardner said he was faster that Bill Terry and more agile and resourceful than George Sisler. "Pretty soon you realize he never misses. He is sure as death."

Dahlgren was an average fielder in the beginning. In 1932, Babe led the league in errors with 30, partly because he played the bag in 187 games. But that still was a dozen more miscues than the first base fielding leader, Sacramento's Dolph Camilli, committed in the same num-

---

> *"Perhaps the niftiest right-handed first baseman of our time."*
> — *Will Connolly about Babe Dahlgren in the San Francisco Chronicle*

---

ber of contests. The durable Dahlgren led again the following season, but cut his miscues down to 24, still twice as many as Camilli. Babe's glove work improved again in 1933, but by then he was recognized as much for the way he wielded the lumber as the mitt.

Dahlgren hit .287, .315 and .302, batted in more than 100 runs annually and showed improved power with 20 home runs the last year. The Boston Red Sox paid $50,000 for Dahlgren, but he hit only .263 and led the league in errors as a rookie in 1935. The Red Sox were thinking pennant and bought Jimmie Foxx to play first base in 1936 and sent Babe to Syracuse.

Dahlgren put up compelling numbers in the International League, batting .318 with 121 RBIs, 31 doubles and 16 homers. He led the circuit with 21 triples and was called up to Boston near the end of the season.

Gehrig held out for more money in 1937 and Yankees owner Col. Jacob Ruppert began looking for first base insurance. He bought Dahlgren and sent him to Newark. When Gehrig agreed to a contract, Newark manager Oscar Vitt was told to let Babe learn other positions. Babe got into 125 games — two thirds at third base — and hit .340 with 18 homers for the champion Bears.

Back with the Yankees, he sat on the bench all season and struggled with a .186 average on the few occasions he got into a game. Only Gehrig's retirement made him a regular.

ELLSWORTH TENNEY DAHLGREN
Born: 6/15/12, San Francisco, CA, BR/TR, 6-foot, 190 pounds

	G	AB	R	H	2B	3B	HR	RBI	SB	AVG.
1931 Miss	58	234	25	57	11	2	1	23	3	.244
1932 Miss	188	722	69	207	40	4	11	101	8	.287
1933 Miss	189	733	98	231	28	9	6	110	4	.315
1934 Miss	186	735	106	222	34	10	20	136	11	.302
1948 Sac	115	379	39	113	21	0	8	41	0	.298
PCL	5	736	2803	337	830	134	25	46	411	26	.296
Majors 12	1137	4045	470	1056	174	37	82	569	18	.261

Babe was a holdout in 1941 when New York shipped him to the Boston Braves for $12,000. The Braves moved him to the Cubs in June and he hit .267 for the year. Chicago sold Dahlgren to the St. Louis Browns conditionally on May 13, but the Browns sent Babe back six days later and he was sold to Brooklyn on the same day. He appeared in only 36 games that year as a fill-in first sacker and pinch hitter.

The Philadelphia Phillies traded Lloyd Waner and Albie Glossop for Babe the following March and, although he hit .287 in 136 games, Dahlgren was shuttled off to Pittsburgh in yet another trade at the end of the year. He hit .289 and .250 for the Bucs and moved on again to his last major league stop with the Browns for 28 games in 1946.

After a year at Baltimore, Dahlgren played the 1948 season with Sacramento and was hitting .298 when an appendix operation in August put an end to his career.

He later scouted for the Kansas City Athletics and Baltimore and was a Kansas City coach in 1964.

CURT DAVIS

The saying goes that hindsight is 20-20, but it's still hard to understand how major league teams left pitcher Curt Davis lingering in the Pacific Coast League past his 29th birthday.

Tall and sinewy, Davis didn't get a chance to show his stuff to a big league crowd until 1934, although he'd already racked up 90 wins in five seasons with San Francisco.

The lanky Davis didn't waste his opportunity, however. Curt stuck around the National League until 1946, winning 158 and losing 131 games before dropping down to the Dodgers' farm clubs in Montreal and St. Paul for his final seasons that closed after his 43rd birthday.

Nicknamed "Coonskin" for his country ways and "Slim" or "Slats" for his angular build, Davis was a late bloomer on the baseball diamond.

Davis grew up on a farm near Salem, Oregon. He played high school baseball, but never thought about becoming a pro. Curt was a self-sufficient youngster who left home at age 17 to work in a lumber camp.

While watching a game in 1925, a friend shouted that Davis could pitch better than the guy on the mound so the manager put him into the game. Curt threw six strong innings and started playing regularly for $15-a-game. His performance eventually won him a raise to $50 per appearance.

A fan in Ashland recommended him to Seals manager Nick Williams, who signed Davis in 1928. San Francisco sent him to Salt Lake City in the Utah-Idaho League with two other good looking youngsters, Val Glynn and Lefty Gomez. Davis went 16-8 and helped Salt Lake City win the championship.

From the time he arrived in San Francisco in 1929, the Seals were a contender and won the title in a post-season playoff against Hollywood in 1931.

Curt Davis

Davis started and relieved in his rookie year, when he went 17-13, but from then on established himself as a key member of the starting rotation. Never a strikeout artist, Curt's forte was control as he mixed his fast ball, sinker and palm ball from a sidearm motion.

Davis was a competent hitter and batted .289 in the PCL with highs of .331 in 1930 and .330 the following season. Against tougher pitching at the major league level, Davis was less dangerous, hitting .203 lifetime. He couldn't be ignored, however, and batted .300 in 1937 and .381 two years later, including five hits in 14 pinch hitting appearances.

Curt's only losing Coast League season came in 1930, when he was 17-18, but he registered a 14-14 mark the following year. Davis had his best year in 1932, winning 22

CURTIS BENTON DAVIS
Born: 9/7/03, Greenfield, MO, BR/TR, 6-foot-2, 185 pounds

		W	L	PCT	G	IP	H	ER	BB	SO	ERA
1929	SF	17	13	.567	41	240	277	106	61	79	3.97
1930	SF	17	18	.486	44	305	389	165	80	103	4.87
1931	SF	14	14	.500	38	236	275	110	56	106	4.19
1932	SF	22	16	.579	44	326	290	81	57	122	2.24
1933	SF	20	16	.556	41	283	340	125	56	86	3.97
PCL	5	90	77	.539	208	1390	1571	587	310	496	3.80
Majors	13	158	131	.547	429	2324	2459	884	479	684	3.42

and losing 16 while leading the league in earned run average (2.24), innings pitched (326) and shutouts (9).

Fans and sportswriters thought he was a lock to go up to the majors, but Curt wore Seals livery again in 1933. There were reports that whenever a scout expressed interest in Davis, the Seals raised the price. The issue became moot after the 1933 season. Davis lost his first nine games, but came on strong for a 20-16 year and was drafted by the pitching poor, seventh place Philadelphia Phillies for $7,500.

The quiet and affable Davis was an immediate star in Philadelphia. The Phillies finished seventh again, but Curt led the staff with a 19-17 record and 2.96 ERA in 51 appearances.

A 16-14 season followed and in May, 1936, Davis and outfielder Ethan Allen were traded to the Chicago Cubs for outfielder Chuck Klein, pitcher Fabian Kowalik and $50,000. Davis finished 13-13. He was ill and had a sore arm the next year, when he was 10-5 in only 124 innings.

The Cubs made one of their worst trades in 1938, sending $185,000 plus Davis, pitcher Clyde Shoun and outfielder Tuck Stainback to the St. Louis Cardinals for Dizzy Dean. The wise-cracking Dean was damaged goods after a toe injury caused him to alter his pitching motion and injure his pitching arm. He brought a 134-55 record to the Cubs, but won only 16 games in four seasons in Chicago.

Davis had two good years with the Cards, winning 12 and 22 games but was off to an 0-4 start in mid-1940 when St. Louis sent him and outfielder Ducky Medwick to Brooklyn in a trade for three players and cash. Davis spent the last six years of his major league career with the Dodgers, compiling a 58-47 record. He lost his only World Series start for Brooklyn in 1941.

FRANK DEMAREE

The 1934 Los Angeles Angels team often is described as the best in Coast League history and sometimes as the greatest minor league aggregation of all-time. The top player on that squad, having the greatest year of his life, was Frank Demaree.

The 23-year-old Demaree arrived in the Los Angeles training camp after being sent down by the parent Chicago Cubs, who had purchased Frank from Sacramento in 1932.

Demaree started for the Cubs in 1933 after outfielder Kiki Cuyler broke his ankle. Frank showed some promise with modest power and a .272 average, but Chicago officials realized that one more year in the minors would help him. When the Cubs called up outfielder Tuck Stainback from the Angels, Demaree was sent to replace him.

Manager Jack Lelivelt's veteran team had won the pennant handily in 1933 and most of the day-to-day players were back for another try. Lelivelt worked on Demaree's swing, attempting to teach him to hit for distance as well as average to take advantage of the attractive power alleys at Wrigley Field.

Helped by a schedule that kept them in Wrigley Field for

the first four weeks of the season — including a series when stadium tenant Hollywood was the "home" team — the Angels jumped off to a 23-5 record and a six-game lead.

Demaree proved to be an outstanding student and by the end of the long home stand was leading the league with a .486 average. He continued his amazing batting pace and remained above .400 into mid-June before cooling off.

The Angels were so far in front of the rest of the pack that Coast League directors ordered a split season and a playoff series against a team of PCL All-Stars if Los Angeles won the second half, which it did quite handily.

Demaree was the Triple Crown champion and run-away winner of the Most Valuable Player Award. He was first in batting average (.383), runs (190), hits (269), doubles (51), home runs (45) and runs batted in (173). His 41 stolen bases ranked fifth. Frank returned to the Windy City in 1935 and began an 10-year big league stay.

Demaree, born Joseph Franklin Dimaria, was raised on a farm in Winters, not far from Sacramento. In high school, Frank starred in baseball, tennis and track, where he was clocked at 10 seconds flat in the 100-yard dash. Frank played shortstop well enough to appear with semi-pro teams around the Sacramento Valley and was converted to the outfield by a manager who wanted to play shortstop himself.

After several trials, Sacramento gave Demaree a contract in 1930 and he hit .228 in 41 games. Frank was one of the Senators' stars as a sophomore, averaging .312 and leading the team in hits (210) and runs batted in (104). He and first baseman Dolph Camilli shared the club's home run title with 16.

Scouts took notice of Demaree and the following year there was considerable interest. Owner Lew Moreing wanted to make sure Frank wasn't drafted at the end of the season, so when the Cubs offered an undisclosed amount of cash for his outfielder, Moreing jumped at the proposal. Demaree took the train to Chicago after hitting .364 and driving in 84 runs in 109 games.

Manager Rogers Hornsby wanted to play Demaree in the outfield every day, but team president William Veeck Sr. did not. After Hornsby was fired and Charlie Grimm took over, Frank hit .250 playing part-time in 23 games.

When Demaree returned to the Cubs from Los Angeles he hit .325, .350 and .324 in three seasons, then fell to .273

Frank Demaree

in 1938 and was traded to the New York Giants.

After hitting better than .300 as a regular for two years, the Giants found little use for Demaree in 1940 and he moved to the Boston Braves on waivers in July. Frank was relegated to the role of utility outfielder with the Braves, St. Louis Cardinals and St. Louis Browns in three more seasons to conclude his career one base hit shy of a .300 lifetime average.

When the Browns dropped him, Demaree found his way to Portland in 1944. But, he had ballooned to 225 pounds and hit .260 in 35 games, leading one writer to say that on the ball field Frank was, "big as a house and twice as useless."

The Beavers employed him again in 1945 largely because no club wanted to let any able-bodied and experienced man go when the player pool had been reduced drastically by World War II. To everyone's surprise, Frank showed up in camp weighing 190. He batted clean-up most of the time and his potent bat and outstanding glove helped the Beavers bring the first pennant to Vaughn Street Park since 1936.

When Frank hit .304 with the Beavers, the Philadelphia Athletics thought he might still have a few major league games left and took him as the first pick in the draft for $7,000. He was on the A's spring roster but was cut before the season began.

Demaree managed Fresno in 1947 and briefly with Wisconsin Rapids in the Wisconsin State League the next

JOSEPH FRANKLIN DEMAREE
Born: 6/10/10, Winters, CA, BR/TR, 5-foot-11.5, 185 pounds

		G	AB	R	H	2B	3B	HR	RBI	SB	AVG.
1930	Sac	41	127	24	29	6	3	1	18	0	.228
1931	Sac	180	674	89	210	41	10	16	104	13	.312
1932	Sac	109	437	71	159	20	6	12	84	6	.364
1934	LA	186	702	190	269	51	4	45	173	41	.383
1944	Port	35	104	12	27	7	0	0	12	2	.260
1945	Port	136	514	87	156	36	3	3	78	5	.304
PCL	6	687	2558	473	850	161	26	77	469	67	.332
Majors	12	1155	4144	578	1241	190	36	72	591	33	.299

year and finished his career as a player-manager for San Bernardino in the Sunset League in 1950. Frank also was a Chicago White Sox scout. After retirement he worked for the United Artists Studio in Hollywood until his death at age 48.

DOM DIMAGGIO

When he first showed up in a San Francisco Seals uniform in 1937, grave doubts were expressed that Dom DiMaggio had the ability to become a Coast League regular.

Skeptics said manager Lefty O'Doul kept him in training camp to cash in on the publicity generated by the fact he was the younger brother of Joe DiMaggio, who had starred in the PCL and moved on to the New York Yankees.

Dom was smaller than the 5-foot-9, 168-pound measurements he would attain in later years and he wore glasses, giving him the bookish appearance that eventually earned him the nickname "The Little Professor." But Dom wasn't disheartened by the criticism.

"I knew I was supposed to have a job only because Joe was a great player," he said. "Joe's example only made me try harder."

The Seals knew about Dom because of Joe and another older ball-playing brother, Vince, who had been sold to the Boston Red Sox after five seasons in the PCL. All three grew up playing at Funston Playground in San Francisco's Marina district near the Italian neighborhood in North Beach. Dom attended Galileo High School, but didn't play on the baseball team, perfecting his skills instead in city leagues.

Dom wasn't in the starting lineup when the 1937 season began. He made a few late inning defensive appearances until mid-April when he blasted a double and three singles in his first start against Sacramento. Dom didn't tear up the league, however, and only a late-season batting surge lifted his average to .306. Strictly a singles hitter, he batted lead-off and led the Seals with 109 runs and 15 steals.

A foot operation kept DiMaggio out of spring training and led to an uneven season in 1938. Before he slumped at the plate during the summer, *San Francisco Chronicle* baseball writer Ed Hughes said, "without a day's spring training he is the best center fielder in the Coast League."

Hughes said Dom did not have the experience to play the outfield like Jigger Statz — acknowledged as the PCL's best — but his speed made up for this deficiency. Dom led Coast League outfielders with 29 assists.

DiMaggio raised his batting average at the end of the season once again, hitting .307. He led the ball club in steals (16) and was second in runs (120), hits (202) and doubles (42).

At least one observer thought DiMaggio didn't earn every hit. Steve George, sports editor of the *Sacramento Union*, remarked that home town scorers helped Dom, who "hits over .300 at home and goes hitless day after day on the road." George prided himself on his own objectivity

and in 1933 had made a controversial scoring decision that kept alive Joe DiMaggio's record hitting streak, which eventually reached 61 games.

O'Doul shortened Dom's stride at the plate, moved him down into the heart of the batting order in 1939 and DiMaggio responded with his best year. The fans thought so, the press thought so, but most of the scouts weren't so sure.

DiMaggio batted .360, losing out to San Diego's Dom Dallessandro, who captured the batting title with a .368

"If he had (brother) Joe's size, he would probably be just as great a ballplayer."
— Scout Charles Chapman
about Dom DiMaggio

---

average. Dom had been hitting near .400 at mid-year when a wrist injury cut 40 points off his average. His 165 runs and 239 hits were the best in the league, which he also led with 27 outfield assists. Dom showed some pop in his bat with 48 two baggers, 18 triples and 14 homers.

The sportswriters voted him the most valuable player and owner Charlie Graham sold him to the Boston Red Sox for a reported $60,000 and players. O'Doul castigated the scouts, saying Dom won at least 40 games for the Seals, "yet not one scout recommended Dominic because he looked frail and wore glasses."

That statement wasn't entirely accurate. Cincinnati Reds scout Charles Chapman, a professor across the bay in Berkeley at the University of California, had written a glowing report that was revealed by the *Oakland Post-Enquire*r after Chapman's death in 1941. Chapman's report summarized Dom's abilities quite accurately.

"He has amply proved that his glasses make no difference," Chapman said. "If he had Joe's size, he would probably be just as great a ballplayer. (There is) no question but that he can do everything well (and is) a great outfielder and a fine base runner, the equal of Joe or Vince in the field, their superior on the bases."

In a 1940 spring training story published in the *Oakland Tribune*, Boston manager Joe Cronin said that he had asked Earl Sheely to compare Dom with Joe Marty, Bobby Doerr and Myril Hoag, three PCL stars who had moved up to the majors. Sheely said Dom was better than either

---

DOMINIC PAUL DI MAGGIO
Born: 2/12/17, San Francisco, CA, BR/TR, 5-foot-9, 168 pounds

		G	AB	R	H	2B	3B	HR	RBI	SB	AVG.
1937	SF	140	496	109	152	33	7	5	46	15	.306
1938	SF	163	659	120	202	42	9	5	60	16	.307
1939	SF	170	664	165	239	48	18	14	82	39	.360
PCL	3	473	1819	394	593	123	34	24	188	70	.326
Majors	11	1399	5640	1046	1680	308	57	87	618	100	.298

Dom DiMaggio (left) with brother Joe at an exhibition game.

Marty or Hoag and had more power than Doerr. Sheely was wrong about Doerr's power, but on the mark with his other comparisons.

The Red Sox were never sorry they bought Joe's little brother. During 10 full seasons in the American League, Dom stood up well in comparisons with Joe, who was with the Yankees during the same period.

Dom couldn't match Joe's batting average or power, but he was an outstanding lead-off batter who scored more than 100 runs six times and led the league twice. The Red Sox moved Doc Cramer out of center field when Dom arrived and DiMaggio more than held his own on defense in the Bean Town outfield.

DiMaggio hit .301 in 108 games as a rookie and led the league in outfield assists for the first of three times during his career. He hit .283 and .286 in two more seasons and then spent three years in the Navy.

The BoSox won the American League title in his first year back from the service with Dom batting .316. He hit better than .300 twice more with a high of .328 in 1950, the same year he led the league in triples and stolen bases. Dom had two lengthy batting streaks during his career, 34 games in 1947 and 27 four seasons later.

DiMaggio set several fielding records, including most chances and put outs for an outfielder in 1948 and led the league in put outs twice.

An eye infection inhibited Dom's play in 1953 and he retired after going to bat three times as a pinch hitter. He retired with a .298 lifetime average.

After baseball, Dom was a success in the business world as the owner of manufacturing plants and founder of two New England banks.

VINCE DIMAGGIO

Although he spent seven seasons in the Coast League and another eight full years in the majors, Vince DiMaggio remains the odd man out when baseball fans discuss the DiMaggio family.

The "other" DiMaggio was a talented outfielder with less all-round skill than brothers Joe and Dom. He showed some power, but struck out an inordinate number of times.

DiMaggio's strikeout marks would not be unusual in today's game, but they dominated discussions about his ability in the 1930s and 1940s. Vince led the National League in Ks a record six times, had 100 or more four times and never finished lower than third on the strikeout chart. He set a league record of 134 in 1938 that stood for 22 years until Philadelphia's Frank Herrera fanned 136 times.

Vince learned to deal with this shortcoming. Casey Stengel, who was his manager in Boston and Oakland, said, "Vince is the only player I ever saw who could strike out three times in a game and not be embarrassed. He'd walk into the clubhouse whistling."

DiMaggio's lifetime batting average of .249 was nearly 50 points lower than Dom's and 76 below Joe's, but his defensive ability was on a par. A great outfielder who could cover acres of territory and field ground balls like a shortstop, Vince led the league in assists three times and had a .981 fielding average — three percentage points higher than either of his brothers.

Two years older than Joe, Vince learned to play ball in San Francisco and was hired by the Seals after a 1931 trial. Sent to Tucson in 1932, he hit .347, led the Arizona-Texas League in homers with 25 and was recalled in time to hit .270 in 59 games.

Vince's most important contribution to the Seals was his recommendation that they sign brother Joe, who played three games at the end of the season and became a three-year regular after that.

Vince started 1933 as San Francisco's center fielder, but hurt his throwing arm and before long lost the job to Joe, who hit safely in a record 61 straight games among other accomplishments.

Released for economy reasons, Vince moved to Hollywood. In 96 games over the season, he batted .333, including .348 with the Stars. Vince became an outfield fixture with the Twinks for two more years and stayed with the team when the franchise moved south to San Diego in 1936.

DiMaggio led the league in games played in the last two seasons of this period and was tops in assists in 1936. After three good seasons at the plate with averages of .288, .278 and .293, more than 100 runs batted in twice and showing evidence of power, Vince was sold to the Boston Braves.

Although he led the league in assists both years, Vince's stay with the Braves resulted in two strikeout championships and batting marks of only .256 and .228.

Sent to Kansas City in the American Association, Vince had the good fortune to play for manager Bill Meyer, who

Vince DiMaggio

changed his swing. Ruppert Stadium was one of the most spacious in baseball, but Vince hit 46 home runs to break the team's record, knocked in 136 runs and hit .290. Cincinnati bought him at the end of the season.

The Reds traded him to Pittsburgh early in 1940 and he spent five years in the Steel City, posting averages between .238 and .267, but earning his way in the outfield. The Bucs swapped Vince to Philadelphia, who turned him over to the New York Giants in a second trade in 1946. The Giants dropped Vince when he went 0 for 25, perhaps the poorest finish to any big league career.

Vince joined San Francisco and hit .264 in 43 games as the Seals won the pennant. DiMaggio was released and joined Oakland after the 1947 season started, appropriately striking out as a pinch hitter in his first time at bat. The fans were dismayed that Stengel would put Vince in the outfield in place of Don Smith, who was hitting well above .300.

"Little in DiMaggio's record indicates he will be a wow with the Oaks, unless as a stop gap until a more consistent hitter comes along," said Clyde Giraldo of the *San Francisco Chronicle*.

Vince played the entire season, hitting only .241 but leading the Acorns with 22 home runs and contributing 81 RBIs.

In June, he hit a line drive homer 400 feet just to the right of the clock near center field in Oaks Park. Reporters said it compared with other tape measure home runs hit at

---

VINCENT PAUL DI MAGGIO
Born: 9/6/12, Martinez, CA, BR/TR, 5-foot-11, 183 pounds

		G	AB	R	H	2B	3B	HR	RBI	SB	AVG.
1932	SF	59	200	35	54	13	2	6	31	2	.270
1933	SF-Hd	96	339	54	113	24	4	11	65	7	.333
1934	Hwd	166	587	89	169	25	3	17	91	7	.288
1935	Hwd	174	659	107	183	36	4	24	112	15	.278
1936	SD	176	641	109	188	43	14	19	102	22	.293
1946	SF	43	129	19	34	10	2	1	21	3	.264
1947	Oak	140	473	80	114	20	4	22	81	7	.241
PCL	7	854	3028	493	855	171	33	100	503	63	.282
Majors	10	1110	3849	491	959	209	24	125	584	79	.249

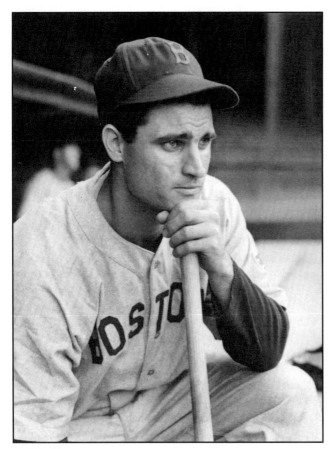

Bobby Doerr

the ballpark by former Oakland sluggers Roy Carlyle and Ernie Lombardi.

DiMaggio spent the last four years of his career as a manager, first at Stockton, where he led the California League with 30 home runs. He played with Pittsburg of the Far West League for three more seasons, posting big numbers in runs, homers, RBIs and batting average and guiding the team to two titles.

BOBBY DOERR

Hall of Fame second baseman Bobby Doerr was a skillful, reliable, durable and consistent second baseman over his long career. When he came into the Pacific Coast League fresh out of Jefferson High School in Los Angeles, the word that best described him was young.

The player recognized as the youngest to appear in the Pacific Coast League is Los Angeles catcher Bill Sarni. At 15 years, 10 months and 10 days of age upon his debut in 1943, Sarni was one of three catchers who backed up regular Bill Holm in 33 games over the course of the season.

When Doerr stepped onto the diamond at Wrigley Field on Aug. 9, 1934, to start earning his first paycheck as a professional with the Hollywood Stars, he was on the threshold of putting his own name in the PCL record book.

Doerr entered that game and the next as a substitute for second baseman Joe Berkowitz and by Aug. 11 was given

the job for the rest of the season. On that day, at age 16 years, 3 months and 25 days, Doerr apparently became the youngest every day player in league history. He played 67 games the rest of the way, hitting .259 and finishing in the middle of the fielding table, but ahead of several veteran second sackers, including Berkowitz.

Robert Pershing Doerr was born a year and a day after America's entry into World War I and his middle name honored the famous commander of the American Expeditionary Force in Europe, General John J. "Black

---

"The most natural second baseman I've seen in many a day. He can't miss."

*— Boston Red Sox manager
Joe Cronin about rookie
Bobby Doerr*

Jack" Pershing.

Baseball scouts started following Doerr's progress when he was 14 and playing for an American Legion team that included catcher Mickey Owen, third baseman Steve Mesner and first sacker George McDonald. This youthful Los Angeles aggregation won the Western regional championship and lost to the eventual national champions from New Orleans.

It was no surprise when Bobby signed with Hollywood, since there was demonstrable baseball talent in his family. Doerr's older brother, Hal, already was catching for Portland.

In the year following his rookie campaign, Doerr teamed with 19-year-old scatter-armed shortstop George Myatt in the Twinks' keystone combination. Each came within one of leading the league in errors at his position as the Stars trailed the league in fielding average and finished fourth in the first half and last in the split season's second half.

Doerr and Myatt held their own at the plate. Doerr averaged .317 — third best on the team — and Myatt batted .311. Doerr was named Hollywood's most valuable player.

With the ball club losing money because of declining fan support and the Los Angeles Angels ordering a 100 percent increase in the Wrigley Field rent, Hollywood owner Bill Lane quit Movieland in 1936 and moved his ball club to San Diego.

Doerr and the team — now renamed the Padres —

ROBERT PERSHING DOERR
Born: 4/7/18, Los Angeles, CA, BR/TR, 5-foot-11, 175 pounds

		G	AB	R	H	2B	3B	HR	RBI	SB	AVG.
1934	Hwd	67	201	12	52	6	0	0	11	1	.259
1935	Hwd	172	647	87	205	22	8	4	74	5	.317
1936	SD	175	695	100	238	37	12	2	77	30	.342
PCL	3	414	1543	199	495	65	20	6	162	36	.321
Majors	14	1865	7093	1094	2042	381	89	223	1247	54	.288

thrived in the new environment. San Diego tied Oakland for second place and Doerr hit .342, fourth best in the league, and led with 238 hits. He had 100 runs, 37 doubles and a dozen triples, improved his fielding and showed a growing ability to range far and wide by leading in assists.

Eddie Collins of the Boston Red Sox visited the West Coast and the first time he watched Doerr, Bobby made four errors. But, the more Collins saw of Doerr, the better he liked him.

The BoSox acquired Doerr and in the 1937 spring camp, manager Joe Cronin pronounced him, "the most natural second baseman I've seen in many a day. He can't miss."

Bobby fielded brilliantly, but when he was hit on the head by a pitch, Earl McNair took over at second base. Doerr averaged .224 in 55 games as a utility player.

His career rolled on for 13 more seasons with the Red Sox and Bobby became one of the best men at his position in the American League. Frequently compared with the other great second baseman of the period, Joe Gordon, Doerr perhaps was the steadier of the two. Doerr made 46 fewer errors than Gordon in 2,300 more fielding chances and Bobby's's career average afield was .980 to Joe's .970.

Doerr led the league in every fielding category except errors, topping the averages four times, put outs in four years, assists in three seasons and double plays in five. He set records for most consecutive games without an error, 73, and most chances without a miscue, 414.

Fenway Park helped Doerr's power totals and he hit 223 home runs with a high of 27 twice and batted in 100-plus runs six times. Bobby usually batted .300 or close to it and his best average was .325 in 1944, the year he won the league's Most Valuable Player Award.

Back from a year in the service, Bobby played in his only World Series in 1946, leading the losing Red Sox with a .409 average. He was a member of the All-Star team eight times.

A bad back forced Doerr to retire after the 1951 season, but he continued to work for the Red Sox as a scout.

AUGIE GALAN

Sore-armed right-handers usually are pitchers, but Augie Galan played the majority of his career in the infield and outfield with a painful limb that didn't prevent him from becoming a star.

One day near his 10th birthday, Augie fell from a tree and cracked his right elbow. Afraid of punishment, Augie told his parents that he had only bruised the elbow. He never was able to straighten out the arm, but learned to throw using his shoulder muscles and performed well enough to play in the outfield.

Although his arm injury was well known and discussed by the *Sporting News* as early as 1935, the baseball paper treated it as big news when the injury led to Galan's classification as 4F and unfit physically to serve in the military in World War II. By 1945, the arm began to give him trouble and the switch-hitting Galan stopped batting right-

handed to ease the pain. His average was unaffected by the change since he always was a better hitter as a lefty.

The injury didn't prevent him from starring in baseball at Berkeley High School, not far from his dad's French laundry. He accepted a San Francisco contract in 1931. The Seals farmed Augie to Globe in the Arizona-Texas League and brought him to camp in 1932.

Two other prospects were supposed to vie for the shortstop job. When one proved a bust and the other was crippled by injuries, Galan took over at the start of the season. The new Seals shortstop got off to an awful start, going hitless in his first 18 at bats in six games and committing three errors.

Manager Lefty O'Doul stuck with the speedy Galan and Augie rewarded his confidence with a .291 average, 122 runs scored and 75 RBIs. Near the end of the year, the Seals gave Galan permission to leave the club early to go on a barnstorming trip to Hawaii, clearing the way for the debut of another rookie at shortstop named Joe DiMaggio.

Often called Frenchy in his PCL days, Galan played shortstop and second base in 1933 as O'Doul made him the clean-up hitter. It was a wise choice and Galan batted .356 on 265 hits with 51 doubles and 102 RBIs. He led the league in runs (164) and triples (22).

The Chicago Cubs came calling with a monumental deal that gave the Seals $25,000 cash and seven veteran players, including several who became the backbone of the ball club for years: pitchers Sam Gibson, Win Ballou, Leroy Hermann and Walter Mails; catchers Larry Woodall and Hugh McMullen and infielder Lenny Backer.

Galan was a reserve in Chicago his first season, but became a regular after that. A series of injuries over the course of 16 years in the majors reduced his playing time and Augie estimated he missed one full season from knee injuries alone.

Galan batted above .300 six times and led the league in steals in 1935 and 1937. His best season was 1935 — the year before his first knee injury — when he batted .314 with a league-leading 133 runs, plus 41 doubles, 11 triples and 12 homers. He was a member of three All-Star teams and played in three World Series, but hit only .138 in 29 trips to the plate.

The Cubs sent Galan to the Angels in August, 1941, and Augie was about ready to retire. His request that Los Angeles officials let him make a deal for himself was refused, but four days later Brooklyn general manager Larry MacPhail called and said he had purchased Augie's

AUGUST JOHN GALAN
Born: 5/25/12, Berkeley, CA, BB/TR, 6-foot, 175 pounds

		G	AB	R	H	2B	3B	HR	RBI	SB	AVG.
1932	SF	183	712	122	207	37	12	6	75	14	.291
1933	SF	189	745	164	265	51	22	9	102	41	.356
1950	Oak	147	447	96	126	25	3	13	72	10	.282
1951	Oak	118	323	69	99	15	1	13	64	4	.307
PCL	4	637	2227	451	697	128	38	41	313	69	.313
Majors	16	1742	5937	1004	1706	336	74	100	830	123	.287

Augie Galan

Joe Gordon

contract for $2,500.

On the verge of becoming a regular again in 1942, Augie was stricken with typhoid fever and finished at .263 in 69 games. He played first base, second base and the outfield for the Dodgers for four more seasons and averaged a steady .318, .307 and .310 in the last three.

Brooklyn traded Augie to Cincinnati, where he hit .314 in 1947. He filled a utility role the following season and was released. His major league career ended with 17 plate appearances with the New York Giants in 1949.

Galan played first base and the outfield and coached with Oakland in 1950 and 1951. He filled a valuable role both years, hitting .282 and .307 to conclude his PCL career with a .313 lifetime mark.

Augie managed the Oaks in 1953, but was fired when the team finished seventh. Galan coached with the Philadelphia Athletics the following season and retired to run a string of meat markets he owned in the Bay Area.

JOE GORDON

Joe Gordon was an outstanding second baseman who fielded brilliantly and hit with power. If Joe's batting average had been 20 points higher he might be in the Hall of Fame.

Joe was called the "best .280 hitter in baseball" in his prime as a major leaguer. Grantland Rice said Gordon, "has shut off more base hits than any fielder I ever saw. He not only is lightning fast with hands and feet, but an acrobat who began practicing that profession years ago."

"Gordon has no weakness in the field," Dan Daniel wrote in the *Sporting News* in 1941. "He will wander to his left, he will move fast to his right, he can come in on slow balls, he will run back as far as anybody. He is a great pivot with a fine arm. Pivoting is an art born in a great second sacker. It requires confidence, mobility and agility and Gordon has them all in acute measures."

Analyst Bill James rates Gordon as the outstanding major league second baseman between Charlie Gehringer and Jackie Robinson.

Gordon began his career in the PCL in 1936 and returned 15 years later to pace the league in home runs. "I thought that year (1951) he was the best player I ever saw in the Coast League," said Bill Conlin of the *Sacramento Bee*, an observer of the league since the 1930s.

Nicknamed "Flash" for the futuristic comic strip charac-

JOSEPH LOWELL GORDON
Born: 2/18/15, Los Angeles, CA, BR/TR, 5-foot-10, 180 pounds

		G	AB	R	H	2B	3B	HR	RBI	SB	AVG.
1936	Oak	143	533	73	160	33	4	6	56	9	.300
1951	Sac	148	485	97	145	24	3	43	136	2	.299
1952	Sac	122	370	39	91	18	0	16	46	5	.246
1957	SF	1	3	0	2	0	0	0	0	0	.667
PCL	4	414	1391	209	398	75	7	65	238	16	.286
Majors	11	1566	5707	914	1530	264	52	253	975	89	.268

ter of the day, Joe played football at Jefferson High School in Portland in the same backfield with future Stanford All-American Bobby Grayson. Although Gordon earned a bachelor's degree at the University of Oregon after he had been in the major leagues, he began his college career as a 140-pound halfback on the freshman football team.

Gordon added 20 pounds by the following spring and was urged to turn out for the varsity. Yankees scout Bill Essick was afraid he'd get hurt playing football and proposed a contract, but Joe refused. Gordon hit .418 for the

---

"I thought that year he was the best player I ever saw in the Coast League."
— *Bill Conlin about Joe Gordon in 1951*

Ducks baseball team, relented and took the $500 bonus.

Sent to spring training with Oakland in 1936, Gordon was told to report to Class A Binghamton. Cocky and confident, Joe refused, saying, "I can't make any money that way." He was kept at camp and got into the line-up when Bernie DeViveiros was injured.

Although Joe spent most of his career at second base, he played shortstop — his college position — for the Oaks. Joe's fielding was adequate and he batted .300 with 33 doubles.

Reassigned to the great Newark team the next year, Gordon batted lead-off, belting 26 homers and compiling a .280 average. "He's better than anybody in the big leagues now with the exception of Gehringer and he'll catch him in a year," said Newark manager Ossie Vitt.

Joe was promoted to the Yankees in 1938, but Frank Crosetti was entrenched at shortstop, so manager Joe McCarthy converted Gordon to second base and released aging Tony Lazzeri.

Gordon anchored the infield for six seasons until he entered military service in 1944. After a .255 rookie season with 25 home runs and 97 RBIs, Joe hit between .276 and .322 before falling to .249 in 1943. He was the American League Most Valuable Player in 1942, winning over Triple Crown champion Ted Williams of Boston.

Joe hit .210 in his first year back from the service in 1946 and after the season was traded to Cleveland by general manager Larry MacPhail, who thought his play was indifferent. Joe teamed with shortstop Lou Boudreau to help the Tribe win the 1948 pennant and defeat the Boston Braves in the World Series

Wide-ranging afield, Gordon grabbed balls other infielders could only wave at and was first in the league in assists three times and errors in four seasons. He hit 24 or more homers six times and drove in 103 or more runs on four occasions. A seven-time all-star, Joe played in six World Series.

After hitting .268 in 11 big league seasons and establishing many fielding records, Joe moved down to the Coast

League as manager of the Sacramento Solons in 1951. He hit .299 and led the circuit in home runs (43) and RBIs (136), both Sacramento records at the time. In mid-year, Sacramento general manager Eddie Mulligan turned down an request from Bill Veeck to hire Joe to manage the St. Louis Browns. Mulligan said Gordon was too big a draw at the gate and Joe also rejected the proposal.

The Solons finished seventh and eighth under Gordon. When his batting average dropped to .246 and his homer production fell to 16 in 1952, Gordon quit at the end of the season.

Joe scouted for Detroit until 1956, when he took over the San Francisco Seals after Eddie Joost was fired. The Seals finished sixth, but Gordon guided them to the pennant in 1957, the Coast League's last year before the National League moved west.

Gordon later managed Cleveland, Detroit and Kansas City. He moved from Cleveland to Detroit when the Indians swapped him for Jimmy Dykes in a trade of managers unique in major league history.

STAN HACK

It took Stan Hack just one season to go from an untested rookie Coast Leaguer to the start of a big league career that would brand him as the best player ever to come out of Sacramento.

San Francisco Missions manager Red Killefer tried unsuccessfully to hire the slender, boyish-looking Hack in 1930. Hack carried around the contract Killefer had sent him for weeks, but Red fell ill and no one pressed Hack to sign.

The 21-year-old graduate of Sacramento High School wasn't sure he was ready for the Coast League, although that winter he led the Sacramento Winter League with a .460 average.

In the spring, Sacramento manager Buddy Ryan invited Stan to come to the Senators camp. Hack took two weeks vacation from his bookkeeping job at the Bank of America and began working out with the team.

The Senators operated in the smallest minor league market in the high minors. One of the primary ways owner Lew Moreing made ends meet was finding and developing talented young players and selling them to major league teams. His 1931 club had other youngsters beside Hack who showed promise — first baseman Dolph Camilli, 24, and outfielders Hank Steinbacher, 18; Frenchy Bordagaray, 20, and Frank Demaree, 20. All four were

---

STANLEY CAMFIELD HACK
Born: 12/6/09, Sacramento, CA, BL/TR, 6-foot, 170 pounds

		G	AB	R	H	2B	3B	HR	RBI	SB	AVG.
1931	Sac	164	660	128	232	36	13	2	37	20	.352
PCL	1	164	660	128	232	36	13	2	37	20	.352
Majors	16	1938	7278	1239	2193	363	81	57	642	165	.301

Stan Hack

sold to the big leagues later.

Hack made the team, but rode the bench in the early going except for a playing a few games out of position in the outfield or as a pinch runner.

Regular third baseman Jimmy McLaughlin was sidelined with a broken thumb. Lenny Backer filled in ably until he was hit on the head by a pitch in late April and put out of the game for the rest of the season. Hack was stationed at third — his natural position — and led the Senators with a .352 batting mark and 128 runs scored. He was unsteady at third base and fielded only .942, the lowest of any full season in his career.

Several teams were interested in Hack, but the Chicago Cubs paid Moreing $50,000 and a player for his contract after the season ended.

Veteran Woody English was at third base when Stan arrived with the Cubs. Stan hit .236 in 72 games, but fielded a miserable .913 and was sent to Albany in the International League in 1933. He improved in all departments and returned to the Windy City.

Just before the season ended, Hack's arm was broken by a batted ball. When the arm didn't heal properly it had to be reset, slowing Stan down when the 1934 season opened. He hit .289 in 111 games, although he faced heavy competition for playing time from English.

Hack fought off Freddie Lindstrom for the third base job the following season with a .311 average and solidified his position. He went on to become the outstanding third baseman of his era as well as an all-fields hitter who drew better than 75 walks a season on average during his last 14 seasons. Stan had speed on the base paths and led the National League in steals in 1938 and 1939.

Until he stopped playing every day after the 1945 season, Hack was a consistent hitter whose average ranged from .282 to .323. Stan hit .301 over the course of 16 seasons in the majors. He never played for any team but the Cubs and was enormously popular with Chicago fans, not only for his dependability and talent, but for his pleasant disposition.

Stan was a money player in every sense of the phrase. He hit .400 in four All-Star game appearances and .348 in four World Series. Baseball analyst Bill James finds it odd that Hack has not received more consideration for election to the Hall of Fame.

After he retired following the 1947 season, Hack managed the Cubs' farm team at Des Moines in the Western League for two seasons, winning a pennant in his debut. He moved to Springfield in the International League in 1950 and came to Los Angeles for three years and two third place finishes.

Hack was set to manage the Angels again in 1954 when he was elevated to the Cubs at the end of March. Manager Phil Cavaretta was fired for telling owner P. K. Wrigley the Cubs were sure second division finishers. Wrigley thought the prediction was "defeatism," but Stan proved Cavaretta right with a seventh place finish.

He had two more teams in the second division, was fired and joined the St. Louis Cardinals as a coach in 1957 and 1958.

MYRIL HOAG

In his Coast League days, Myril Hoag gained some notoriety for the size of his feet and the controversy surrounding his purchase by the New York Yankees.

Hoag's tiny tootsies weren't what you'd call the talk of the league since the fleet-footed outfielder could cover plenty of ground for Sacramento. But, his feet were smallest in the PCL and the fact that one was a size 4 and the other a 4 1/2 meant that he had to have wear custom made baseball spikes.

His 1930 sale to New York touched off a rhubarb that was not resolved until it went all the way to the commissioner's office.

Hoag was only one element of the brouhaha, which centered on Sacramento's acquisition of pitcher Fay Thomas from Baltimore before the season started in a complicated and apparently illegal transaction.

Thomas was a powerful right-hander who went on to a long career in the Coast League. He was 18-20 for the Senators in 1930.

Hoag was batting .377 at mid-year and major league scouts were after him. However, Sacramento owner Lew Moreing had made a grievous error before the season, agreeing to a secret proposal from Yankees scout Bill Essick to take Hoag for $25,000 plus Thomas.

When Cleveland's Cy Slapnicka offered $50,000 and four good players and New York Giants manager John McGraw said he'd give $60,000, Moreing knew he'd made a terrible mistake. Moreing tried to send Thomas back to New York. He contended the Yankees didn't have a legitimate option on Hoag, because they farmed Fay to the Senators illegally instead of selling him to Sacramento for $5,000, as had been announced.

Thomas wrote to Baseball Commissioner Kenesaw Mountain Landis, who could have declared him a free agent, a circumstance that would have permitted Thomas to make his own deal for perhaps $15,000. When Landis read the riot act to Moreing over the telephone, the Sacramento owner quickly accepted $40,000 from the

Myril Hoag

Yankees for Hoag and bought Thomas.

Hoag wasn't a five-figure player when he broke in with Sacramento in two games late in 1926. But the 18-year-old from nearby Davis had performed well in the Sacramento Valley League and had good blood lines. His father, Tracy, had played in the outlaw California League.

Sacramento sent Hoag to Twin Falls in the Utah-Idaho League in 1927 where he hit .305 in 55 games. Recalled late in the year, Myril was overpowered by PCL pitching in four games. He sat out 1928, but came to training camp the following spring ready to compete for an outfield position. Hoag won a starting spot and began to show the league that he belonged.

"Hoag is as stylish an outfielder as you will see in any league," raved the *San Francisco Chronicle's* Ed Hughes. "He has speed, he is a marvelous fielder and he throws like a shot and on the mark. He has only to do some hitting to have the scouts on his trail."

Myril and shortstop Ray French liked to demonstrate their arm strength for early arrivals at Sacramento's Moreing Field by standing near the right field fence and throwing balls against the screen behind home plate.

Although he was well down on the fielding table, Myril covered a lot of ground and his 2.59 total chances per game was just behind the 2.68 registered by legendary Los

MYRIL OLIVER HOAG
Born: 3/9/08, Davis, CA, BR/TR, 5-foot-11, 180 pounds

		G	AB	R	H	2B	3B	HR	RBI	SB	AVG.
1926	Sac	2	3	0	1	0	0	0	2	0	.333
1927	Sac	4	16	0	3	1	0	0	0	0	.188
1929	Sac	116	414	47	116	25	2	6	54	5	.280
1930	Sac	188	725	148	244	57	9	17	121	19	.337
PCL		4	310	1158	195	364	83	11	23	177	24	.314
Majors		13	1020	3147	384	854	141	33	28	401	59	.271

Angeles center fielder Jigger Statz. In 116 games, Myril hit .280 with 25 doubles.

His last year in the Coast League saw Hoag produce a well-rounded set of stats. He topped Solons regulars with a .337 average and was among the league leaders in runs (148), doubles (57) and RBIs (121). Myril teamed with outfielders Frank Osborn and Brick Eldred to give Sacramento one of the league's best fielding trios.

Hoag was almost exclusively a utility outfielder with the Yanks. But he played that role well enough to stick with

---

"He has only to do some hitting to have the scouts on his trail."
— Ed Hughes about Myril Hoag

---

the Bronx Bombers for seven seasons and collect three World Series checks.

He averaged 67 games annually in New York and suffered a severe brain concussion in a 1936 collision with Joe DiMaggio. The following season was his best as Myril made a remarkable recovery and hit .301 in 106 games.

In the five-game World Series against the Giants, he started and hit .300. Attempts to convert Hoag into a pitcher failed, although he later took the mound in three games with the St. Louis Browns and Cleveland Indians.

The Browns got Hoag in a trade late in 1938 and he became a regular, batting .295 and .262 in St. Louis and .255 with the Chicago White Sox in 1941. Myril enlisted in the Air Force in 1942 and concluded his career with the White Sox and Cleveland after the war.

Hoag moved to Florida, where he played and managed successfully. He took up pitching seriously in 1947 while managing Gainesville, compiled a 71-24 record over four seasons and threw a 1948 no-hit game against St. Augustine. He led the league in batting twice.

Hoag asked for his release after the 1949 season. Myril became a trucking company executive and spent more time on the golf course, where he was always regarded as one of professional baseball's best players.

FRED HUTCHINSON

No Coast League pitcher ever had a better rookie year in baseball than Fred Hutchinson.

Only 18 years old when the 1938 season began, Hutch took the league by storm and led manager Jack Lelivelt's Seattle Rainiers to a second place finish. They wound up 3 1/2 games behind the team fielded by Lelivelt's former employer, the Los Angeles Angels.

The Rainiers were rated as a second division ball club before the season started. The *San Francisco Chronicle's* Will Connolly placed Seattle sixth in his preseason prognostications and warned that, the "pitching is doubtful unless a 14-game winner is acquired."

Fred Hutchinson

Hutchinson, a man-sized 6-foot-2, 190-pounder, gave the team more wins than that, grabbing a league-leading 25 victories, losing only seven and compiling the PCL's best earned run average of 2.48. Fred completed 29 of 35 starts and pitched 290 innings, the league's third highest total.

A sportswriters panel for the *Sporting News* voted Hutchinson the most valuable player over runner-up second baseman Eddie Mayo of Los Angeles. At year's end, the *Sporting News* named Fred the Minor League Player of the Year. It was a great season for any player, but a remarkable one for a youngster little more than a year away from Seattle's Franklin High School.

After graduation, Fred joined the Yakima team run by former Seattle manager George Burns in the semi-pro Timber League. Fred's performance was outstanding and Detroit tried to sign him. Hutchinson's physician father demanded a $5,000 bonus. When the Tigers refused, Fred inked a $2,500 Seattle contract which carried a promise

---

FREDERICK CHARLES HUTCHINSON
Born: 8/12/19, Seattle, WA, BL/TR, 6-foot-2, 190 pounds

	W	L	PCT	G	IP	H	ER	BB	SO	ERA
1938 Seat	25	7	.781	35	290	241	80	99	145	2.48
PCL 1	25	7	.781	35	290	241	80	99	145	2.48
Majors 11#	95	71	.572	242	1465	1487	606	388	591	3.72

Pitched 10 seasons and in 1941 appeared only as a pinch hitter.

that he would receive a 20 percent share of the purchase price by any big league club.

Hutchinson was ineffective in his debut against San Diego in the season's opening series at Lane Field. He took the loss after being knocked out of the box, surrendering three runs on two hits and three walks in two-thirds of an inning. By early May, Hutchinson had settled down and demonstrated that he had skill and poise. *San Francisco Chronicle* baseball writer Ed Hughes said he was, "green, but plenty tough, just as Walter Johnson was at this age."

"The boy is the greatest student of the game and pitching I have ever met."
— Manager Jack Lelivelt about teenager Fred Hutchinson

On May 28, Hutchinson racked up a 19-4 win over the Seals and showed his batting ability with three hits in five at bats including a double, home run and five runs batted in. Always a good hitter, Fred batted .313 for the year.

"If he keeps his health and avoids accidents, Hutchinson is a cinch to go to the majors and it will not be long," said Hughes in his game account.

Fred continued to register wins. Hutch gained his 10th victory on June 16 with a 7-0 whitewashing of Portland that ended the team's eight-game losing streak. Hutch tossed another shutout five days later and beat San Diego, 1-0, before 13,000 spectators. It was the season's largest crowd. Over the course of the campaign, the Rainiers averaged nearly 10,000 whenever the schoolboy sensation took the mound at home.

On Aug. 12, Fred celebrated his 19th birthday with victory Number 19, a 3-2 win over San Francisco before 16,354 happy fans.

Hughes speculated that Seattle owner Emil Sick would not sell Hutchinson after the season because the kid was such a drawing card. Lelivelt disagreed, saying he wanted the youngster to go to a big league team for players who would make the Rainiers pennant contenders for years to come. Although a half a dozen big league clubs were after the Rainiers too sell the youngster, Lelivelt predicted nothing would happen until the winter meetings.

The *Los Angeles Times* described Hutch as, "the most brilliant young pitcher ever to break into the Coast League" and credited his accomplishments to the knowledge he was absorbing from roommate Kewpie Dick Barrett and physical attributes seldom seen in one so young.

Lelivelt agreed and in a *Sacramento Bee* feature story about the boy wonder the manager said Hutchinson had knowledge about pitching usually found in a player with 18 years of experience, not 18 years of age.

"The boy is the greatest student of the game and pitching I have ever met," Lelivelt declared. Hutch threw his ordi-

nary fast ball and curve from a straight overhand delivery and had supreme control. He had "the greatest change of pace I have ever seen," Lelivelt added.

Around the league, fans marveled at his cool-headed approach to the game. For years, fans told the story of the game where Hutch got into trouble with Portland's hard-hitting Johnny Frederick coming to the plate. Fred called time out, walked to the dugout and took a long drink of water. He returned to the mound and gave up two runs, but preserved a 5-3 win.

L. H. Gregory of the *Portland Oregonian* asked Hutch after the game if he'd left the mound to steady his nerves. Not at all, said Hutch. "I was thirsty."

Hutchinson was ineffective in the post-season playoffs in 1938, losing twice as Seattle was ousted by fourth place San Francisco, four games to one.

There were questions about his fast ball, but Detroit — which had refused to give him a $5,000 bonus before the season — paid Seattle cash and four players in a package estimated worth between $50,000 and $80,000. The players were outfielder Jo Jo White, infielders George Archie and Tony Piet and relief pitcher Ed Selway.

True to Lelivelt's hope, White and Archie provided a foundation for a Seattle championship in 1939. White stayed on through 1941 as the Rainiers took two additional titles and first baseman Archie was on the team in 1940, when he was the PCL's most valuable player.

Hutch went 6-13 in his first two seasons in Detroit, showed he needed more experience and was sent to Toledo and Buffalo in the next two years. He remained in Buffalo in 1941, compiling a 26-7 record. The war intervened and Hutch didn't return to baseball until 1946 when he started a seven-year stay with the Tigers in which he never had a losing season.

His best year was 1947, when he compiled an 18-10 mark. Fred's career record was 95-71 and he continued to hit well, batting .263 with 91 appearances as a pinch hitter.

Fred began his managerial career when Red Rolph was fired with the Tigers in eighth place in 1952. Hutch became a successful manager, compiling an 830-827 record in 12 seasons.

Hutchinson, nicknamed "the Big Bear" by broadcaster Joe Garagiola for the way he paced in the dugout, worked with the Tigers two more seasons then quit when the club refused to offer him a two-year contract. He turned down a one-year pact, saying, "I'm not going to compromise my principals."

Hutchinson went home to Seattle, led the Rainiers to the league title in 1955, and was hired to manage the St. Louis Cardinals. With his team in fifth place on Sept. 17, 1958, Stan Hack replaced him.

Hutch returned to Seattle in 1959 and the Rainiers were eighth when Fred was hired to manage Cincinnati on July 8. Two years later the Reds won the National League, but lost to the New York Yankees in the World Series.

Fred had a legendary temper, but he left the game at the ballpark and was easy-going elsewhere. Yogi Berra told a story about Hutch's well-known locker room antics.

"When we followed Detroit into a city," Yogi said, "we could tell how Hutch fared. If we got stools in the dressing room, we knew he had won. If we got kindling, we knew he had lost."

While visiting his family in Seattle at Christmas, 1963, Fred was examined by his physician brother, who said Fred had cancer. Later it was diagnosed as terminal. The courageous Hutchinson returned to manage Cincinnati in 1964 and continued with the team until August, when he took a leave of absence. He died in Florida on Nov. 12, 1964.

"He was a man's man," said Stan Musial, who played for the popular manager in St. Louis. "If you couldn't play for Hutch, you couldn't play for anybody."

INDIAN BOB JOHNSON

Indian Bob Johnson was a powerful and productive hitter who led Portland to its first pennant in 18 years in 1932 and won promotion to the majors, where he struggled for recognition with teams that finished near the bottom of the standings.

The big outfielder smacked at least 21 homers annually in the first 13 years of his career. Johnson showed consistency during his first nine seasons in the big leagues by averaging 27 four-baggers, 102 runs, 107 RBIs and 86 walks each year.

Extra base power and run production were his strong suits. While managers everywhere were eager to find mobile outfielders who had those capabilities, Johnson couldn't even win a contract in the Pacific Coast League in his younger days.

Part Cherokee Indian, Bob was born in Oklahoma, but moved to the Pacific Northwest with his family when he was a youngster. He ran away from home at 15 and eventually became a firefighter in Los Angeles, where he played for the department's strong team. The powerfully built Johnson tried out as a pitcher with the Los Angeles Angels, but was rejected.

When his brother, Roy, won a job with San Francisco, Bob asked Seals manager Nick Williams for a trial. Williams said he couldn't use an outfielder. Johnson received the same reply from Hollywood skipper Ossie Vitt.

Bob Johnson

Art Griggs took him on at Wichita in the Western League in 1929. He moved to Pueblo, hitting .273 with 16 homers before Portland's Ted Turner picked him up at mid-season for $12,000. Bob batted .254 the rest of the year with the Beavers.

Johnson showed progress in 1930, hitting .265 with 21 homers and 93 RBIs for the lowly Beavers. He blossomed the following two seasons when Portland moved up in the standings as a contender in 1931 and champion in 1932. Portland tried Johnson at first base and second base because he was so error-prone in the outfield. It finally became clear that Bob's hitting offset any defensive deficiencies and he eventually became a capable fielder.

Johnson was fourth in the league with 22 homers in 1931, averaging .337 and knocked in 94 runs. The following season Bob hit .330 with 43 doubles, 29 homers and 111 runs batted in.

Connie Mack was preparing to sell off his aging stars on the Philadelphia Athletics. Mack took Johnson, third baseman Pinky Higgins and outfielder Lou Finney from Portland to fill some of the holes created by the departure of Al Simmons, Jimmy Dykes and Mule Haas.

After finishing first or second for six straight years, the A's fell to third in 1933 with Johnson showing promise at .290 with 21 home runs. As Mack continued to sell such stars as Mickey Cochrane, Lefty Grove and Rube Walberg, Philadelphia dropped to fifth in 1934 and never rose above seventh during Johnson's remaining eight years with the team.

Johnson was a consistent performer who belted 30 or

ROBERT LEE JOHNSON
Born: 11/26/06, Pryor, OK, BR/TR, 6-foot, 180 pounds

		G	AB	R	H	2B	3B	HR	RBI	SB	AVG.
1929	Port	81	264	42	67	16	3	5	27	6	.254
1930	Port	157	401	91	133	25	3	21	93	5	.265
1931	Port	141	504	108	170	37	5	22	94	12	.337
1932	Port	149	545	105	180	43	1	29	111	9	.330
1947	Seat	130	342	44	101	28	1	7	50	6	.295
1948	Seat	59	145	17	41	7	0	5	23	1	.283
PCL	6	717	2301	407	692	156	13	89	398	39	.301
Majors	13	1863	6920	1239	2051	396	95	288	1283	96	.296

PCL PICTORIAL

Stan Hack

Marv Owen

Bob Johnson

Joe Bowman

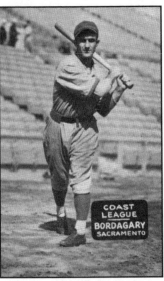

Frenchy Bordagaray

more homers three times with a best of 34 in 1934 — the year he had a 26-game hitting streak — and whose batting average ranged as high as .338.

Bob tied the American League record in 1937 with six RBIs in a 13-run inning, knocking in two with a double and another four on an inside-the-park grand slam. During his career, he produced the only hit to break up three no-hit games.

Johnson was traded to Washington in 1943 and hit .265 with seven homers before the Senators sold him to the Boston Red Sox. Fenway Park was more suited to his right-handed power than Griffith Stadium and Johnson responded with 17 home runs, 106 RBIs and a .324 average.

When his totals declined in 1945, Bob was cut from the roster, joined Milwaukee in the American Association the next season and moved to Seattle in 1947. Although his weight was up around 200 and he had slowed, Johnson shared the outfield with lefty Edo Vanni and hit .295 in 130 games. He became a Seattle coach and part-time player in 1948.

Johnson managed Tacoma in the Western International League to a seventh place finish the next season, hitting .326. After a year out of baseball, he bid farewell for good in 1951, playing 21 games with Tijuana in the Southwest International League.

EDDIE JOOST

Two things stand out when you inspect Eddie Joost's record in the Coast League and The Show. He didn't hit for a high average, but he was an outstanding fielder.

This fluid shortstop played 22 years against the best competition and averaged only .247 at the plate, including .239 in the majors. Joost stuck around all those years because he carried one of the best gloves in baseball.

"He was a hell of a shortstop, the steadiest I ever played with," said former teammate Ferris Fain. "He had a great arm, great range and was real sure-handed. Eddie didn't hit much, but he had a good eye and got lots of walks".

Joost's ability to draw walks nearly 16 percent of his times at bat boosted his major league on base percentage to .361, offsetting the minuscule batting average. The last six years be played regularly in the majors, Joost averaged nearly 119 walks per year, with a 1949 high of 149 in 144 games.

There was some pop in Joost's bat in his later years. Eddie equaled his entire major league career's home run total when he blasted 13 in his first campaign with the Philadelphia Athletics in 1947. Although he batted only .206 that season, he received two first place votes for the American League's Most Valuable Player Award. He averaged 19 homers-a-year for five more seasons as a regular.

Eddie had neither a great glove nor many offensive weapons when he started in professional baseball in 1933.

Joost played on an American Legion team sponsored by Joe Baerwald, owner of the San Francisco Missions team. New York Yankees scouts Joe Devine and Bill Essick were interested in Eddie, but he opted for the Missions because his father felt Baerwald should have the first crack at his son's services.

Joost signed at age 17 with the stipulation that he'd continue attending Mission High School until June, then join the team. He got into 25 games, hit .250 and made five errors at shortstop.

After playing briefly at Omaha the following year, Eddie appeared in seven more games with the Missions. The Missions let third sacker Eddie Mulligan go in 1935 so Joost could find a place in the lineup. Baerwald reasoned that the youngster had some sale value while the 40-year-old Mulligan was near the end of his PCL career. Joost responded with a creditable showing at third base and hit .287. Most observers felt he was a natural shortstop, but the Missions had Clyde Beck in that spot and he was the best fielder in the Coast League.

"He was a hell of a shortstop, the steadiest I ever played with."
— Ferris Fain about Eddie Joost

Shortly after the 1936 season opened, the *San Francisco Chronicle's* Ed Hughes reported Baerwald had rejected a Chicago White Sox offer for Joost because Missions manager Willie Kamm couldn't afford to let him go.

Hughes described Joost as, the "best prospect on the team and one of the best young infielders in the league. It is a cinch he will be grabbed by a major league club for next year although he is not 20 years old."

Hughes noted that Joost was eligible for the major league draft because he had been with the team four seasons. Joost averaged .286 while playing 126 games at third and 40 at shortstop and was acquired by Cincinnati.

Joost hit .154 with the Reds in 13 games at the end of the year and was sent to Syracuse in the International League in 1937 and to Kansas City in 1938.

Back with Cincinnati for two seasons, Joost was a reserve until the middle of 1940 when the regular shortstop, spectacular but erratic Billy Myers, jumped the team because of personal problems. Joost played 78 of his 88 games at shortstop and averaged .216 while Myers batted only .202. Joost played all seven games of the World Series at second base, hitting .200 in the win over Detroit.

Myers was traded away at the end of the year and the shortstop position became Joost's for two years. He was sent to the Boston Braves with cash and a player for shortstop Eddie Miller, who led the league with only 13 errors in 748 tries while Joost was last among shortstops with 45 miscues. Joost hit .185 with the Braves in 1943, sat out a year while expecting to be drafted into the Army and came back in 1945 to play 35 games after suffering a broken toe and broken wrist.

Joost had an effervescent personality and when he was with the Reds joined with Bucky Walters — another former Missions player — to form the practical joker team in the clubhouse. But, he also was high-strung, had an explosive temper and an attitude that some feared might cost him his big league job.

Joost said he was called up to umpire Babe Pinelli's hotel room after one game. Pinelli, a San Francisco native

EDWIN DAVID JOOST
Born: 6/5/16, San Francisco, CA, BR/TR, 6-foot, 175 pounds

		G	AB	R	H	2B	3B	HR	RBI	SB	AVG.
1933	Miss	25	64	8	16	0	1	0	1	0	.250
1934	Miss	7	14	0	2	0	0	0	0	0	.143
1935	Miss	147	533	72	153	32	6	1	83	8	.287
1936	Miss	167	668	120	191	40	7	6	72	36	.286
1956	SF	6	12	0	2	0	0	0	0	0	.167
PCL		5	352	1291	200	364	72	14	7	156	44	.282
Majors		17	1574	5606	874	1339	238	35	134	601	61	.239

Eddie Joost

Cookie Lavagetto

whose on field temperament once rivaled Joost's, told Eddie that he was getting a bad name and should take steps to curb his tantrums.

"I changed my tactics from then on and found the umpires treated me differently," Joost said. "I might have been sold down the river if it hadn't been for Pinelli's little talk."

Joost lost his big league job in 1946 when he was shipped to Rochester in the International League. It turned out to be a move that changed his career for the better. Joost had his eyes examined and was told he needed glasses. Improved vision helped Eddie top the league in fielding and hit .275 with 35 doubles, 19 homers and 101 RBIs.

The Philadelphia Athletics bought Eddie, who led the league in put outs four times and in errors only once through his last year as a regular. In late 1947 and early 1948 Joost established an American League record of 41 consecutive errorless games at shortstop. His power totals and bases on balls added to the mix that made him one of the league's most productive shortstops.

He managed the team in 1954, but was fired when the Athletics moved to Kansas City. Joost closed his major league career with the Boston Red Sox in 1955 and became manager of their San Francisco farm team the following year.

The Seals struggled and Joost had several run-ins with the umpires. Shortly after the team came out of a nine-game losing streak, Eddie got into a dispute over a call at second base and was thumbed from the game. He threw the

ball over the wall at Seals Stadium in disgust. Joost had been in trouble with Red Sox farm director Johnny Murphy, who fired Eddie and replaced him with Joe Gordon.

COOKIE LAVAGETTO

When Cookie Lavagetto's name comes up among major league baseball aficionados, the name Floyd "Bill" Bevens inevitably follows.

The event that joined them in baseball history was the 1947 World Series between the Brooklyn Dodgers and the New York Yankees.

Lavagetto was a utility infielder with the Dodgers, playing out the string of his 10-year major league career. Bevens had pitched successfully during the previous three seasons with the Yankees, but was 7-13 in 1947 and making his final appearances in a big league uniform.

They faced each other in Game 4 in one of the most dramatic finishes of any Fall Classic game. Bevens was wild, walking eight batters, but still had a 2-1 lead and a no-hitter going into the last half of the ninth inning at Ebbets Field.

With one out, Carl Furillo drew the ninth walk off Bevens and was replaced by pinch runner Al Gionfriddo after the Dodgers made their second out. Gionfriddo stole second and Yankees manager Buck Harris broke one of baseball's cardinal rules by ordering Pete Reiser walked intentionally to put the winning run on base. Eddie Miksis ran for Reiser.

Lavagetto, 34, was sent up to bat for Eddie Stanky and turned out to be an unlikely hero. He had hit .261 in 41 games, but was only 4 for 17 (.235) off the bench.

Cookie provided the Dodgers with an unexpected victory by lashing an outside pitch off the right field wall for a double that bounded away from the outfielders as Gionfriddo and Miksis raced home to win the game.

It was Cookie's final major league at bat, but not his last in baseball. He returned to Oakland, where he had started his career, for three more seasons in the Pacific Coast League.

Lavagetto was a skinny kid not long out of Oakland's Technical High School when big league scouts saw him play in an All-Star game against some major leaguers. They wanted to pick up Lavagetto, but his mother refused to give permission, feeling her 18-year-old son shouldn't leave home. She had no objection to signing a contract with the local PCL club, so Lavagetto joined the Oaks.

Lavagetto, known as Harry at that time, received his nickname from teammates who called him "Cookie's boy," because he had been hired by Oakland president Victor "Cookie" Devincenzi.

Lavagetto made his first appearance in an unsuccessful pinch hitting role on April 9, 1933. Manager Ray Brubaker used him as a late inning substitute at second base, third base and shortstop for about a month. He won a starting job at second base in mid-May and played well above expectations. Cookie batted as high as .330 before finishing at .312. He showed modest power and was one of three Oaks to bat in 100 or more runs.

Pittsburgh acquired Cookie for the 1934 campaign, but he was thought to be a year or two away from being ready for the big leagues. The Pirates had traded away second baseman Tony Piet and expected veteran infielder Tommy Thevenow to fill his spot in the starting lineup.

When third baseman Pie Traynor developed a sore arm, Thevenow filled in for him and manager George Gibson surprised Lavagetto by using him at second in 87 games. The feeling that Lavagetto needed more experience was correct as he hit only .220. Cookie continued in a utility role for two more years with the Bucs, batting .290 and .244.

Lavagetto escaped part-time duty in 1937 with the Brooklyn Dodgers, where he was sent in a trade for pitcher Ed Brandt. The next five seasons were his best. Cookie

averaged .279 and 74 runs batted in per year as the Dodgers' third baseman and made the National League All-Star squad twice.

After Pearl Harbor was bombed, Cookie became the first Dodger to enlist and served four years in the Navy. He played 88 games at the hot corner for Brooklyn in his first year back in 1946, but hit a meager .236 and was relegated to the bench the following season.

Brooklyn sought waivers on Lavagetto early in 1948 and Cookie joined the Oaks after the season started, but in time to help manager Casey Stengel and his veteran team of "Nine Old Men" collect the city's first pennant in two decades. Cookie shared third base with Dario Lodigiani and batted .304. He played with the Acorns two more years, batting .290 and .286 as a full-timer in 1949 and 1950.

Brooklyn called the following season and Cookie returned to the majors as a coach with the Dodgers through 1953. When Brooklyn skipper Chuck Dressen had a disagreement over salary and left the Dodgers to return to manage Oakland, Cookie went along.

Cookie became a Washington coach in 1955 and succeeded Dressen as manager of the Senators after the season began in 1957. Lavagetto stayed on when the team moved to Minnesota in 1961 and was dismissed in June. Cookie's teams had one fifth place and four eighth place finishes.

JOHNNY MOORE

It didn't seem to matter to Johnny Moore whether the opposing pitcher was in the Coast League, some other minor league or the National League. He hit them all for 22 years.

The chunky New Englander was an amazingly consistent batter. Between 1924, when he broke into Organized Baseball with New Haven of the Eastern League, until 1945, when he finished as a pinch hitter for Los Angeles and Chicago, Moore averaged .314. His lifetime batting average was .307 in the majors and .326 in the PCL.

In spite of this consistency — or perhaps because of it — Moore drew little notice in the newspapers that reported on the teams he played with. He seems to have been there every day, doing his job in a quiet and workmanlike manner.

Perhaps he was confused with one of the many other Moores who played in the majors at the same time he did. It was the most common name in the big leagues in 1934, when Joe (Giants), Randy (Braves) and Gene (Cardinals) all roamed the outfield and Austin "Cy" Moore pitched for the Phillies.

There were no other Moores on Eastern League diamonds when Johnny broke in with a .323 average in 31 games. He stayed in the circuit three more years before gaining a promotion to the Chicago Cubs late in 1928. Moore was used sparingly by the Cubs in 1929 and went to their Los Angeles farm club the following season.

The great 1927 San Francisco outfield of Earl Averill,

HARRY ARTHUR LAVAGETTO
Born: 12/1/12, Oakland, CA, BR/TR, 6-foot, 170 pounds

		G	AB	R	H	2B	3B	HR	RBI	SB	AVG.
1933	Oak	152	509	83	159	29	8	7	100	18	.312
1948	Oak	86	286	54	87	16	1	3	38	1	.304
1949	Oak	142	459	76	133	23	1	6	58	2	.290
1950	Oak	143	490	81	140	18	0	8	66	3	.286
PCL		4	523	1744| 294	519	86	10	24	262	24	.298
Majors		10	1043	3509| 487	945	183	37	40	486	63	.269

Johnny Moore

Bobo Newsom

Roy Johnson and Smead Jolley hit a combined .373 and often is mentioned as the PCL's best offensive unit, but L.A.'s 1930 trio of Moore, Jigger Statz and Wes Schulmerich isn't far behind. Their .362 average was generated by Moore's .342, Jigger Statz at .360 and Wes Schulmerich at .380. A fourth outfielder was G. W. Harper, who batted .308. Moore tossed in 45 doubles, 26 homers and 101 RBIs and was third among in outfielders in fielding.

Johnny played a reserve role with Chicago at the beginning of 1931, but was returned to Los Angeles in June when the Cubs called up Vince Barton, who was hitting .302 with 17 homers. Barton's major league career con-

cluded with the Cubs the following season after he hit a meager .233 in 102 games.

Moore averaged a blazing .366, just three percentage points behind PCL leader Ox Eckhardt of the Missions, and returned to Chicago to spend six seasons in the National League. After a .305 season with the Cubs in 1932, Johnny and three teammates went to Cincinnati in a trade for Babe Herman. Moore's worst major league season followed as he hit .263 and was swapped to Philadelphia early in 1935. He averaged .330 for the year.

Moore finished his big league career with .323, .328 and .319 averages, but returned to Los Angeles in 1938 to join the Angels for eight more seasons. He hit well, made more than three errors in a season only once and ranked among the top five in fielding average every year but one.

After hitting in the low .300s for three years, Johnny won the Coast League batting title with a .331 mark in 1941, striking out only a dozen times in 474 at bats. He missed a month with injuries, but muscled up for 10 triples and 18 homers and batted in 100 runs. Johnny finished second in the batting race with a .347 mark in his last season as a starter as the Angels lost the pennant to Sacramento on the last day of the season.

After two seasons as a reserve, the 43-year-old Moore came to his last year in baseball as a first base coach and pinch hitter. Johnny had 23 hits in 65 plate appearances coming off the bench for a .354 mark, prompting Los Angeles manager Bill Sweeney to call Johnny the best pinch hitter he ever saw. One of his hits was a grand slam

JOHN FRANCIS MOORE
<u>Born: 3/23/02, Waterville, CT, BL/TR, 5-foot-10.5, 175 pounds</u>

		G	AB	R	H	2B	3B	HR	RBI	SB	AVG.
1930	LA	142	546	120	187	45	2	26	101	15	.342
1931	LA	80	317	66	116	34	4	6	69	8	.366
1938	LA	140	492	81	150	33	7	21	86	2	.305
1939	LA	131	491	83	148	24	5	17	99	2	.301
1940	LA	120	380	41	118	20	2	9	69	2	.311
1941	LA	134	474	77	157	31	10	18	100	2	.331
1942	LA	134	487	59	169	28	6	7	85	3	.347
1943	LA	81	217	22	63	11	1	1	31	1	.290
1944	LA	85	120	11	39	9	0	3	30	2	.325
1945	LA	71	65	5	23	4	0	4	26	0	.354
PCL	10	1118	3589	565	1170	239	37	112	696	37	.326
Majors	10	846	3013	439	926	155	26	73	452	23	.307

off Portland's Ad Liska, a blow the veteran hurler said was the first one off his submarine pitch.

The Cubs called Moore up to pinch hit six times late in the season. He got one hit and retired.

Johnny had hung around the game long enough to see his son, John Jr., break into pro baseball as a Piedmont League outfielder in 1944. After retiring as an active player, Moore scouted for the Braves and Expos until 1970.

BUCK/BOBO NEWSOM

After the lords of baseball created Dizzy Dean to amuse and delight National League fans, they evened things up by sending Bobo (aka Buck) Newsom to the American League.

Sporting News publisher J. G. Taylor Spink summed up Newsom in 1940 as, "garrulous, boisterous, breezy, verbose, loquacious. He has been called the Great Pop-Off, rightful successor to Jerome Hanna Dean, the Big Mouthpiece, but regardless of how he strikes you personally, you have to admit that Louis can pitch."

Newsom was named Buck by an uncle in his youth in South Carolina and called himself Bobo as he became a baseball senior citizen.

Newsom won 211 major league games, but the true measure of his considerable pitching ability lies in the loss column, where he finished with 222. Only a truly talented pitcher is allowed to perform often enough to taste defeat that often. More than half of the 22 pitchers ahead of him on the all-time loss list are in the Hall of Fame.

Newsom's career stretched over a quarter century and his time in the majors nearly matched that. He toed a big league slab as early as 1929 and as late as 1953, his last year in baseball. Bobo's itinerary reads like a travelogue of major league cities from the 1930s through the 1950s — Brooklyn (twice), Chicago, St. Louis (three times), Washington (five times), Boston, Detroit, Philadelphia (twice) and New York. He never received a pay check in Cincinnati, Cleveland or Pittsburgh.

Beyond the numbers, his unquestioned talent and an audacious personality the equal of any in the game, Bobo had a major flaw. Fast, smart and the master of confusing windups, he was erratic on the mound. "One day Newsom belongs in the class with the great pitchers," said reporter Frank Yeutter. "The next day he's lucky to get by the first inning against sandlot competition."

Buck began deep in the bushes in 1928, but was fired by Greenville in the Eastern Carolina League for blowing a lead after playing cards all night. Newsom wired fourth place Wilmington in same league and said he could win pennant if they'd hire him. Sure enough, Buck went 15-3 and Wilmington took the title.

Brooklyn bought him late in 1929 after he compiled a 19-18 record for Macon in the Sally League. He pitched 12 innings with the Dodgers in 1929 and 1930, was released and went back to the minors.

Buck did well at Little Rock in 1931 and was drafted by

the Chicago Cubs. On his way to Chicago to meet with owner William Veeck Sr. that winter, he drove off a cliff in the Smoky Mountains and broke his leg. The leg was broken again when a mule kicked him. After he recovered, the Cubs used him as a batting practice pitcher and farmed him to Albany.

Chicago shipped Buck to Los Angeles in 1933 as part payment for outfielder Tuck Stainback and Newsom had one of the best seasons of his career.

With the help of *Los Angeles Times* sportswriter Bob Ray — who penned many an exorbitant quote during the season — Newsom's reputation for braggadocio grew. When Newsom shut out Seattle in L.A.'s third game of the year, Ray quoted him as saying manager Jack Lelivelt should have pitched him in all three contests. "But, maybe you shouldn't print that," Buck added, "because Lelivelt might think I'm trying to tell him how to run his club."

Buck continued winning until Sacramento shelled him in mid-April. Newsom's record showed more wins than losses as the season rolled along. Frequently striking out opposing batters in double digits, Buck also walked more than his share.

Hollywood snapped his eight-game winning streak in July, but Buck launched another. He pitched a club record 15th straight wins and was one shy of Frank Browning's 1909 league record of 16 in-a-row when San Francisco stopped him in 11 innings near the end of September.

Newsom was the league's most valuable player as the Angels walked off with the pennant. He led in wins (30 with 11 losses), games pitched (56), innings (320) and strikeouts (212). His earned run average was 3.18.

The St. Louis Browns took him in the draft for $7,500 and he had a 16-20 record with a sixth place team, including pitching no-hit ball for 9 2/3 innings against the Red Sox before giving up a bad hop single to Roy Johnson that beat him in the 10th.

During that game, Buck defied manager Rogers Hornsby's rule never to throw a strike on an 0-2 count. He tossed one to Wes Ferrell, who didn't swing, but was called out by umpire Bill McGowan. Ferrell blew his top and argued Bobo would never throw a strike in that situa-

LOUIS NORMAN NEWSOM
Born: 8/11/07, Hartsville, SC, BR/TR, 6-foot-3, 200 pounds

		W	L	PCT	G	IP	H	ER	BB	SO	ERA
1933	LA	30	11	.732	56	320	328	113	124	212	3.18
PCL		1	30	11	.732	56	320	328	113	124	212	3.18
Majors	20	211	222	.487	600	3762	3769	1664	1732	2082	3.98

PCL PICTORIAL

Ted Williams

Ferris Fain

Babe Dahlgren

Augie Galan

Frank Demaree

tion because of Hornsby's edict. When Ferrell's brother, Rick, joined in, McGowan threw them both out of the game. They were fined for the rhubarb and Bobo was docked $50 by Hornsby.

Newsom got off to a slow start in 1935 and was sold to Washington in May for $40,000. After 11-18 and 17-15 records for the second division Senators, Boston took him in a trade midway through 1937 and he finished 16-14.

The Red Sox traded him back to the Browns in October. Before climbing on the train to Cleveland for the 1938 opener, St. Louis president Don Barnes said he'd buy Newsom a new suit if he won. After the Browns' victory, Barnes reminded Buck of his offer. "Hell, Mr. Barnes," said the ever confident Newsom, "I ordered that suit before we left St. Louis."

Although the Browns finished seventh, Bobo had a 20-16 record and led the league with 330 innings pitched.

Newsom was part of a 10-player trade with Detroit the following year and won 20 games again. The Tigers took the 1940 pennant with Newsom's 21-5 record built on a 13-game winning streak, proving what he could do playing for a decent team. The streak ended when Bobo broke his thumb, but continued to pitch anyway. Earlier in his career he had finished a game after his knee cap was broken by a line drive.

Buck won the World Series opener over Cincinnati and was ready to celebrate when he learned that his dad, who was in attendance, had suffered a heart attack. He died the next day. Newsom dedicated his Game 5 start to his father and beat the Reds, 8-0. He lost in the seventh game, 2-1.

Buck was a disappointing 12-20 with a 4.61 earned run average the following season and when he refused to accept a huge pay cut in 1942, the Tigers sold him to Washington for $40,000. His ERA ballooned to 4.92 and his won-lost was 11-17 before the Senators took a financial loss and sold Bobo for $25,000 to Brooklyn, which was in a close race against St. Louis.

A reporter asked Cardinals general manager Branch Rickey why he didn't block the sale. "I did not bid for Newsom," he replied, "because I was afraid I'd get him."

Newsom had a different attitude. "Old Bobo's here. Stop worrying," he told manager Leo Durocher. But, Bobo and Leo were incompatible and while he was leading the staff with nine wins in July, 1943, Newsom was traded to the Browns for a pair of pitchers who had one win between them. Bobo described it as, "the dirtiest deal I ever got."

Newsom returned to Washington before the year was done and continued bouncing around the American League, generating 46 wins and 59 loses, including seven key victories for the pennant-bound Yankees in 1947.

He moved to the New York Giants in 1948, spent three years in the Southern League and returned to the Senators in April, 1952. He lasted two months and moved on to the Philadelphia Athletics, where he completed his career the following season.

MARV OWEN

Although Marv Owen developed into a fine major league third baseman, he hardly got a tumble at the hot corner in his rookie year in Seattle.

The Indians played him at all four infield positions, but most of his 138 games were spent at shortstop (82 games), second base (30) or his college position, first base (23).

Veteran Fritz Knothe had third base locked up when Marv arrived in May, 1930, after graduating from Santa Clara University. Owen joined the Indians in San

Marv Owen

Francisco where Seattle was playing seven games against the Missions. Marv appeared in six games and played all four infield spots as manager Ernie Johnson — the second baseman — juggled the lineup to look at his latest acquisition. Owen became a regular when shortstop Chick Ellsworth was injured.

Owen didn't find a permanent home at third base for three more years, but he acquitted himself well at the other positions, finishing with no errors at first base and among the league's fielding leaders.

Johnson regarded the rangy Owen as a first class prospect, a view shared by teams in the big leagues and the PCL that had pursued Marv during his college career. There was one report that Connie Mack offered to give Marv a $1,000 bonus and pay his way through Harvard University.

Marv stayed at Santa Clara University not far from where he grew up in San Jose. After being named the most valuable player in his college league in 1929, the soft-spoken Owen was looking forward to being captain of the 1930 team. But, Owen made a bad mistake before his senior year, agreeing in writing to join Seattle, which had ties to the Detroit Tigers.

Owen was assured that his college eligibility would not be jeopardized so long as he didn't actually sign a contract to play professionally. College officials disagreed and banned him from playing in 1930. Marv kept involved with the college nine as its coach.

Seattle president Bill Klepper said he gave Marv $2,000

to sign and promised $2,000 more when he reported after graduation. It was a good deal for Marv, but an even better one for Klepper, who sold Owen to Detroit for $25,000 and two players the following September. The Tigers liked Marv's style afield and his .300 average with 24 doubles and 16 steals were definite pluses.

When Owen joined the Tigers in 1931, the Portland scenario was repeated and he was shuttled among the four infield positions, playing primarily at third base and shortstop. His .223 batting average in 105 games convinced the Tigers that he needed more experience and he was sent to the International League.

Marv started at Toronto, but moved to Newark after 45 games when Detroit broke off relations with Toronto. Owen was pleased to be with the pennant-bound Bears. Marv split the season between second and third, hit .317 with 92 RBIs and was near the top in doubles and triples. The *Sporting News* named him the league's most valuable player.

Marv returned to the Motor City in 1933 and was the Tigers third baseman for five years. He hit .317 in his best season in 1934, when he drove in 96 runs, the lowest among the Tiger infield of Hank Greenberg (139), Charlie Gehringer (127) and Billy Rogell (100). Owen drove in 105 two seasons later, when he batted .295.

Marv didn't hit well in his two World Series, going 3 for 49, but he was a central figure in a famous incidents in the 1934 series against St. Louis. With the Cardinals leading, 9-0, in the seventh game, Ducky Medwick slid into Marv at third base and the men arose ready to fight, but were separated before any blows were landed. When Medwick went to left field in the bottom of the inning, the home town Tigers crowd showered him with garbage of all sorts and Baseball Commissioner Kenesaw Mountain Landis ordered Ducky removed from the game to restore order.

Owen was traded to the Chicago White Sox in December, 1937. He played there two seasons and finished his big league career in 20 games with the Boston Red Sox in 1940.

Marv started a six-year stay at third base for Portland in 1941. The Beavers were last for two years and fourth the next, but Marv was a major contributor in all three campaigns, hitting .299, .303 and .308. Injuries limited him to 73 games the last year.

Owen became Portland's manager in 1944 and led the Beavers into second place, their best finish in nearly a decade. Owen headed the league in fielding for the second time since his return and averaged .290.

The following season was his most satisfying. The Beavers won their first pennant since 1936 as Marv batted .311 with 40 doubles and 83 RBIs. His greatest achievement was at the hot corner where he made only six errors and fielded .985, still the Coast League record for third basemen in at least 150 games.

Marv was back at the helm in 1946, but many veterans had returned from the war to bolster rosters around the league and Portland tied Seattle for the cellar. Owen hurt his ankle just before the season began and he appeared in only 39 games, hitting .155. Portland president George Norgan fired him after the season.

Marv wasn't out of work long. Back home in San Jose, the Red Sox had added a farm club in the California League and Owen was its manager. The team finished in the first division four of five years before he retired and became a scout for the Tigers.

MONTE PEARSON

Monte Pearson's wildness, rather than his great curve ball or run-of-the-mill fast ball, was what kept the batters off balance and reluctant to dig in against him at the plate.

The tall right-hander walked more batters than he fanned throughout his career, but had a winning record almost every one of his 13 years in Organized Baseball.

Monte had 100 big league wins and 61 losses in regular season play and was a perfect 4-0 with three complete games in four World Series starts with the New York Yankees in the late 1930s.

Monte's family moved from Oakland to Fresno when he was 12. He was a baseball star as both a pitcher and hitter in high school and was performing in a semi-pro league when scout Phil Koerner obtained his signature on an Oakland contract in 1929.

The Oaks dispatched Monte to Bakersfield in the California State League and Pearson played some games in the outfield and pitched 101 innings for a 6-6 record.

Oakland sent Pearson to Phoenix in 1930, but recalled him quickly and put Monte in the bullpen. He went 3-2 in 24 appearances and produced a 5.77 earned run average.

Pearson was in the starting rotation in 1931 and showed enough potential on his way to a 17-16 season that Cleveland took an option on his services in mid-July. The Indians had sent pitcher Fay Thomas to the Oaks earlier in the year and he became part of a package to which Cleveland added $35,000 for Pearson in September.

Once again, Monte's ERA of 4.46 was fairly high even for the run-happy Coast League. His control improved and, while he led the loop with 123 bases on balls, Pearson's 158 strikeouts was the league's third highest total.

Cleveland farmed Monte to Toledo and recalled him late in the year to pitch eight innings in as many games without

MARVIN JAMES OWEN
Born: 3/22/06, Agnew, CA, BR/TR, 6-foot-1, 175 pounds

		G	AB	R	H	2B	3B	HR	RBI	SB	AVG.
1930	Seat	138	443	67	133	24	7	3	55	16	.300
1941	Port	144	501	68	150	38	6	1	70	3	.299
1942	Port	147	535	52	162	27	7	3	66	5	.303
1943	Port	73	260	27	80	12	2	0	32	1	.308
1944	Port	131	449	40	130	27	2	1	63	9	.290
1945	Port	163	566	88	176	40	3	1	83	10	.311
1946	Port	39	103	8	16	1	1	0	5	0	.155
PCL		7	835	2857	350	847	169	28	9	374	44	.296
Majors		9	1011	3782	473	1040	167	44	31	497	30	.275

Monte Pearson

a decision. He split 1933 between the two cities again, going 11-5 with the Mud Hens, but returning to Cleveland in July for a 10-5 record and the league's best ERA (2.33). Pearson won a place on the American League's All-Rookie team.

After an 18-13 year in his first full season in the majors, Pearson fell back to 8-13 in 1935 and was packaged with rookie pitcher Steve Sundra in a swap with the New York Yankees for temperamental pitcher Johnny Allen.

Results of the trade were even the first year as Pearson won 19 and Allen 20, but Allen went 15-1 in 1937 while Pearson's record was 9-3 in 145 innings.

Fred Lieb said New York owner Col. Jacob Ruppert told him confidentially that, "we made this deal to get Sundra. We felt Allen was a better pitcher than Pearson, but we disguised our hand." Sundra was regarded by New York scouts as the best pitching prospect in the minors, although his record was undistinguished.

Pearson continued to produce for New York in 1938, going 16-7 with 10 straight wins and a no-hit victory over Cleveland. He was 12-5 the next year, but slipped to 7-5 in 1940 when he tore a shoulder muscle in his final season in the Big Apple.

MONTGOMERY MARCELLUS PEARSON
Born: 9/2/09, Oakland, CA, BR/TR, 6-foot, 175 pounds

		W	L	PCT	G	IP	H	ER	BB	SO	ERA
1930	Oak	3	2	.600	24	53	57	34	30	25	5.77
1931	Oak	17	16	.515	40	234	260	116	123	158	4.46
1941	Hwd	0	1	.000	1	5	6	4	3	0	7.20
PCL		3 20	19	.513	65	292	323	154	156	183	4.75
Majors	10	100	61	.621	224	1430	1392	635	740	703	4.00

The Yankees sent Monte to Cincinnati for third baseman Don Lang and $20,000 in 1941, but he was cut after throwing only 24 innings.

Monte hooked up with Hollywood, pitched five ineffective innings for a loss and returned home to Fresno, where he sold real estate until his death in 1978.

JIM TOBIN

Jim Tobin was a home town boy who got away from the Oakland Oaks initially, but still made his Pacific Coast League debut with the Acorns on his way to fame as a pitcher who could swing a bat with power.

Tobin was a scrawny kid at Roosevelt High School in East Oakland, the same school that produced Ferris Fain nine years later. Jim attended a baseball school sponsored by the Acorns and officials saw enough potential to send him to Bisbee-Douglas in the Arizona-Texas League. When the circuit went out of business in late July, Tobin had the best winning percentage, .818, on nine wins and a pair of losses.

The Oaks didn't recall Jim, so he went home and pitched with a semi-pro team. The New York Yankees signed Tobin in 1933 and moved him across the country where he split the season between Binghamton and Wheeling for a combined record of 16-10. He batted .279 at Wheeling and showed the first real evidence of power by blasting three home runs in 86 at bats. Tobin returned to Binghamton the following season. He was 15-10 on the mound and hit .250 with 10 doubles and three home runs.

The Yankees gave Tobin a trip home in 1935. Jim responded with an 11-8 record for Oakland up to July 14, when he tore cartilage in his left knee while backing up third base on an outfield throw and was out for the rest of the season.

The Oaks lost a potent bat that had produced a .294 average with six doubles and four home runs. Ed Hughes praised Tobin in the *San Francisco Chronicle* and pointed out that, "many teams in the Coast League would like to have him and play him regularly, not as a pitcher."

Bad luck continued to haunt Tobin. An appendix operation kept him from reporting on time to the Yankees spring camp in Florida and his hopes of ascending to the American League failed to materialize. Back with Oakland, Tobin picked up where he left off, appearing in 72 games with 37 mound appearances and a 16-8 record. While he hit no homers, Tobin contributed three doubles, three triples and a .261 average.

New York wanted to send Jim back to Oakland again in 1937, but he refused to report and arranged a deal with Pittsburgh that was agreeable to the Yanks.

Tobin spent nine years in the Big Time, three with Pittsburgh and six more at Boston before being sent to Detroit early in his final season in 1945. His pitching record was 105-112, a creditable showing considering seven of the clubs he played with finished sixth or seventh.

Except for his first year with Pittsburgh, when he was

Jim Tobin

used as a reliever, and 1940, when a knee injury limited him to 15 pitching appearances, Jim pitched at least 145 innings-a-year and worked 238 or more five times. Another shoulder injury may have cost Pittsburgh the pennant in 1938 as Tobin won 14 games for the second place Pirates.

Jim was out of favor with Braves manager Casey Stengel, who relegated him to mop up relief chores in 1941. Tobin had been working on a knuckle ball which he began to master in June, when his record was 2-4. Moved into the rotation, Tobin went 17 games without being knocked out of the box and finished 12-12. The following season he topped the league with 288 innings and 28 complete games for a 12-21 record.

Tobin began throwing his knuckler sidearm in 1944 and it paid big dividends. Two of his 18 wins were no-hitters, a

nine inning shutout of Brooklyn on April 27 — in which he hit a home run — and a five inning whitewashing of the Phillies two months later. In between those gems, Tobin was the loser to Clyde Shoun's 1-0 no-hitter when he gave up a home run to Cincinnati's Chuck Aleno.

As a hitter, Jim achieved some home run records, but his lifetime average was only .230, padded appreciably by a .441 mark (15 for 34) as a rookie. He hit 17 four-baggers in his career, including six in 1942. That season he pounded three straight homers in May to set a record for pitchers. Jim also hit another the day before.

Tobin was sold to Detroit in 1945 after Braves owner Lou Perini accused the outspoken pitcher of being the ringleader of a group of six players who did not care if the team won. Other teams must have believed he was a troublemaker because Jim passed through waivers before winding up with the Tigers.

Detroit won the American League pennant, but Tobin did not appear in the World Series. Tigers general manager George Trautman tried to sell Tobin to many clubs with no takers and told Jim he'd place him with Dallas if Tobin couldn't make a deal for himself. Jim signed a Seattle contract.

When Tobin came back to the PCL in 1946, he split a 10-10 season between the Rainiers and champion San Francisco and was released again. After pitching semi-pro ball in the Bay Area, Tobin signed with Oakland in August, 1948, and played for his second straight pennant-winner. He even pitched the final out against Sacramento to give the Oaks their first title since 1927. Jim pitched four shutout innings in 1949 to record his last victory for the Acorns.

In retirement, the outgoing and fun-loving Tobin was a bartender.

BUCKY WALTERS

Bucky Walters didn't look like anything out of the ordinary on the mound when he began his career, but he could hit so managers stationed him in the infield for the first six years of his life as a pro. National League batters wished he had stayed there.

Walters showed promise at second and third base, but it was a catcher who persuaded Walters to trade his bat for a toe plate.

The year was 1934 and Walters was a rookie with the Philadelphia Phillies. After watching Bucky's throws whiz across the diamond from third base, veteran catcher Jimmy Wilson — who was in his first year as manager — asked Walters near the end of the season if he'd like to pitch a little.

Walters threw seven innings and gave up only one earned run in two games, but went home thinking about how to improve his .260 batting average.

During the winter, the Phillies swapped Dick Bartell to the New York Giants for four players including third baseman Johnny Vergez. Wilson told Bucky his best shot at the

---

JAMES ANTHONY TOBIN
Born: 12/27/12, Oakland, CA, BR/TR, 6-foot, 185 pounds

		W	L	PCT	G	IP	H	ER	BB	SO	ERA
1935	Oak	11	8	.579	23	152	160	70	59	68	4.14
1936	Oak	16	8	.667	37	230	252	112	65	110	4.38
1946	Se-SF	10	10	.500	29	157	177	70	43	42	4.01
1948	Oak	2	1	.667	10	44	41	11	10	11	2.25
1949	Oak	1	0	1.000	2	4	2	0	1	1	0.00
PCL	5	40	27	.597	101	587	632	263	178	232	4.03
Majors	9	105	112	.484	287	1899	1929	619	557	498	3.44

majors was as a pitcher because he had a great arm and fast ball and could learn the rest. Bucky took Wilson's advice and the result was a 198-160 lifetime record on the mound.

Walters — whose father's nickname also was Bucky — attended Germantown High School near Philadelphia but didn't play ball there. After earning a reputation as a good infielder in the minors, he was purchased by the Boston Braves.

He played nine games with Boston at the end of 1931, but was sent down to Montreal in 1932. Walters was recalled again by the Braves, but hit only .187 in 22 contests.

As part of their acquisition of infielders Dick Gyselman and Al Wright from the San Francisco Missions in 1933, the Braves optioned Walters to the Coast League team.

Bucky had his best year at the bat, stroking the ball for a .376 average with 32 doubles, 16 four-baggers and 92 RBIs in 91 games. He batted fourth and was the league's top fielder at the hot corner for the seventh place Missions.

Big days were common for Walters. He had four hits in four trips twice and was four for five on two other occasions. The capper for his season came June 10, when he cracked a minor league record five straight doubles in the first of two games against San Francisco and came back with a two for two performance in the second game.

Boston Red Sox general manager Eddie Collins toured the Pacific Coast League looking for talent and acquired Walters and two Seattle players, Mel Almada and Fred Muller. Bucky cost the Red Sox $20,000 plus infielder Bernie Friberg. Walters was sold to the Phillies in June and hit .256 in 52 games for the year.

Bucky had a 38-53 record in three-plus seasons when the Phillies sent him to Cincinnati midway through 1938 for pitchers Spud Davis, Al Hollingsworth and $50,000. It was one of Cincinnati's best trades as Walters stood out with a team that won pennants in the next two seasons and was a first division club for four more.

He topped the league with 27 and 22 wins with the champions and did it again with 23 in 1944. Bucky registered 160 victories and 107 defeats during his career in Cincinnati and was 2-2 in World Series play. Walters pitched a one-hit contest against the Braves in 1944, losing a perfect game to Connie Ryan's single.

Bucky received many honors. He played in five All-Star games and took the Most Valuable Player Award in 1939,

Bucky Walters (left) with Jimmy Wilson

when he had a 27-11 record and topped the league in innings pitched (319), strikeouts (137) and ERA (2.29).

That same year, a *Sporting News* poll of sportswriters named him as the best all-around player in the majors over Joe DiMaggio and 41 other stars. He received 14,074 of a possible 15,000 points for ability, dependability, application, team value, popularity, initiative, aggressiveness, courage, fellowship and deportment.

Walters managed Cincinnati to seventh place finishes in 1948 and 1949. He led Milwaukee to the American Association pennant in 1952 after replacing Charlie Grimm, who was promoted to manage the Braves. Bucky also coached with the Boston and Milwaukee Braves and the New York Giants.

TED WILLIAMS

Ted Williams was a lot of things in his career — brash, cocky, boisterous, obscene, brusque, a real pain to newsmen and fans. But, most of all, he was the best hitter baseball ever saw.

If he hadn't lost the better part of seven seasons to injuries and military service in World War II and the Korean War, Williams might rank first in many batting categories where he only resides near the top. When averages and percentages that don't require long service are considered, Williams' excellence is evident. He's seventh in batting average (.344), first in on base percentage (.483),

---

<u>**WILLIAM HENRY WALTERS**</u>
<u>Born: 4/19/09, Philadelphia, PA, BR/TR, 6-foot-1, 180 pounds</u>

	G	AB	R	H	2B	3B	HR	RBI	SB	AVG.
1933 Miss	91	362	74	136	32	1	16	92	7	.376
PCL	1	91	362	74	136	32	1	16	92	7	.376

Majors (Converted to pitcher in the major leagues)

	W	L	PCT	G	IP	H	ER	BB	SO	ERA
PCL	(Did not pitch in the Pacific Coast League)									
Majors 19#	198	160	.553	428	3104	2990	1139	1121	1107	3.30

Pitched 16 seasons and in 1931 to 1933 appeared only as an infielder.

Ted Williams

second in slugging average (.634) and first in walks ratio (20.76)

Playing for only the Boston Red Sox in a career that spanned the years from 1939 to 1960, Ted led the American League in hits (six times), doubles (twice) homers (four times), RBIs (four times), walks (eight times) and won seven batting titles. His home run totals were adversely affected by Fenway Park, which inhibits left-handed power.

Ted obviously had some potential, but wasn't considered a lock for stardom in his youth. Growing up in San Diego, the gangly Williams went to Hoover High School because it was new and provided the best chance to make the baseball team. Ted was so skinny that he wore three pairs of socks to make his legs look muscular. He carried 205 pounds on his 6-foot-3 frame at the peak of his career and was dubbed "The Splendid Splinter."

Ted liked to ride the streetcar to the San Diego harbor with his buddy and future PCL catcher Del Ballinger to go fishing, a pastime that filled many leisure hours most of his life. Most of his time was spent on a playground near his home where director Rod Luscomb pitched so Ted could perfect his picture perfect swing. Those countless hours on the playground now named in his honor paid off and the scouts took notice, although some wanted to send him to the lower minors because of his skinny build. Los Angeles proposed a contract, but Ted's father rejected the offer.

San Diego, a team newly arrived from Hollywood, got Ted for $150-a-month when high school closed in June,

1936. The month was nearly over when Ted signed the contract on the kitchen table of a neighbor's home, but the Padres gave him the entire amount. It was a welcome bonus for a Great Depression kid from a family of modest means.

Ted got into his first game the next day at Lane Field as a pinch hitter. In an inauspicious start, Sacramento's Cotton Pippen struck him out on three pitches. The following Friday against Los Angeles, Williams pitched in relief before he was knocked out of the box and sent to left field. His pitching wasn't much to talk about, but he had two singles in two tries.

Manager Frank Shellenback kept Williams in the outfield and he appeared there 42 times, often as a late inning replacement. He hit .271 in 107 plate appearances without a home run. His first round-tripper of the season came on Sept. 15 against Oakland's Willie Ludolph in the post-season playoffs. Williams called it the greatest thrill of his rookie season.

Williams failed in a pinch hit try on opening day in 1937, but hit his first regular season home run off Stew Bolen of the Missions a week later. Ted would hit 586 more before his career concluded. Shellenback placed Williams in the lineup occasionally in the early going, but Ted gradually got more playing time.

Playing in 138 games, Williams posted 24 doubles and 23 home runs while batting in 98 runs with a .291 average. The Boston Red Sox bought his contract in December.

When he came to training camp in the spring, Ted showed plenty of self-confidence and not a little arrogance. When a teammate said, "Wait'll you see Jimmie Foxx hit," Williams replied, "Wait'll Jimmie Foxx sees me hit." But, the Red Sox brass judged "The Kid" was unready for the big leagues and sent him down to Minneapolis.

With exceptional eyesight and coordination and a swing that drew the rapt attention of players and fans alike when he was in the batting cage, Williams made it clear he would be back at the top soon. He led the American Association in batting (.366), runs (130) homers (43) and RBIs (142).

Throughout his career, Williams was never more than an average outfielder with a so-so arm, but it was different story with the bat in his hands. There he was simply superb.

THEODORE SAMUEL WILLIAMS
Born: 8/30/18, San Diego, CA, BL/TR, 6-foot-3, 205 pounds

		G	AB	R	H	2B	3B	HR	RBI	SB	AVG.
1936	SD	42	107	18	29	8	2	0	11	2	.271
1937	SD	138	454	66	132	24	2	23	98	1	.291
PCL	2	180	561	84	161	32	4	23	109	3	.287
Majors	19	2292	7706	1798	2654	525	71	521	1839	24	.344

		W	L	PCT	G	IP	H	ER	BB	SO	ERA
1936	SD	0	0	.000	1	1	2	—	1	0	—
PCL	1	0	0	.000	1	1	2	—	1	0	—
Majors	1	0	0	.000	1	2	3	1	0	1	4.50

He set numerous records and hit three homers that are frequently recalled — one to win the 1941 All-Star game, another off a Rip Sewell blooper pitch in the 1946 All-Star contest and a third in his last major league at bat.

A Triple Crown winner in 1942 and 1947, Williams remains the last major leaguer to reach the batter's ultimate plateau of .400 with a .406 mark in 1941. He'd have been the most valuable player that year, but the award went to a fellow ex-Coaster named Joe DiMaggio, who hit in 56 straight games for the Yankees. Ted gathered MVP awards in 1942 and 1949, was second in the voting four times and third another year. He was the *Sporting News* Player of the Year in 1941, 1942, 1947, 1949 and 1959 and the Player of the Decade of the 1950s.

After his playing career ended, Ted managed Washington and Texas for four seasons and demonstrated that he was a fine hitting instructor. His teams were below average, finishing as high as fourth only once, so Ted retired to Florida and his fishing pole.

When he was indicted into the Hall of Fame in 1966, Ted said, "Today I feel humility and pride, because God let me play the game and be good at it."

Ted's stated goal had been to have people say, "There goes Ted Williams, the greatest hitter that ever lived." There is ample evidence that he was exactly that.

"Wait'll Jimmie Foxx sees me hit."
—*Ted Williams*

WARTIME AND POST-WAR

LUKE EASTER

Luke Easter was just a rookie in 1949, but he may have set a record for putting fans in the seats at Pacific Coast League ballparks.

Clean-up hitter Easter had some help, of course. San Diego presented a powerful offensive aggregation that led the PCL in home runs and runs batted in and was second to Oakland in team batting.

The Padres' featured attractions were Easter and Max West, who led the league in runs (166), total bases (369), home runs (48), RBIs (166), walks (201) and strikeouts (109).

Easter's own numbers might have surpassed those of everyone, including West, but the big first basemen appeared in only 80 games before he was forced to the bench with a bad knee that required surgery. When he quit in mid-June, Easter had 25 homers, 92 runs batted in and was leading the league with a .363 batting average.

The giant first baseman was sort of a mystery man when he was arrived at the San Diego training camp on option from Cleveland. Black players were still a novelty in baseball, although the Padres had employed African-American catcher John Ritchey, who grew up in San Diego and integrated the Coast League by joining the club in 1948.

Like others of his race, Luke was barred from Organized Baseball by the unwritten "gentlemen's agreement" among the white owners. This ended in 1946 when Brooklyn general manager Branch Rickey signed Jackie Robinson to a contract with the Dodgers' farm club in Montreal. Robinson joined Brooklyn the following season.

Easter and many other black prospects were products of the professional Negro Leagues. After 13 months of military service in 1942 and 1943, Easter sought a job with black professional teams, but was rejected for being "too big" to be a baseball player. Luke finally joined the Cincinnati Crescents in 1946 for $350-a-month. He played outfield and first base with the Homestead Grays for two more seasons. Incomplete statistics for his years with the Grays show a .336 average in 434 times at bat with 23 homers.

Baseball men and reporters generally believed the level of play in the Negro Leagues was well below that in the National and American leagues. They were unsure about Easter's potential, but were awed by his size. When the 6-foot-4, 240-pound Easter got ahold of a bat, they became positively enthusiastic about his ability.

Easter tore up San Diego's opposition in spring games, striking out rarely and showing a tremendous ability to get good wood on the ball as he complied a .474 average with four home runs. "I never saw a smoother swinger from the left side and that includes (Ted) Williams," said Oakland pitcher Charlie Gassaway.

"Most of the outlandish stories about Easter are true," said Bob Stevens of the *San Francisco Chronicle*. "A few have been embellished, though in the main the anecdotes stand up." One of those stories was about the day Luke poked a home run into the center field bleachers at the Polo Grounds in New York, more than 450 feet from home plate.

Against Hollywood early in the year, Easter hit a low line drive that made the pitcher duck. The ball continued to rise until it hit the center field wall, 400 feet away.

In addition to his obvious batting talent, Stevens found Luke was proficient in the field and very fast on his feet. Others said he was better than Mickey Vernon, who was manning first base for Cleveland. This may have been an exaggeration in light of the fact that Easter ended the PCL season last in fielding among first sackers who played in a significant number of games.

But hitting, not handling a fielder's glove, was what made Easter so popular with the fans. When he came to the ball club, San Diego president Bill Starr talked to Easter about the intolerance and discrimination he would face in the Coast League and especially in San Diego, which was a conservative Navy town. Luke said he wasn't worried.

"Mr. Starr," Luke said, "when I hit that ball a long way, everybody likes me."

His teammates felt pretty much the same way before they got to know Easter, who was a likable guy aside from

---

LUSCIOUS LUKE EASTER
Born: 8/4/15, St. Louis, MO, BL/TR, 6-foot-4.5, 240 pounds

		G	AB	R	H	2B	3B	HR	RBI	SB	AVG.
1949	SD	80	273	56	99	23	0	25	92	1	.363
1954	SD	56	198	43	55	8	1	13	42	1	.278
PCL	2	136	471	99	154	31	1	38	134	2	.327
Majors	6	491	1725	256	472	54	12	93	340	1	.274

Luke Easter

capped by a crowd of 23,366 for the series-ending double-header and a new Sunday record in San Francisco. Another 5,000 fans were turned away at the gate and hundreds more stood on car roofs or climbed trees in nearby Franklin Park to catch a glimpse of the game and it's biggest star. The crowd in the ballpark was only 242 tickets short of the club record set in a 1946 weekday game against the Seals' hottest rivals, the Oakland Oaks.

Easter limped along for three weeks, the leg bothering him so much that Luke winced when he stepped on the

---

*"When I hit that ball a long way,
everybody likes me."*
— Luke Easter

---

brake in his car. When the Padres rolled into Oakland for a seven-game set on June 14, Luke was on the field and the fans were in the stands. Oaks Park in Emeryville held fewer than 15,000, but 10,915 turned out for the Tuesday night game. Luke blasted six balls out of the park in a pregame hitting exhibition.

Crowds of similar size filled the seats the rest of the week, culminating in a turnout of 14,706 — largest of the year for the Acorns — for the Sunday twin bill. Easter responded with a home run in the first game and three hits including a homer and double in the second. Sadly, it was his last appearance in a Padres uniform as he went under the knife before the end of the month.

Easter came back near the end of the year, playing 21 games for Cleveland, hitting .222 with no home runs in 45 at bats.

The next three years were good ones for Easter. He played at least 127 games annually for the Indians, averaging .280, .270 and .263 with between 27 and 31 home runs, including a 477-foot shot considered the longest ever hit in Cleveland Municipal Stadium. But, Luke broke his foot in 1953 and never recovered, appearing in only 68 games with a .303 average and seven homers.

In 1954, he played 56 games for San Diego, posting a .278 average with 13 four-baggers. Easter just wasn't the same and the next year he hit .283 with 30 homers at Charleston in the American Association. Easter found a home in Buffalo of the International League, where he became a "folk hero" in 1956, according to Buffalo baseball historian Joseph M. Overfield.

The Bisons bought him from Charleston and gave him the first base job. Crowds turned out in record numbers and the team was saved from moving elsewhere. In three-plus years, Luke hit 114 home runs and led the league twice. He left Buffalo in 1959 and spent the rest of that year and five more with Rochester. He coached there from 1963 through 1965 and in Cleveland in 1969.

The best remembered Buffalo home run came on June 14, 1957, when Luke hit a Bob Kuzava fast ball over the center field scoreboard, a couple of houses and onto a street an estimated 550 feet away.

his batting prowess. "It looks like he's our meal ticket," said one Padre. "So long as his big bat drives in runs and brings people into the park, we're on his side."

And he did bring them into the park. The Padres were a good draw everywhere they went as word spread around the league that Easter was worth the price of admission. At home, the team packed in a record 493,780 paid admissions for the year.

Hobbled by the painful leg, Easter came to San Francisco in late May for a series against the Seals. Reporters asked if he planned to take time off to rest his knee in hopes an operation might not be necessary. Luke played anyway, explaining, "San Francisco hasn't seen Luke Easter and I think it should."

The fans responded with good turnouts at every game,

It was vintage Easter and Luke himself was vintage. Although Easter claimed to be 27 when he entered the Coast League in 1949, Luke actually was born Aug. 4, 1915. So, Easter was 33 when he debuted and almost 42 when he hit that big home run in Buffalo.

Easter died tragically in 1979. Working as a union steward in Cleveland, he was carrying a shopping bag filled with money from checks cashed for co-workers at a bank in Euclid, Ohio. When he was accosted by two men, Luke refused to give up the bag and was killed by shotgun blast to the chest.

FERRIS FAIN

The question after Ferris Fain's first three full seasons in the Pacific Coast League was: who is the REAL Ferris Fain? Was it:

1) The San Francisco rookie who hit a meager .238 in 1940?
2) The kid they called "Cocky," who rapped out 201 hits for a .310 average in 1941?
3) The puzzled and disappointed 22-year-old who batted .216 and was benched in favor of a replacement from Tacoma in 1942?

San Francisco team officials and fans had to wait three years to learn the answer. Fain went into the Navy after the 1942 season and didn't show up again until spring training in 1946. Time to grow and mature was just what Ferris needed.

Manager Lefty O'Doul had few doubts about the ability of the slender southpaw who stood deep in the batters box when Ferris joined the Seals out of Oakland's Roosevelt High School in the summer of 1939. Fain had received major league offers, but thought he had a better chance to succeed with an independent ball club. Fain later revealed the Seals paid him $200-a-month under the table so he wouldn't play prep football in his senior year and risk injury.

Fain sat on the bench as a rookie, absorbing baseball at the professional level. Ferris got into a dozen games and hit .212 and while he showed amazing agility around the first base bag, Fain's inexperience was evident in his eight errors.

Everyone liked the way he fielded and he was compared with Hal Chase, regarded by many as the epitome of the modern first sacker. Fain had the same feline grace and judgment as Chase and showed exceptional range. Throughout his career, he almost always led the league in errors, but was at or near the top in assists.

Because he was a gambler on the field, Fain often made sensational plays. One in the 1946 PCL All-Star game at Seals Stadium stands out. Playing deep at the edge of the infield grass with Loyd Christopher on second base, Fain fielded a rifle shot grounder from Steve Mesner. Instead of making the easy play at first, he fired the ball across the diamond to cut down Christopher at third by a yard. Hollywood manager Jimmy Dykes, who had been in pro-

fessional baseball 30 years, said Zeke Bonura was the only other man he ever saw make that play.

Fain's glove wasn't all that kept him in baseball but his hitting was inconsistent in the early years. San Francisco was a poor team that finished seventh in 1940, but its executives were willing to put the kid at first base in hopes he would develop.

Fain began the 1940 season as an understudy and got into the lineup when veteran Jack Burns was injured. He played 146 games and hit .238. O'Doul told Ferris after the

---

"I miss him more than any other player I ever had and that includes Joe DiMaggio."
— Lefty O'Doul about Ferris Fain

---

season not to worry because the first base job was his. Fain said later he was an inch taller and 20 pounds heavier at 5-foot-11 and 180 pounds when he arrived in camp in 1941 and knowing that he had the job let him relax and concentrate on hitting.

Ferris produced a .310 average with 27 doubles and led the league in walks (96) and runs scored (122) as the Seals rose to fifth place. O'Doul tried unsuccessfully to make a pull hitter out of Fain and for the rest of his career he was recognized as a singles hitter with a good eye at the plate and an elevated on base percentage. His shining season prompted talk the Seals would realize $50,000 to $75,000 when they sold Ferris to a big league team.

When the 1942 season rolled around, Fain was 21 and an established star on a Seals team that had high hopes of contending for the pennant in the first season after Pearl Harbor. Injuries ruined the team's hopes of climbing out of the second division and Fain did nothing to help the cause.

Fain was nicknamed Cocky by trainer Bobby Johnson, not because of his demeanor or hair-trigger temper, but because his eyes didn't seem to meet. The moniker also recognized that Fain was becoming a confident hitter. That confidence began to wane from the start of the season.

Fain was batting .167 after a month and O'Doul was considering recalling Chuck Henson, a .359 hitter at

---

FERRIS ROY FAIN
Born: 5/29/21, San Antonio, TX, BL/TL, 5-foot-11, 180 pounds

		G	AB	R	H	2B	3B	HR	RBI	SB	AVG.
1939	SF	12	33	4	7	2	0	1	8	0	.212
1940	SF	146	446	64	106	21	7	7	50	3	.238
1941	SF	174	649	122	201	27	8	5	66	8	.310
1942	SF	162	519	57	112	17	4	4	53	3	.216
(1943, 1944, 1945 - Military Service)											
1946	SF	180	615	117	185	35	6	11	112	24	.301
1956	Sac	70	147	18	37	6	0	0	16	0	.252
PCL	6	744	2409	382	648	108	25	28	305	38	.269
Majors	9	1151	3930	595	1139	213	30	48	570	46	.290

Ferris Fain

finished second in the 1912 Kentucky Derby and later was a flyweight boxer, looked upon Lefty as a father figure. O'Doul thanked Ferris for doing a great job and presented him with a 16-gauge shotgun, which Fain said he always treasured.

Connie Mack, the penurious Philadelphia owner, watched his expenses because the ball club had languished in seventh or eighth place 12 of the previous 13 seasons. Fain was happy to be in the majors, but complained that he nearly had to take a pay cut when he went up from the Seals. San Francisco paid him $5,500 with a $1,000 bonus at the end of the year. Mack offered $6,000, but eventually raised it to $6,500 after Ferris protested.

Fain earned his pay with the A's, winning American League batting titles in 1951 (.344) and 1952 (.327 with a league-leading 43 doubles). He averaged 110 bases on balls in his first seven seasons, including one year with the Chicago White Sox, where he was traded in 1953. He walked nearly 19 per cent of the time, placing him fifth all-time in that category.

Knee problems reduced him to part-time service with the White Sox, Detroit and Cleveland in 1954 and 1955 and he left the majors with a lifetime batting average of .290.

Fain returned to the Coast League as a player-coach with Sacramento in 1957, but it was not a happy experience. He was hired for $7,500 by the club's general manager over the objections of manager Tommy Heath, who wanted Chuck Stevens.

Ferris was used less and less as the season progressed, hitting .252 in 70 games. Fights on and off the field contributed to his release at the end of the year.

LARRY JANSEN

Only 28 men ever won 30 or more games in the Pacific Coast League. Larry Jansen was the last to accomplish it.

The fact that nearly three-quarters of the 30-game winners played before 1912 makes Jansen's 1946 feat even more significant.

Jansen's last season with the San Francisco Seals produced more than just 30 wins for the slender Dutchman. Larry led the Coast League in victories and came within three wins of the league record by chalking up a 13-game winning streak that ended in mid-August.

Jansen was tops in winning percentage with an .833 mark and an earned run average of 1.57 that broke the Coast League record of 1.61 set in 1943 by Sacramento's Clem Dreisewerd. This does not include the 1.48 ERA Vernon's Jack Quinn authored in the abbreviated 1918 season.

Jansen led the Seals to the pennant and a win in the playoffs. Sportswriters who voted for the *Sporting News* Most Valuable Player Award thought Oakland first baseman Les Scarsella — who missed two months with an injury but batted .332 — deserved the prize more than Larry.

Jansen probably didn't care. At age 26, he was back in baseball after nearly two years of working on his farm and

Tacoma. Ferris continued to collect his infrequent hits on weak grounders and bloop flies over the infield.

Henson arrived in early June. The competition made Fain rally a bit and his average rose to .215 by the end of July. It stayed there the rest of the year. Fain finished as one of the PCL's worst hitting regulars at .216 in 164 games with only 112 hits and 25 extra-base blows.

Fain went off to war and played service ball, first at McClelland Field team near Sacramento — a team he managed to an 80-20 record — and in 1944 with the Hickam Field Bombers in a Hawaiian military league. Ferris led the league in batting with a .385 average and made the All-Star squad.

When Fain came back from the war, he had gained confidence and was ready to show what he could do. The season started with spring training in Hawaii, where reporters learned that Ferris had held his own against major league players in the island's service league. It was a fast circuit and Fain's team was loaded with such big time talent as Joe DiMaggio, Joe Gordon and Mike McCormick.

Called "Burrhead" for his haircut and personality, the hard-working Fain hit well most of the year, leading the Seals to the pennant and a victory in the post-season Governor's Cup playoffs. He led the league in runs scored (117) and runs batted in (112) while hitting .301 with 129 walks.

After Fain was drafted for $10,000 by the Philadelphia Athletics, O'Doul moaned — with possibly just a little bit of hyperbole — that he was a "$100,000 ball player (and) I miss him more than any other player I ever had and that includes Joe DiMaggio."

After the season, Fain went to see O'Doul, who he admired deeply. Fain, whose own dad was a jockey who

was headed for a job with the New York Giants in 1947. It had been a long trip to the big time.

Jansen was one of eight kids who grew up on the family farm in Oregon. He played on the town team and when San Francisco came north for a series in Portland in 1938, the team's manager arranged a tryout with the Seals. Jansen was invited to spring training in 1939, but turned down an offer of $100-a-month to play at Tucson and returned to the farm.

Boston Red Sox scout Ernie Johnson eventually signed him to a contract, but left blank the name of the club where he would be assigned. Jansen didn't hear from the Red Sox the following spring so he wrote to Baseball Commissioner Kenesaw Mountain Landis, who made him a free agent. Jansen wired San Francisco manager Lefty O'Doul and was invited to try out. O'Doul hired Larry and shipped him to Salt Lake, where he had a 20-7 record and led the Class C Pioneer League with a 2.19 ERA.

Promoted to the Seals in 1941, Jansen proved to be an enigma. At his 6-foot-2, 190-pound full grown height later on, Jansen was considered slender. When he arrived at San Francisco in 1941 he had an even less imposing physique.

His fast ball — what there was of it — didn't impress anyone. But, his demeanor, pitching style and control did. Early in the year, Larry beat Oakland in under an hour and a half while throwing just 96 pitches. He followed that up with another win of the same duration over Portland. Veterans often worked fast and tossed few pitches, but Jansen was only 21.

Sportswriters compared him with "Dead Pan Joe" DiMaggio — a former Seal of some celebrity — who did not pop off, minded his own business and never did anything whimsical that passed as personality. On the mound, Jansen was all business and batters were unnerved by his style. They came back to the bench after striking out mumbling, "he ain't got nothing." Jansen's "nothing" resulted in a 16-10 record and a 2.80 ERA for the fifth place Seals.

Jansen explained his lack of speed by saying he wasn't sure he had Class AA talent at the beginning of 1941, so he emphasized control. After coach Larry Woodall taught him the slider, Jansen said he was certain that, "I have what's

Larry Jansen

needed to win in this league."

Great things were expected from Larry in 1942, but he struggled. His ERA ballooned to 4.32 and he won 11 and lost 14. The critics grumbled that Jansen wouldn't make it to the majors, because he lacked a fast ball. Most of Jansen's problems were physical, however, and he suffered from both a heel infection and fractured cheek bone after being hit by a ball in training camp. He was hospitalized with influenza in May, missed almost a month and lost 15 pounds.

San Francisco officials hoped he'd recover in 1943, but they never found out. The Draft Board classified Jansen 1A and he would have gone into military service except for an exemption for working on his farm, which provided food for the war effort. Jansen was out of baseball for two years, but returned to the Seals late in 1945 after World War II ended to post a 4-1 record. His 30-win season followed.

Jansen had a great rookie year in the National League. With a 21-5 record, he led the league in winning percentage (.808) and his 3.16 ERA was seventh, a good ranking

LAWRENCE JOSEPH JANSEN
Born: 7/16/20, Verboort, OR, BR/TR, 6-foot-2, 190 pounds

		W	L	PCT	G	IP	H	ER	BB	SO	ERA
1941	SF	16	10	.615	32	238	220	74	75	70	2.80
1942	SF	11	14	.440	32	173	222	83	39	46	4.32
		(1943 - Suspended; 1944 - Voluntarily Retired)									
1945	SF	4	1	.800	7	55	63	25	12	34	4.09
1946	SF	30	6	.833	38	321	254	56	69	171	1.57
1955	Seat	7	7	.500	26	137	147	51	26	66	3.34
1956	Seat	11	2	.846	24	98	85	28	20	59	2.58
1957	Seat	10	12	.455	30	180	185	63	25	82	3.15
1958	Port	9	10	.474	22	158	142	55	24	85	3.13
1959	Port	1	0	1.000	11	24	26	7	4	11	2.62
1960	Port	3	0	1.000	9	18	11	3	6	13	1.50
PCL	10	102	62	.622	231	1402	1355	445	300	637	2.86
Majors	9	122	89	.578	291	1767	1751	703	410	842	3.58

considering he worked in the Polo Grounds. The Giants hit 221 homers and rose from the cellar to fourth place.

Over the next four seasons, Larry won between 15 and 23 games annually, the high mark coming in 1951 when the Giants took the playoff series against Brooklyn in the game won by Bobby Thomson's stunning home run. Jansen did not do well in the World Series, losing two games in 10 innings pitched with a 6.30 ERA.

He went 24-29 in three more years and returned to the PCL with Seattle in 1955 to compile a 7-7 record. Larry followed with an 11-2 mark that won him another brief trip to the majors with Cincinnati. Jansen went 2-3 and was sent back to the Rainiers in 1957. His production diminished over the next four seasons with Seattle and Portland as he combined pitching with coaching.

Jansen was pitching coach for the San Francisco Giants from 1961 through 1971, helping to develop Hall of Fame hurlers Juan Marichal and Gaylord Perry, and with the Chicago Cubs for two more seasons.

JACKIE JENSEN

Jackie Jensen and Olympic diving champion Zoe Ann Olsen drove away from their celebrated 1949 wedding ceremony in a yellow Cadillac convertible with red leather seats that Jensen received as a bonus for signing a three-year, $75,000 contract with Oakland a few months earlier.

A decade later, Jackie's successful major league career was interrupted and finally ended because of a crumbling marriage and his fear of flying.

Jensen was a sports hero in his home town long before he stepped onto a major league baseball diamond. A star baseball, football and basketball player at Oakland High School, the blond and muscular Jensen came to the University of California's Berkeley campus in 1946 after 19 months of Navy service. Although 230 candidates were out for the football squad in the first post-war season, Jensen was an immediate star with the Golden Bears.

The first time he touched the ball in Cal's opening game against Wisconsin, the Golden Boy shook off five tackles in a dazzling 56-yard punt return for the Bears' only score. Cal was 2-7 in his freshman year, but Jensen was chosen to play in San Francisco's annual post-season East-West Shrine All-Star game.

Cal improved to 9-1 in 1947 under new head coach Lynn "Pappy" Waldorf and went to the Rose Bowl the following season with a 10-0 record. Jensen was the star fullback of both squads, a swift, powerful and deceptive runner who

JACK EUGENE JENSEN
Born: 3/9/27, San Francisco, CA, BR/TR, 5-foot-11, 190 pounds

		G	AB	R	H	2B	3B	HR	RBI	SB	AVG.
1949	Oak	125	467	63	122	21	7	9	77	5	.261
PCL		1 125	467	63	122	21	7	9	77	5	.261
Majors		11 1438	5236	810	1463	259	45	199	929	143	.279

"We will not pay an exorbitant price."

— Yankees owner Del Webb after trying to sign college star Jackie Jensen

gained All-America honors in his junior year when he rushed for a school-record 1,010 yards and a 7.4-yard average. He was fourth in voting for the Heisman Trophy that season.

Jensen also was a baseball All-American in 1947 and led Cal to the first NCAA College World Series championship over Yale, which featured future President George Bush at first base.

As the end of the 1949 school year approached in May, there was speculation Jensen would sign a baseball contract rather than return to the football team, which would go undefeated in the regular season and lose to Ohio State in the Rose Bowl.

Columnist Rube Samuelsen of the *Los Angeles Times* predicted the 22-year-old Jensen would turn pro with Oakland, not only because other former Cal stars had started out with the Oaks, but because club owner Clarence "Brick" Laws' son was one of Jackie's fraternity brothers. Samuelsen's speculation proved correct. At the Alpha Delta Phi house, the brothers joked that Bill Laws was, "majoring in Jensen."

On May 25, Jensen met with New York Yankees owner Del Webb and scout Joe Devine at the Palace Hotel in San Francisco. The *San Francisco Chronicle* reported Jackie had been offered between $35,000 and $40,000 to join the Bronx Bombers.

"We will not pay an exorbitant price," said Webb. "After all, Jensen still is of unknown major league quality."

Brick Laws signed Jensen the next day, "for a bonus in excess of $5,000," and Jackie debuted in the Oaks outfield as a seventh inning replacement for Maurice Van Robays. Wearing the number 36 he made famous on the Memorial Stadium turf, Jensen flied to left field in the eighth and hit a hard line drive to the third baseman in the tenth as the Acorns lost to Seattle in 12 innings.

Jensen chose the Oaks because he was afraid to accept a major league bonus contract. Under the rule in effect at the time, bonus players could not be farmed out immediately and Jensen feared he would languish on the bench if he wasn't ready to play at the big league level. Jensen was subject to the $10,000 major league draft, but Laws believed he could sell Jackie for more than that before the Oct. 15 draft.

Jackie got three hits the next night. On June 4, after Zoe Ann's parents announced their 17-year-old daughter and Jensen would marry in the fall, Jackie hit two home runs against San Francisco, the second one winning the game in the ninth inning.

Jensen hit .261 in 125 games with nine homers and 77 runs batted in as the Oaks finished second to Hollywood

Jackie Jensen

by five games. Manager Chuck Dressen worked to correct his rookie's flaws in the outfield, where Jensen had a strong arm, but often showed poor judgment on flies, and to teach him to hit the curve and change of pace. Jensen improved in all departments by the end of the season.

Two days before the draft, Laws sold Jensen and second baseman Billy Martin — another local product from Berkeley High School — to the Yankees for a reported $100,000 and players.

When he arrived in New York, Jensen was looked upon as the successor to his boyhood idol, Joe DiMaggio. Although he was inexperienced, the Yankees had to keep him on the roster in 1950 as a bonus player. They farmed him out to Kansas City in 1951 and sold him to Washington the following year. Jackie's big league abilities came to the fore that year when he hit .280 with 10 home runs and 82 RBIs. After a second year with the Senators produced similar power numbers with a .266 average, Jensen was sold to the Boston Red Sox.

Fenway Park's Green Monster in left field was a much better target for his right-handed power than the distant fences at Washington's Griffith Stadium. From 1954 to 1959, Jensen averaged 26 homers and 111 runs batted in annually, leading the league in RBIs three times. He was atop the American League once in stolen bases (22 in 1954) and triples (11 in 1956) and made the All-Star team

five times. His best year was 1958 when he hit .286 with 35 home runs and 122 RBIs and beat out pitcher Bob Turley for the Most Valuable Player Award.

While he had success on the field, problems in his private life were becoming intolerable. Zoe Ann did not like living in Boston with their three children while Jackie traveled with the Red Sox, so she maintained her home near Lake Tahoe's sports and gambling resorts.

Jensen had shown no extraordinary signs of discomfort accompanying the Cal football teams on flights. But, his dislike of air travel increased as his big league career progressed. Jackie took sleeping pills, but was wide awake once the plane's engines roared into life. He began riding the train on Red Sox road trips and once even drove from Boston to Detroit. Jensen's fear of flying turned into a full-blown phobia by the end of 1959.

This fear, coupled with domestic problems caused by long separations from his family, led Jensen to quit baseball. He sat out the 1960 season but returned to the Red Sox at age 34 the following spring. He quit the team in Cleveland on April 29 before a scheduled flight to Kansas City.

Jensen rode the train home and drove with Zoe Ann to Las Vegas, where he went through several sessions with nightclub hypnotist Arthur Ellen before rejoining the team in Los Angeles. After playing out the season — hitting a career low .263 with only 13 homers and 66 RBIs in 137 games — Jackie retired.

Jensen's parents had divorced when he was a child and Ellen said Jackie's fear of flying was an excuse to cover up his desire to go home and patch up his own marriage.

Jensen and Zoe Ann divorced, remarried and divorced again. Jackie moved to Nevada, remarried, worked at several jobs and completed work at the University of Nevada for his bachelor's degree. He was the baseball coach at Cal from 1974 to 1977, then moved to Virginia. The only player ever to appear in an East-West football game, a Rose Bowl, a baseball All-Star game and a World Series died of a heart attack in 1982.

BILLY MARTIN

Billy Martin was the kind of leader many baseball men wanted on their side out in the field or down in the dugout. Many others didn't.

"He was a fresh punk, but what a competitor," said Brick Laws, owner of the Oakland Oaks and the man who gave Billy his start in baseball.

Not everyone liked Martin or appreciated his relentlessly aggressive personality. One reporter described him as, "a mouse studying to be a rat."

Billy's bluster and pugnacious style — sometimes combined with alcohol — often got him in trouble. As a Coast League rookie, he fought with Hollywood infielder Lou Stringer. In the majors, Martin had famous on field fights with St. Louis Browns catcher Clint Courtney and Chicago pitcher Jim Brewer, who later was awarded $10,000 in

PCL PICTORIAL

Billy Martin (left) and Jackie Jensen

Larry Jansen

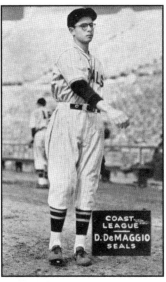

Dom DiMaggio

Vince DiMaggio

Eddie Joost

court for a broken jaw. One nationally-televised confrontation with star outfielder Reggie Jackson took place in the Yankees dugout in 1977. Billy was fined and/or suspended frequently for run-ins with players and umpires.

Off the field, Martin and Mickey Mantle, Yogi Berra and other teammates were involved in a brawl at New York's Copacabana nightclub. Martin was fined $1,000 and traded to Kansas City soon after. He had fights and other altercations with fans, bar patrons, sportswriters and a marshmallow salesman. Billy's arm was broken in a

hotel battle with pitcher Ed Whitson.

Billy was fired from every one of his record five managerial jobs with Minnesota, Detroit, Texas, New York and Oakland. His legendary love-hate relationship with Yankees owner George Steinbrenner culminated in his ouster four times.

Despite all this turmoil, Billy was a smart and hustling, if light-hitting infielder, for 16 years and a skipper for 17 more, including 16 in the majors. Martin's teams won five division titles and split a pair of World Series appearances.

Billy Martin (left) and Vic Raschi celebrate Martin's 1952 World Series homer.

His record as a manager was 1,253 wins and 1,013 losses. Martin was chosen America League Manager of the Year in 1974 (Texas), 1976 (New York), 1980 and 1981 (Oakland).

Martin was a tough kid from Berkeley when the Oaks obtained his signature on a contract in 1946. His given name was Alfred, but his Italian grandmother called him "Belli" (pretty), which became Billy. Given the size of his ample nose, often compared with Ernie Lombardi's and later reduced by surgery, Martin did not qualify as pretty. But the Oaks hired him to field and hit, not win beauty contests.

When he joined the team, general manager Cookie Devincenzi bought him a suitcase and gave him a salary advance.

"It was the first suitcase I ever owned," said Martin. "I was ready to wrap my shirts in a paper bag. Socks and handkerchiefs I'd stuff in my pockets."

Billy was sent off to Idaho Falls in 1946 and to Phoenix the following season. He led the Arizona-Texas League in batting (.392), hits (230), doubles (48) and RBIs (174). Although he couldn't handle PCL pitching in 15 games at the end of the year, Billy was invited back in 1948.

The scrappy little infielder became a favorite of manager Casey Stengel, who saw potential under the rough exterior and liked his versatility and aggressive style of play. Called "Kid" for his age or "Horn" for his nose, Billy hit .277 in 132 games as the youngest member of the "Nine Old Men" who won a pennant for Oakland. Stengel said Martin was the "find of the year."

Stengel took over as Yankees manager in 1949 and was replaced in Oakland by Chuck Dressen, who told the *San Francisco Chronicle* that Martin was, "one of the best infield prospects I've seen in years."

Martin had trouble making the double play. He stepped on the bag with his right foot, forcing an extra step before he could pivot and throw. Some sportswriters said the Oaks should station him at third base, but Dressen disagreed.

"Why waste him at third," askemd Dressen. "He has good, fast hands and speed afoot. He can cover ground. Only one in a thousand has these qualities."

When Cookie Lavagetto joined the Acorns in May, he

ALFRED MANUEL MARTIN
Born: 5/16/28, Berkeley, CA, BR/TR, 5-foot-11.5, 165 pounds

		G	AB	R	H	2B	3B	HR	RBI	SB	AVG.
1947	Oak	15	53	3	12	3	0	0	5	0	.226
1948	Oak	132	401	60	111	28	2	3	42	7	.277
1949	Oak	172	623	90	178	27	3	12	92	11	.286
PCL	3	319	1077	153	301	58	5	15	139	18	.279
Majors	11	1021	3419	425	877	137	28	64	333	34	.257

became Billy's roommate and self-appointed tutor on the art of playing second base. Martin appeared in 158 games at second and 18 more at shortstop, finishing near the bottom of both fielding tables.

But, he was a decent hitter, batting .286 with a dozen home runs, 90 runs scored and 92 batted in. At the end of the year, the Oaks sold Martin and outfielder Jackie Jensen to the Yankees for $100,000 and players.

Billy split 1950 between Kansas City and New York and was a reserve with the Yankees again in 1951. He broke

---

"He was a fresh punk, but what a competitor."
— Oakland owner Brick Laws about Billy Martin

---

into the lineup as a regular and was made team captain in 1952, then missed all of 1954 and most of 1955 while serving in the Army. After starting for New York in 1956, the Copacabana incident sent him to the Kansas City Athletics in the first of six moves that transferred him to Detroit, Cleveland, Cincinnati, Milwaukee and Minnesota.

His playing career over in 1962, Billy became a Minnesota scout and later a Twins coach before he was hired as Denver's manager in 1969. He was back in the majors the following season as Minnesota's skipper. Although the Twins won the division, his relationship with owner Calvin Griffith was contentious and Martin was fired. Success, followed by his discharge, was the pattern of Martin's entire career as a manager.

Martin was successful as a player in five World Series with the Yankees, banging out 33 hits in 28 games for a .333 average. His shoe-string catch of Jackie Robinson's bases loaded pop up ended an inning and saved the 1952 series for New York. A year later he set a record with a 12 for 24 series and a .500 batting average.

Martin was a member of the Yankees' front office in 1989 when he was killed in a Christmas Day automobile accident near his home.

GEORGE METKOVICH

If airlines were as competitive in the 1940s and 1950s as they are today, George Metkovich would have collected lots of frequent flier miles traveling back and forth between the Coast League and the big leagues.

The hard-hitting outfielder-first baseman went up from the PCL in 1943, came back down in 1948, returned to the majors the following year, was sent down in 1950, climbed up to the big leagues again a year later and fell back for the last time in 1955.

He was a starter and a reserve for a decade in The Show, hitting .261 in 1,055 games. Between major league appearances, George helped Oakland win Coast League pennants in 1948 and 1950, was the most valuable player in 1950

and captured the league's batting title (.355) in 1955.

George played most of his debut year in 1939 at Fulton in the Kitty League, where he hit .313. Metkovich was on the Detroit farm club's roster early in 1940 when Baseball Commission Kenesaw Mountain Landis made him and 90 other Detroit players free agents. He signed with the Boston Braves and was sent to Evansville in the Three I League, where he tore knee ligaments and hit only .227 in 60 games. George spent two more seasons in Boston's minor league system.

George didn't make it to the Braves, but received his nickname, "Catfish," from Boston teammates in a spring training accident. Metkovich stepped on a catfish while trying to pull the hook from its mouth and a barbed fin went through the crepe sole of his shoe. The wound became infected and he limped for weeks.

A graduate of Fremont High School in Los Angeles, Metkovich was a next door neighbor of Bobby Doerr, who was a close friend of George's brother, Chris.

Classified 1A in the draft in 1943, Metkovich refused to report to the Braves camp. He wanted to be sent to a team on the West Coast and threatened to keep working at his job in a Los Angeles aircraft plant to stay near his pregnant wife and widowed mother. Landis ruled Metkovich could not be optioned, so the Braves sold him to San Francisco for $500, agreeing that $4,500 more would be paid if he stuck with the Seals.

Metkovich became one of the most publicized pieces of diamond merchandise in the Coast League. One San Francisco writer called him the Seals' best left-handed batter since Paul Waner in 1925 and the best prospect since Joe DiMaggio in 1935. He started in the outfield and wound up playing first base when Gus Suhr went out with an injury.

Under manager Lefty O'Doul's guidance, Metkovich's batting average improved to .325. O'Doul compared George's throwing ability with that of DiMaggio, Tris Speaker, Chick Hafey and Duffy Lewis. "I've never seen (an arm) to equal it for accuracy," Lefty said.

Metkovich played 11 weeks on the West Coast before the Boston Red Sox offered $25,000 and outfielder Dee Miles to take him to the American League. It was the first time in memory that owner Charlie Graham had sold a player for immediate delivery. It probably wouldn't have

---

GEORGE MICHAEL METKOVICH
Born: 10/8/21, Angel's Camp, CA, BL/TL, 6-foot-1, 185 pounds

		G	AB	R	H	2B	3B	HR	RBI	SB	AVG.
1943	SF	71	268	43	87	12	8	3	38	4	.325
1948	Oak	134	500	116	168	23	7	23	88	9	.336
1949	Oak	77	285	50	96	13	5	14	50	9	.337
1950	Oak	184	739	152	233	34	8	24	141	23	.315
1955	Oak	151	532	94	178	21	2	17	79	10	.335
1956	Vanc	132	489	73	144	24	5	6	43	9	.294
1957	SD	24	90	13	24	4	1	1	8	0	.267
PCL	7	773	2903	541	930	131	36	88	447	64	.320
Majors	10	1055	3585	476	934	167	36	47	373	61	.261

George Metkovich

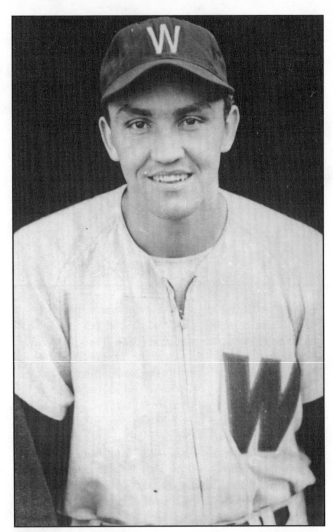

Irv Noren

happened, but Graham needed the money immediately to make a huge payment on the Seals Stadium mortgage.

George was a Boston regular for three seasons. He finished 1943 at .246 and elevated his average to .277 the following year, which was highlighted by a 25-game hitting streak. He slumped to .260 in 1945 and became a utility outfielder on the pennant-winning 1946 team. George was sold to Cleveland, where he hit .254 in 1947 and was shipped to Oakland along with pitcher Les Webber the following May in a deal that brought pitcher Will Hafey to the Indians at the end of the 1948 season.

The Oaks almost didn't get Metkovich from Cleveland. The St. Louis Browns had agreed to swap Johnny Berardino for George and $50,000 during the winter, but Metkovich was not sent because of an injured shoulder. When he reported to Oakland, George declared his arm was sound.

Metkovich joined a team that was notable for its lineup of major league veterans. At 26, George was one of the younger members of the "Nine Old Men" who won the pennant. The right field bleachers at Oaks Park were less than 300 feet from the plate down the foul line, ideal for the southpaw Metkovich. He belted 23 home runs, more

than twice the number he had ever hit in nine previous seasons. He averaged .336 and batted in 88 runs.

Casey Stengel had gone to the New York Yankees and Chuck Dressen was managing the Oaks in 1949. Metkovich was having a banner year in late May — .337 average, 14 homers and 50 RBIs — when he was sold to the Chicago White Sox in one of several deals reporters said were designed to remake the Oaks into the kind of team Dressen wanted. The price tag was $40,000 plus outfielder Earl Rapp and first sacker Gordon Goldsberry.

George batted .237 for Chicago and came back to Oakland the next year. He had his best all-around season, hitting .315 with 24 home runs, 152 runs scored and 141 runs batted in to capture his MVP award and win a trip to Pittsburgh. After two-plus seasons with the Pirates, George was included in a 10-player swap with the Chicago Cubs,

"I've never seen (an arm) to equal it for accuracy."
— Lefty O'Doul about
George Metkovich

where he was used as a reserve and was sold to Milwaukee at the end of 1953. He ended 10 years in the big leagues hitting .276 in 68 games with the Braves.

Metkovich came back to the Oaks again in 1955 to hit a league-topping .335 with 17 homers. When the Acorns abandoned Oakland for Vancouver the following season, Metkovich went along and hit .297 in his last year of full-time duty.

In 1957, Metkovich was in San Diego, where he batted .267 in 24 games and took over as manager from Bob Elliott early in the year. He piloted the Padres to fourth and second place finishes and was replaced by Jimmie Reese in his last year in baseball in 1960.

IRV NOREN

When Irv Noren heard the Dodgers were sending him out again in 1949, that was bad news. When Brooklyn officials said he was headed for Montreal, that was worse and Noren balked.

Irv had roamed the bushes in Brooklyn's minor league way stations from Santa Barbara to Fort Worth since his discharge from the Army in 1946. Noren thought he deserved a shot at the big leagues.

Noren threatened to leave the Vero Beach training camp with his wife and daughter and head home to Pasadena, where his father ran a bakery. When Dodger general manager Branch Rickey heard Noren might take a walk, he suggested the 24-year-old outfielder could play with Hollywood.

If Noren's rebellion had happened a year earlier, playing for Hollywood would not have been an option. But, the Dodgers and Stars had approved a working agreement the previous winter, so Noren packed his bags and headed west.

It was a great opportunity for a player who had moved from Jamestown, N.Y., when he was 12 and had grown up following the Coast League and its local entries, the Stars and Los Angeles Angels.

Noren was an outstanding athlete at Pasadena High School where he played baseball, but excelled at basketball. He was the region's prep basketball player of the year in 1943 and later starred at Pasadena Junior College. Irv was offered basketball scholarships by several colleges, including UCLA, USC and Kentucky.

The service called, but after his discharge Irv returned to junior college — where he once scored 37 points in a Compton tournament game — and played professional basketball during the winter. His first pro experience was with the Red Devils, a local quintet that included Jackie Robinson on its roster. Noren did well in games against visiting Eastern teams including the Chicago Gears, who featured 6-foot-10 star center George Mikan. Noren joined the National Basketball League's Gears the following season and the team won the playoffs after finishing third in the regular season.

While Noren was a fine player on the hardwoods, base-ball was where he was going to earn a living.

He had done well in the California League with Santa Barbara. He hit .363 and led the Class C league in hits, doubles, triples and RBIs. He followed up with two seasons at Fort Worth, where he batted .323 and won the Texas League's Most Valuable Player Award in 1948.

There were doubts about some aspects of Noren's game when he arrived in Hollywood. Manager Fred Haney feared Irv might not be fast enough to patrol center field. A few great catches by the rookie convinced the skipper that Noren knew how to play the outfield even if he didn't have blinding speed.

Haney liked Noren's arm strength and felt that only a foolish base runner would attempt to take advantage of him. Irv led the league in fielding and was tops in assists with 30, the first time that many had been recorded by a PCL player since 1936.

As the season opened, Irv was learning to hit the fast ball and trying to correct his tendency to undercut the ball. "For a player of his experience, he's coming along faster than could be expected," Haney said.

Even Haney underestimated Noren, who took over the league lead in batting in late June when Luke Easter went out for the rest of the year with a knee injury. Irv wound up at .330, second only to batting champion Artie Wilson of Oakland, who hit .348. Noren belted a career high 29 home runs to tie Frank Kelleher for the team lead and knocked in 130 runs.

Haney said he was the best player in the league, rookie or veteran. The sportswriters agreed and voted Noren the league's MVP. Irv could run, hit, throw and — as the *San Francisco Chronicle's* Will Connolly said — was, "a pleasure to watch."

In spite of these accolades, Brooklyn couldn't find a place for Noren in its outfield. The incomparable Duke Snider was in center and Carl Furillo was a fixture in right, but the left field spot was manned by a committee. Still, the Dodgers thought so little of Noren that they sold him to Washington for $70,000 and a player.

Noren later said he heard Rickey had to unload a number of minor leaguers for cash to pay off losses incurred by the Brooklyn Dodgers football team, which had won only eight games in three All-America Conference seasons and had been forfeited to the league.

Noren thrived at Griffith Stadium in 1950. Irv led the club in just about every batting department, hit .295 and topped the American League in outfield assists. After two

IRVING ARNOLD NOREN
Born: 11/29/24, Jamestown, NY. BL/TL, 6-foot, 190 pounds

	G	AB	R	H	2B	3B	HR	RBI	SB	AVG.
1949 Hwd	180	678	134	224	40	6	29	130	10	.330
1962 Haw	76	135	13	32	3	0	4	25	0	.237
1963 Haw	16	15	2	4	1	0	0	1	0	.267
PCL 3	272	828	149	260	44	6	33	156	10	.314
Majors 11	1093	3119	443	857	157	35	65	453	34	.275

more years, Noren and infielder Tommy Upton were swapped to the Yankees for outfielders Jackie Jensen and Archie Wilson, pitcher Spec Shea and infielder Jerry Snyder.

Irv fit in well with manager Casey Stengel's platoon system, sharing the outfield with Mickey Mantle, Gene Woodling and Hank Bauer. His best year was 1954, when he hit .319 and made the All-Star squad. The following year was his last as a more-or-less every day player and Irv hit .253.

Noren moved to Kansas City in 1957, then on to the St. Louis Cardinals and the Chicago Cubs before making his last major league stop with the Los Angeles Dodgers in 1960.

After being out of baseball for a year, Noren returned to the Coast League as manager of the Hawaiian Islanders in 1962 and 1963. Later he scouted for the Washington Senators, managed Niagara Falls in the New York-Pennsylvania League and was a coach for five seasons with the Oakland A's and Chicago Cubs.

ANDY PAFKO

Sportswriters called him "Handy Andy" or less frequently, "Dandy Andy." They thought it was clever, because it rhymed.

If Andy Pafko's first name had been Edward, they could have manufactured a more accurate piece of verse and called him, "Steady Eddie."

Throughout his long career in the minors and the National League, Pafko showed good power, usually producing 20 to 30 doubles and 15 to 30 home runs. His batting average never was too high or too low, generally ranging between .280 and the low .300s.

Even in 1943, his only year in the Pacific Coast League, Pafko was remarkably consistent from start to finish as he led in hits (215), runs batted in (118) and batting average (.356). He played in all 157 games with Los Angeles and showed decent speed along with a strong, accurate arm that placed him among the top five players in outfield assists.

With only Johnny Moore back from the 1942 outfield, new manager Bill Sweeney had some concerns about his fly chasers. He was not worried about right field, patrolled by the 22-year-old Pafko.

In his first full season in a Class AA league and in only his third full season as a professional, Andy took charge of the Coast League in several offensive categories from the beginning.

Andy Pafko

ANDREW PAFKO
Born: 2/25/21, Boyceville, WI, BR/TR, 6-foot, 190 pounds

		G	AB	R	H	2B	3B	HR	RBI	SB	AVG.
1943	LA	157	604	109	215	31	13	18	118	13	.356
PCL		1 157	604	109	215	31	13	18	118	13	.356
Majors	17	1852	6292	844	1796	264	62	213	976	38	.285

Ken Raffensberger

He collected one hit in five tries in an unusual Sunday opener won by the Angels in a slugfest over the Oakland Oaks before a record first day crowd at Wrigley Field. Two days later, Andy broke out with his first home run and six RBIs in another win over the Acorns.

Pafko was near the top of the league stats sheets from then on. By mid-May, his batting average was hovering near .400 and Andy trailed only Hollywood's Johnny Dickshot, who was in the midst of a 33-game hitting streak.

Los Angeles dominated the standings, winning 21 straight games from April 28 through May 19 to break the league record of 19 set by the Angels in 1939.

A week later, Pafko's average soared above .414 and rose to .419 at the end of the first week in June. Andy led the way all season in RBIs and was near the top in home runs, finishing with 18, second behind teammate John Ostrowski's league-leading 21.

At the end of the season, the no-contest pennant race was won by Los Angeles with a 110-45 record and a 21-game lead over second place San Francisco. But the Seals took the playoffs after Los Angeles was upset by four straight losses to third place Seattle in the opening round.

Pafko still had some things to celebrate at the end of the year. The *Sporting News* named him the Coast League's most valuable player and he won promotion to the Chicago Cubs.

Pafko hadn't wanted to come to Los Angeles before the season started. One of six children in a Wisconsin farm family, he was the first child born in America after his parents came from Czechoslovakia. His high school had no baseball team, so Pafko played for a town team.

Andy joined Eau Claire in Northern League in the spring of 1940, but was let go the same day when officials discovered they had too many players on the roster. Andy went home and was recalled late in the season to hit .209 in 20 games.

In a full season with Green Bay of Wisconsin State League the following year, Pafko was second in batting with a .349 average. Milwaukee bought Andy and took him to spring training in 1942 before farming him out to Macon. He hit .300 and led the South Atlantic League with 18 triples.

Pafko hoped to stay close to home in Milwaukee. Andy nearly quit baseball the following winter when he saw a newspaper story that said he had been sold to Los Angeles. But Andy wasn't temperamental and he had a competitive spirit so he made the best of his trip out west.

Chronic high blood pressure kept Pafko out of the service during World War II, so when the call came from the Chicago Cubs at the end of his season in Los Angeles, Andy moved up and hit .379 in 13 games.

The 1944 season was a learning year for Pafko as he batted .269. Andy and the Cubs both broke out of the doldrums together in 1945. Pafko hit .298 with 110 RBIs and gained a spot on the *Sporting News* All-Star squad. The Cubs took their first pennant since 1938, but lost to Detroit in the World Series in seven games. Never a good post-

season hitter, Andy batted .214 in the first of his four series.

In five more seasons, Pafko solidified his position as a Chicago favorite. He batted better than .300 three times with a career high of .312 in 1948 and popped 36 homers in 1950, when he averaged .304 with 92 RBIs.

Pafko was part of a eight-player trade the following June with Brooklyn, which won the 1952 championship. The Dodgers dealt him to the Milwaukee Braves, where he finished his career, playing in World Series in his last two seasons, 1957 and 1958.

He continued with Milwaukee for three years as a coach and later managed in the minors and scouted for Montreal.

KEN RAFFENSBERGER

If Ken Raffensberger pitched for major league clubs that were as successful as his Coast League teams there's no telling what kind of career numbers he would have posted.

The big Pennsylvania Dutchman was a respected National League hurler for most of his 15 years, although his lifetime record of 115-154 does not appear to be anything special.

The big southpaw's luck was all bad in the big leagues and he had the misfortune to pitch with a string of teams that finished in the second division during the 1940s and 1950s. Day-to-day achievements were scarce, but winning the 1944 All-Star game and pitching four one-hitters were his greatest baseball thrills.

Raffensberger first attracted the attention of major league talent hunters in the early 1930s when he pitched his American Legion team to the Pennsylvania state championship. Raffy continued working in semi-pro leagues until 1937, when he signed with the St. Louis Cardinals and joined their Eastern Shore League affiliate in Cambridge, Maryland. Ken fanned 183 and posted an 18-6 mark.

The hard-working Raffensberger went to Rochester in 1938, leading the league with 53 games pitched and winning 15 of 25 decisions. After a brief trial with the Cards, Ken returned to Rochester in 1939 and split 30 decisions evenly.

The Chicago Cubs acquired Ken in a trade for Gene Lillard, Steve Mesner and cash. Raffensberger pitched with the Cubs and St. Paul in the American Association for two seasons before being shipped to Los Angeles in 1942.

The Angels were seventh in 1941 and had brought many

KENNETH DAVID RAFFENSBERGER
Born: 8/8/17, York, PA, BR/TL, 6-foot-2, 185 pounds

		W	L	PCT	G	IP	H	ER	BB	SO	ERA
1942	LA	17	18	.486	51	242	258	93	51	138	3.46
1943	LA	19	11	.633	35	244	228	58	53	134	2.14
PCL		2	36	29	.554	86	486	486	151	104	272	2.80
Majors	15	119	154	.436	396	2152	2257	860	449	806	3.60

George Metkovich

Harry Simpson

Irv Noren

Albie Pearson

Cookie Lavagetto

new players into camp. The rebuilding job paid off as Los Angeles took over first place at mid-season behind a lineup of solid hitters and the strong arms of a pitching staff led by workhorses Raffensberger and Ray Prim.

The Angels looked like a sure thing going into the season's final week when they built a four game margin with five games left against second place Sacramento. The Solons whipped staff ace Prim (21-10) in a rare relief appearance on Thursday, shelled Raffensberger on Friday and won the last three games to take the pennant in a remarkable comeback.

Ken finished the season 17-18, leading the Seraphs in games pitched (51) and strikeouts (138) with a 3.46 earned run average. The Cubs left him in L. A. for another season and put him on the only pennant-winning team of his career.

The Angels took the 1943 championship by 21 games over second place San Francisco, dominating the PCL like no other team since the great Los Angeles club of 1934.

Unlike the ball club, Raffensberger got off to a slow start. Relegated to the bullpen part of the time, Ken contributed three wins to the team's record 21-game win streak, but was the losing pitcher on May 20 when Hollywood ended the skein with a 4-2 victory.

Ken came on strong the rest of the season and produced a 19-11 record with the league's third best ERA of 2.14. He led Los Angeles with 134 strikeouts.

Raffensberger didn't have a killer fast ball so he relied on his curve and later a slider plus good control to pile up strikeouts by keeping the batters off balance. He averaged 1.93 walks per game in the Coast League, slightly above his 1.88 per game ratio in the majors (45th all-time).

Ken's contract was purchased by the Philadelphia Phillies and he lost his lone start with them late in the season. Raffy was off to a 9-4 record in 1944 when he gained his only trip to the All-Star game. Raffensberger finished 13-20 for the Phillies, a team he rated worse than the Angels he had played with the year before.

Raffensberger lost his only three decisions in 1944, when he served in the Navy most of the year. After an 8-15 record in 1945 and a 2-6 start the next year, Philadelphia traded him to Cincinnati.

The Reds were as poor on the field as the Phillies. Over six seasons — Raffensberger's peak years — Cincinnati finished an average of 30 games out of first place. Ken averaged 14 wins and 15 losses during the period.

"I didn't have much support," he said in an interview in *Sports Collectors Digest*. "With the clubs I was on, you had to pitch your best every time out . . . (and) practically had to shut out the other team to stay in contention." Twenty-five of Ken's 83 victories with the Reds between 1948 and 1953 were shutouts and he led the league in whitewash jobs in 1949 and 1952.

Reserved and modest, Raffensberger said batters kidded him, "that I don't have a fast ball (and) I don't have a curve ball. All I got, I guess, is confidence in myself to get that ball over." But, nobody hit him consistently and Stan Musial called Raffy the toughest pitcher he ever faced.

Ken stepped on a baseball and injured his ankle in the 1954 spring camp, never fully recovered and was released. He pitched for Havana in the International League and in his birthplace in York, Pennsylvania, in the Piedmont League. Raffy managed teams in the Evangeline and Three I leagues for two more seasons and retired.

EDDIE WAITKUS

A few baseball players are etched in our memories by some defining moment — Lou Gehrig giving his retirement speech at Yankee Stadium, Babe Ruth gesturing before hitting a home run in the World Series, Fred Merkle failing to touch second base as the winning run scores.

Eddie Waitkus is remembered for being shot in a hotel room in 1949 by a deranged female fan in a scene that was reprised in a movie based on author Bernard Malamud's novel, *"The Natural."*

Ruth Ann Steinhagen fell in love with Waitkus while watching him play for the Chicago Cubs. The smooth-fielding first baseman was traded to the Philadelphia Phillies after the 1948 season. Steinhagen, 19, missed watching Eddie regularly from the stands at Wrigley Field, although she continued to talk about him constantly and built a shrine of his photos in her bedroom.

Steinhagen purchased a second hand .22 caliber rifle and went to the Edgewater Beach Hotel, where the Phillies were staying during a trip to Chicago in June.

She sent a note to the front desk asking Waitkus to come to her room because she had "something important" to discuss with him. Waitkus didn't know the woman but thought she might be "a friend of a friend" so he went. When he arrived around midnight to inquire what she

---

"You're not going to bother me any more."
— *Deranged fan Ruth Ann Steinhagen when she shot Eddie Waitkus*

---

wanted, Steinhagen went into a hallway and returned with the rifle.

"You're not going to bother me any more," she said, and pumped a bullet into his chest.

"I knew I would never get to know him in a normal way," she later told the staff at a court-appointed behavioral clinic. She reasoned, "if I can't have him, nobody else can. And then I decided I would kill him." Steinhagen was kept in an Illinois mental institution for several years.

Waitkus, who was having his best year with a .306 average in 54 games, missed the rest of the season. The bullet ripped through a lung and lodged in a muscle near his spine. Eddie was hospitalized in Chicago for weeks and for a time doctors weren't sure whether he would ever play again.

The ordeal "was really rugged," Waitkus told *Sporting News* publisher J. G. Taylor Spink. "If I thought I had to go through the same thing again, the many operations, the fears, the uncertainty, the mental torture, I think I would rather die."

Waitkus recovered from his wound and returned to the Phillies in 1950 to hit .284 — a percentage point below his lifetime average — for the pennant-winning Whiz Kids. He was named the comeback player of the year.

Waitkus grew up in Cambridge, Massachusetts, where he lived near former major league first baseman Jack Burns, who showed neighborhood kids how to play baseball. As a left-hander, Waitkus was a natural choice to play first base. Eddie gained national recognition in 1938 when he was chosen as the first sacker on the All-Star team at

---

EDWARD STEPHEN WAITKUS
Born: 9/4/19, Cambridge, MA, BL/TL, 6-foot, 170 pounds

		G	AB	R	H	2B	3B	HR	RBI	SB	AVG.
1942	LA	175	699	108	235	40	8	9	81	7	.336
PCL	1	175	699	108	235	40	8	9	81	7	.336
Majors	11	1140	4254	528	1214	215	44	24	373	28	.285

Gene Woodling (left) with manager Al Lopez

Eddie Waitkus

the national semi-pro tournament in Wichita.

Scout Jack Doyle signed him to a Chicago Cubs contract and he was sent to Moline in the Three-I League, where he batted .326 with a dozen triples in 1939. He spent two years at Tulsa in the Texas League, hitting .303 the first year and going four for five with a double and triple on the final day to pace the league in hits, doubles and triples. Waitkus batted .293 the following season and was promoted to Los Angeles in 1942.

Waitkus never had great power, but he was rarely fooled by a pitch and had sufficient speed afoot to keep from being doubled up on ground balls. Los Angeles manager Jigger Statz said Waitkus had the ideal temperament for a ballplayer because nothing bothered him and he was a great team player.

At first base, his stretch and reach were considered phenomenal and he had great range and a fine instinct for positioning. In his year in the Coast League, Eddie fielded .994 — a percentage point above his average in 11 seasons in the big leagues — to finish second behind Sacramento's Jack Sturdy.

Waitkus' batting average with the Angels was a shade below .300 by the end of May. It was .336 two months later and reporters were beginning to write about a batting title. Teammate Johnny Moore and Portland's Ted Norbert were ahead of him, but it wasn't clear that either would meet the minimum 450 at bats required by the league to qualify for the crown.

Waitkus continued his consistent hitting, finishing with a .336 average, a league-leading 235 hits plus 40 doubles and 81 runs batted in for the Angels. Both Norbert and Moore made the necessary trips to the plate with Norbert the runaway title winner with a .378 average.

Eddie was accorded team MVP honors by the Los Angeles press corps. Following the end of the season he enlisted in the Marines and served three years.

Upon his discharge, Waitkus joined the Cubs at their spring camp on Santa Catalina island. Phil Cavaretta appeared to have a secure hold on the first base job at the start of the season. By the end of April, manager Charlie Grimm decided he had to find a place in the lineup for Eddie's bat and Cavaretta was shifted to right field.

Injured during the season, Waitkus played in 113 games and was the Cubs' best hitter at .304. He recorded .292 and .295 averages the next two years and was traded to the Phillies along with pitcher Hank Borowy after the 1948 season.

Although Waitkus came back strong in 1950 with the Whiz Kids, his average dropped to .257 in 1951, but rose to .289 in 1952, his last year as a full-time player. Waitkus was sent to Baltimore and closed out his career with the Phillies at the end of 1954.

GENE WOODLING

When Gene Woodling hit .385 in 1948, he joined a distinguished list of San Francisco Seals who preceded him among the Pacific Coast League's batting champions.

Excluding the Seals' first two bat kings from the Dead Ball Era, Henry Melchoir (.298 in 1909) and Royal "Hunky" Shaw (.281 in 1910), Woodling's figures stack up well against those of Paul Waner (.401 in 1925), Smead Jolley (.397 in 1927 and .404 in 1928), Earl Sheely (.403 in 1930) and Joe Marty (.359 in 1936).

Although he wasn't held in particularly high regard as an outfielder when he arrived at the training camp, it was hard to ignore the husky Woodling's minor league batting feats.

Gene had a long history of success with the bat in the lower reaches of Organized Baseball. At age 25, with two years of military service and three brief and unsuccessful appearances with Cleveland and Pittsburgh behind him, Woodling was ready to make a serious run for another chance in the majors.

Growing up on the mean streets of Akron, Ohio, during the depths of the Great Depression probably helped his development. "I was raised right in the shadow of the Goodyear Tire Co.," he said. "Looking back on it, living in a rough neighborhood probably was the best thing for me. It made me tough when I needed to be tough."

That attitude helped him greatly in 1948, when a severe injury threatened to stop his rush toward the PCL batting title.

Woodling had been involved in batting races before. In his first year as a professional in 1940, he hit .398 at Mansfield to take the Ohio State League crown. He moved

to the Michigan State League the following year, winning a second batting championship with a .394 average.

Promoted to Wilkes-Barre in the Eastern League in 1942, Gene hit only .192 in 39 games and missed most of the year when he broke a leg sliding. Woodling showed his prowess with the timber again the following season with the same team, taking the title with a .344 mark. The Indians gave Woodling a taste of major league play for eight games at the end of the year.

Back from two years in the service in 1946, he averaged .188 with Cleveland and at the end of the season was swapped to Pittsburgh for catcher Al Lopez. The Pirates sent him to Newark. Gene hit .289 with the Bears and moved west as part of the deal that sent pitcher Bob Chesnes from the Seals to the Pirates. Woodling was happy to be in the high-paying PCL, because it meant a $1,000 raise over his former major league paycheck.

Although his throwing arm was regarded as merely adequate, by the end of the first six weeks of play there was no doubt about his overall talent.

"This Woodling is spectacular, a standout" said Bob Stevens in the San Francisco Chronicle. "(He is) the only REAL major leaguer I have seen in the circuit so far."

At the time Stevens typed those words, Gene was batting .372 and had been in and out of the league lead in hitting since opening day. Seals manager Lefty O'Doul — one of baseball's great batting instructors — had worked on his swing and Gene no longer drove the ball up the middle of the diamond for long outs, but was pulling pitches consistently.

Although he was playing in spacious Seals Stadium and had never hit more than eight triples or eight home runs in his career, Woodling ended the season with a league-leading 13 triples plus 22 homers and 107 runs batted in. These totals would have been higher, but on May 23 he made an awkward slide and tore ankle ligaments. Gene didn't reappear in the lineup until he pinch hit on July 2 and didn't play regularly again until July 8.

Woodling limped noticeably, but his batting eye never faltered because Gene had taken batting practice every day his foot was in the cast. He rapped out hits in 17 straight

EUGENE RICHARD WOODLING
Born: 8/16/22, Akron, OH. BL/TR, 5-foot-9.5, 195 pounds

		G	AB	R	H	2B	3B	HR	RBI	SB	AVG.
1948	SF	146	524	121	202	22	13	22	107	6	.385
PCL		1	146	524	121	202	22	13	22	107	6
Majors	17	1796	5587	830	1585	257	63	147	830	29	.284

games and by mid-August boosted his average to .403 before falling back to his final .385 mark. It was the best average by a PCL batting champ since Ox Eckhardt of the Missions hit .399 in 1935 and the *Sporting News* named him Minor League Player of the Year.

Woodling's absence may have cost San Francisco the pennant. The Seals battled Oakland down to the wire, with the Oaks winning the title by two games over their trans-bay rivals.

Gene thought Detroit would buy him, but the New York Yankees acquired him instead. Woodling got lots of work in 1949, partly because Joe DiMaggio was injured in the spring and didn't play until late June. Gene spent five seasons playing for Casey Stengel, often platooning with other outfielders as the Bronx Bombers won the World Series each year with Woodling batting .318 in post-season play.

Woodling was hurt much of 1954 and the New York brass figured it was time to move the 32-year-old outfield-er. In November, Gene was included in a record 18-player trade that took New York and Baltimore more than two weeks to complete. The major players were pitchers Don Larsen and Bob Turley and shortstop Billy Hunter, who went to New York, and Woodling, infielder Willie Miranda plus catchers Hal Smith and Gus Triandos, who wound up with the Orioles.

Although the Yankees are usually regarded as big winners in the trade, Woodling didn't stick around long enough to find out. He was sent to Cleveland at mid-season and hit .257 for the year.

Woodling had his finest major league year with the Indians in 1957, hitting .321 with 19 homers, but was sent back to the Orioles the following April in another trade. Gene stayed in Baltimore for three seasons, moved to Washington and finished with the New York Mets in 1962.

After his playing days were done, Woodling coached with the Orioles and was a scout for the Yankees.

END OF A GREAT ERA

BOB BOYD

When Bob Boyd got a chance to play regularly, a .300-plus batting average usually followed.

Boyd was a black player who toiled four years in the Negro Leagues before breaking into Organized Baseball and then traveled around the minors for six more seasons before sticking with Baltimore.

Boyd was 28 years old by then and past his prime. He batted between .309 and .318 in four of the next five seasons and finished his major league career with a .293 average in nearly 700 games.

When Boyd arrived in training camp in 1951 as the first black to get that far with the Chicago White Sox, there was no question about Bob's fielding, but manager Paul Richards was unsure about his ability to hit. He evidently put little stock in Boyd's history as a batter. Bob had averaged .339 or better during his stay in the Negro Leagues and .373 at Colorado Springs in the Western League the previous season, his first in Organized Baseball.

"Boyd can really handle that mitt around first base," Richards told reporters. "I know he's good enough defensively for the big leagues and has real speed. Whether he can hit remains for the future."

The soft-spoken Boyd said, "I could always hit," and set about to prove it at a level above Class A.

The southpaw was on the small side to play first base, but had been stationed there since childhood. Bob grew up in New Albany, Mississippi, and moved to Memphis to live with his father after his mother died. Boyd returned home after three years of Army service and was working in a warehouse when he tried out for the Memphis Red Sox of the Negro American League.

Line drives were a specialty that later earned him the

Bob Boyd

nickname "Rope" and at his tryout Bob ripped the ball to all fields and was hired on the spot. He batted .339, .376 and .375 in the league and showed unusual power by driving a ball into the left field stands at Comiskey Park, joining Ted Williams and Larry Doby as the only left-handers to accomplish the feat.

Sacramento's new playing-manager, Joe Gordon, coveted Boyd's services and the White Sox agreed to send him west on option. Batting clean-up, Bob got two hits including a home run as the Solons whipped Hollywood on opening day.

Boyd and Gordon carried the club as far as they could, but Bob's speed and high average plus Gordon's team record 43 homers and 136 RBIs weren't enough. Sacramento finished seventh.

Bob chased Seattle's Jim Rivera — another White Sox

ROBERT RICHARD BOYD
Born: 10/1/26, Potts Camp, MS, BL/TL, 5-foot-10, 170 pounds

		G	AB	R	H	2B	3B	HR	RBI	SB	AVG.
1951	Sac	145	555	82	190	32	11	5	64	41	.342
1952	Seat	161	641	100	205	29	18	3	75	33	.320
1963	OC	67	223	19	56	12	1	2	23	0	.251
1964	OC	9	8	1	0	0	0	0	0	0	.000
PCL	4	382	1427	202	451	73	30	10	162	74	.316
Majors	9	693	1936	253	567	81	23	19	175	9	.293

Lee Walls

Jim Grant

farmhand — all season long for the batting championship. Helped by a 26-game hitting streak, Bob averaged .342 and finished second in the batting race to Rivera by 10 percentage points. Bob led the PCL with 41 stolen bases and had 11 triples for third place. In the field, he was first in put outs, assists and errors.

Recalled to the ChiSox for a late season appearance, Boyd returned to the PCL in 1952. Sacramento officials tried to get him back, but he was sent to Seattle. Although Boyd was hospitalized with ulcers late in April and missed three weeks of the season, he edged out teammate Artie Wilson by four percentage points for the batting crown with a .320 average, the lowest champion's mark since 1916. His 33 steals was second and he was a runaway winner for the triples title with 18.

Boyd split 1953 between Chicago, Charleston and Toronto. He was hitting poorly with the White Sox in 1954 when they shipped him to Houston where he averaged .321. Bob was assigned to Houston again in 1955 and balked. Boyd told the club that he was going back to the Negro Leagues, but those circuits did not resume play after 1954 and he had no other option. Bob had another fine year in the Texas League with a .310 average.

Boyd was convinced he'd have stayed in the majors long before then if he'd been white. When Richards drafted him at Baltimore, Bob was surprised. Although he respected the Texan as a manager, Boyd said Richards' comments made it clear, "he didn't like blacks."

Boyd hit better than .300 with little power once he played regularly. After his average declined to .265 in 1959, the Orioles replaced him with slugger Jim Gentile the following season. Confined mainly to a pinch hitting role, Bob responded with a .317 average.

Boyd's major league career closed after appearances in Kansas City and Milwaukee and he returned to the minors in Louisville, San Antonio and two trips to Oklahoma City, then a Coast League franchise. Bob batted .251 in 67 games in 1963 and was hitless in eight tries the following season. He played in the Caribbean winter leagues until 1957 and later scouted for the Orioles.

MUDCAT GRANT

Because Mudcat Grant had a reputation as a pretty good hitter, San Diego manager Bob Elliott toyed with the idea of employing the powerful pitcher in the outfield early in 1958.

Grant, "is conceded to pack more power at the plate than any other member of the squad," said Phil Collier of the *San Diego Union* in a spring training story.

Mudcat had produced a .325 average the previous season in Reading and had hit five homers the year before that in Keokuk. But, the real attraction was his pitching arm, since he registered a 21-5 record in his debut with Fargo-Moorhead in 1954 followed by 19-3 in Keokuk and 12-13 at Reading along with high strikeout numbers annually.

Elliott abandoned the notion of penciling Grant into the lineup as a fly chaser and started him out in the bullpen. Elliott kept him there even after Mudcat's winning performance in a pregame home run hitting contest. Grant was awarded a $25 gift certificate for smacking two homers off 15 pitches, one more than teammate Bill Pinchard and Hollywood sluggers Dick Stuart and R. C. Stevens.

Mudcat got his first mound decision, a loss, on May 3, when he pitched the last 8 1/3 innings of a 15-inning contest at Vancouver. He surrendered nine hits while walking seven and striking out seven.

Mudcat was whiffing batters at a rate of better than one per inning when Elliott was fired in mid-May and replaced by George Metkovich.

If was a fortuitous change for Grant, whose nickname referred to a type of catfish he caught as a child in the swamps near his Florida home. Metkovich — whose own nickname was Catfish — decided Grant would better serve the Padres as a starter. Grant lost his first outing a week after Metkovich took over, fanning eight in a seven-inning twilight game against San Francisco. He walked none and KO'd six in another seven-inning game a week later, beating Los Angeles for his first win.

Grant lost a decision in relief a few days later, but on June 6 tallied his second win by pitching 15 strong innings and scattering six hits with 14 strikeouts as the Padres beat Sacramento. Grant evened his record with a 13-strikeout win over L.A. and later took eight straight to produce 15 wins in 19 decisions the rest of the way to finish 18-7. He struck out 178 batters in 218 innings, walked 102 and had a 2.13 ERA.

Grant had planned to attend college when he was a youngster. Since he'd starred as an all-state prep football quarterback and basketball forward, there might have been some interest among recruiters, but college athletic opportunities for blacks in the segregated South were limited to the Negro schools and he wound up working in a lumber mill.

Cleveland scout Fred Merkle offered him a tryout and at the end of spring training Mudcat signed a minor league contract and went off to the Class C Northern League to start a career that led him to the Indians in 1958 after his great season at San Diego.

Six good years as a Cleveland starter followed. His best season was 1961, when he went 15-9. Grant struck out more than 100 batters three times for the Indians, with a high of 157 in 1963.

Midway through 1964, the Indians sent Grant to Minneapolis in a trade and he finished the year 14-13 with a 3.67 ERA, his best in the majors to that time.

The following season was tops in Mudcat's career. The Twins grabbed the pennant and Grant headed the

Jim Grant

American League in wins (21), percentage (.750) and shutouts (6). He won two of three decisions in the World Series, but the Twins fell to the Los Angeles Dodgers in seven games.

Mudcat never reached those heights again. He pitched two more seasons in Minnesota then bounced around the majors as a reliever with five different teams. His best parting shots were 24 saves with the 1970 Oakland Athletics and two key wins that helped Pittsburgh capture the National League's Eastern Division title later that year. He was through at the end of 1971 with a 145-119 career record. Grant's wildness had been checked as he matured and he wound up with 849 walks and 1,267 strikeouts in 2,441 innings.

Grant pitched for Iowa in the American Association in 1972, then retired to become a Cleveland baseball broadcaster. Later, he had a show business career as a singer with a group called Mudcat and the Kittens.

SAM JONES

Sam Jones had a long, sad face, a toothpick in his mouth and threw a fast ball as overpowering as anyone in the 1950s. Like many pitchers who relied on his number one pitch, he also suffered from a pronounced case of wildness.

Sam's strengths and weaknesses were demonstrated dramatically in 1955 when he was with the Chicago Cubs. He pitched a no-hit game against Pittsburgh, walking six and

JAMES TIMOTHY GRANT
Born: 8/13/35, Lacoochee, FL, BR/TR, 6-foot-1, 186 pounds

		W	L	PCT	G	IP	H	ER	BB	SO	ERA
1957	SD	18	7	.720	34	218	169	56	102	178	2.31
PCL		1	18	7	.720	34	218	169	56	102	178	2.31
Majors	14	145	119	.549	571	2441	2292	985	849	1267	3.63

fanning seven. The poker-faced Jones loaded the bases on three passes in the ninth inning, then struck out Dick Groat, Roberto Clemente and Frank Thomas.

Jones tossed a seven-inning no-hitter for the San Francisco Giants against St. Louis in September, 1959, in a game washed out in the eighth by rain. Two months earlier, a controversial eighth inning ruling by scorer Charlie Park in Los Angeles deprived Sam of another no-hitter against the Dodgers.

Over the course of his major league career, the rangy redhead averaged more than four walks and seven strikeouts per game on his way to a 102-101 record. He was the National League's strikeout champion three times and was among the leaders in other years.

Jones grew up in Ohio, where he played football and basketball in high school, but learned to play baseball on his neighborhood's vacant lots. His family moved to West Virginia in 1943 and he lied about his age so he could get a job after school. The Army drafted Sam when he was in the 11th grade, believing he was 18.

Jones liked military life at a Florida air base, where he pitched on the base team and a civilian Negro team which played a spring exhibition against the Cleveland Buckeyes of Negro American League. Buckeyes manager Quincy Trouppe watched as Jones "struck out about everybody on our team," and urged Sam to join the ball club when his military hitch was up.

Sam took the advice and played two years with the Buckeyes. The pay was spotty and in 1949 Jones joined a semi-pro team in Rochester, Minnesota, which paid him $800-a-month on time, every time. Sam won 18 in-a-row in a fast league and went 24-3.

Cleveland general manager Hank Greenberg offered him a tryout. Greenberg was amazed by what he saw from a 23-year-old who had never played in Organized Baseball. "He had an overhand curve and a sidearm curve," Greenberg said. "And speed. What speed."

Jones agreed to join the Cleveland organization and went to Wilkes-Barre in the Eastern League with Greenberg's promise to bring him up in two years ringing in his ears. Sam received no bonus, but Cleveland had been his favorite team as a child and he only wanted to make it to the Big Time with the Indians.

After a 17-8 year at Wilkes-Barre with a 2.71 ERA and a league best 169 strikeouts, Jones got off to a fast start with the Padres, winning four of five decisions by the end of April. He was striking out batters at a rate of better than one an inning and most of his games were low hit affairs. The Padres produced little offense and finished with the

Sam Jones

PCL's lowest batting mark while averaging only four runs per game. Jones lost numerous games by one run as he finished third with a 2.76 ERA and a 16-13 record.

The *Los Angeles Mirror* called Sam "a poor man's Bob Feller" and San Diego business manager David Starr said he was the best pitcher in Padres' history. Jones led the PCL with 267 innings pitched, 175 walks and 246 Ks, just short of Frankie Dasso's all-time team strikeout mark of 253 set in 1944.

Sam hurt his arm pitching in Puerto Rico that winter and the Indians farmed him to Indianapolis early in 1952. He only pitched 71 innings all year and was back in Indianapolis for two more seasons. The second year his 15-8 mark, plus a 14-win winter season in Puerto Rico convinced the Chicago Cubs that his arm had recovered and they acquired him along with outfielder Gale Wade and $60,000 in a swap for Ralph Kiner.

While Kiner played one more year before retiring, Jones launched the most productive part of his 12-year career. After two losing seasons with the lowly Cubs, he was traded to St. Louis, where he won 12 and 14 games before moving on to the San Francisco Giants in 1959.

The West Coast seemed to agree with Jones and he posted a 21-15 record and led the league with a 2.82 ERA. The *Sporting News* selected him as the National League's outstanding pitcher. Seasons of 18-14 and 8-8 followed before declining skills turned Sam into a relief pitcher in his final three years with Detroit, St. Louis and Baltimore.

SAMUEL JONES
Born: 12/14/25, Stewartsville, OH, BR/TR, 6-foot-4, 192 pounds

		W	L	PCT	G	IP	H	ER	BB	SO	ERA
1951	SD	16	13	.552	40	267	179	82	175	246	2.76
PCL		1	16	13	.552	40	267	179	82	175	246	2.76
Majors	12	102	101	.502	322	1644	1403	655	822	1376	3.59

When Sam couldn't cut it in the majors, he still had enough ability to pitch effectively in relief with Columbus in the International League for four more seasons. Jones died of cancer in 1945.

DALE LONG

Long-ball power put Dale Long in the record book, but so did two appearances behind the plate with a catcher's glove on his right hand.

The big slugger blasted eight home runs in eight consecutive games with Pittsburgh in 1956 to establish his first major league mark.

His record homer splurge in 1956 came against some good pitchers, including Warren Spahn and Carl Erskine. He hit his first off Chicago's Jim Davis on May 19, then popped homers in both games of a double-header the next day and five more in the following five games through May 28.

Two years later, Dale appeared behind the plate for the Chicago Cubs to become the first left-handed throwing catcher of modern time.

Branch Rickey, the Pittsburgh general manager who had been a catcher during three seasons in the major leagues, was the innovator who thought Dale might be the man to break baseball's tradition that a southpaw isn't suitable to be used behind the plate. Long was drafted by the Pirates in 1950 and when he showed up in camp the following spring, manager Bill Meyer said Rickey wanted to convert him to catcher.

"But, I'm left-handed," protested Long. Meyer, a former receiver, agreed there must be some misunderstanding and checked with Rickey. The general manager assured Meyer there was no mistake and said he'd already ordered three of the odd right-handed catchers mitts for the Long.

Dale had been touring the minors as a first baseman and outfielder since receiving his Navy discharge in 1944 and was happy for the opportunity to make a major league ball club at any position.

Stooping behind the plate was torture for Long, however, and his knees were sore and swollen. When he didn't make it as a backstop, Long was acquired on waivers by

Dale Long

the St. Louis Browns, who played him in 34 games before Bill Veeck bought control of the team and shipped him to San Francisco.

It was the 11th stop on Long's extended tour of America's minor leagues that began in 1942. Long was a prep football phenom and coach Curly Lambeau wanted to sign him for the Green Bay Packers. His mother objected, but was willing to let her underaged son play professional baseball.

Dale moved slowly through the lower minors until 1948, when he arrived at Lynn in the New England League. His .302 average, 18 homers and 119 RBIs won a promotion to the Eastern League, where he batted .288 and .287 in two seasons and led the circuit in doubles (35) the first year and homers (27) and RBIs (130) the second. That's when Pittsburgh drafted him.

After Long arrived in San Francisco in 1950, manager Lefty O'Doul worked on his hitting, but Dale batted only .266 with four homers in part-time duty. O'Doul promised Dale that he could catch the last game of the year, if the Seals escaped the cellar with a win in the first game of a Sunday twin bill against Sacramento. But, the Seals lost the opener and Dale never donned catcher's togs in the Coast League.

Drafted again by the Pirates, Long was dispatched to New Orleans in 1951, where he was runner-up to home run

---

RICHARD DALE LONG
Born: 2/6/26, Springfield, MO, BL/TL, 6-foot-4, 205 pounds

		G	AB	R	H	2B	3B	HR	RBI	SB	AVG.
1951	SF	36	128	10	34	4	1	4	23	0	.266
1953	Hwd	172	599	106	163	34	7	35	116	5	.272
1954	Hwd	129	410	69	115	27	5	23	68	3	.280
PCL		3	337	1137	185	312	65	13	62	207	8	.274
Majors		10	1013	3020	384	805	135	33	132	467	10	.267

		W	L	PCT	G	IP	H	ER	BB	SO	ERA
1953	Hwd	0	0	.000	1	1	0	0	4	1	0.00
PCL		1	0	.000	1	1	0	0	4	1	0.00
Majors (did not pitch in the major leagues)

champ Frank Thomas with 33 while hitting .254. Hollywood was his next stop and the last one of his minor league odyssey.

Dale played two years with the Stars and contributed to a pennant the first season and a tie for the title in 1954. Playing in Gilmore Field was a disadvantage for the southpaw swinger, but it didn't stop him from showing off his long range power.

Although he got off to a slow start in 1953, manager Bobby Bragan stuck with him and Dale led the league with 116 runs batted in and 35 home runs — a Hollywood record by a left-handed batter playing at Gilmore. He was fourth in runs with 106, averaged .272 and was picked as the PCL's most valuable player.

If Dale had repeated his performance the following season, the Twinks might have won in a walk. Instead, Long's back ached all year, his home run production fell to 23 and he knocked in only 68 runs with a .280 average in 129 games. Hollywood and San Diego deadlocked for first place and the Stars lost a one-game playoff.

Long returned to the Big Time in 1955 with Pittsburgh at age 29 and played nine seasons. He never hit for a high average — .298 in 1957 with the Pirates and Cubs was his best — but Dale's power kept him in the lineup until 1963 with those teams as well as San Francisco, Washington and the New York Yankees.

MINNIE MINOSO

Three words crowd out all the others when Minnie Minoso comes to mind: talent, enthusiasm and longevity.

A black man from Cuba, Minnie entered Organized Baseball late. He first broke into Cleveland's lineup at age 26 in 1949, just two years after teammate Larry Doby had smashed the American League's color line.

Minoso continued playing regularly in the minors until he was 50 and made his last appearance as a major league pinch hitter when he was 57 in 1980. Baseball Commissioner Fay Vincent refused to allow Minnie another major league appearance in 1990, but Minoso had one more at bat in 1993 in the independent Northern League.

Little was known about Minoso when he arrived in San Diego in 1949 and one early newspaper story misidentified him as Puerto Rican.

Jackie Robinson had become the first modern black to play in Organized Baseball in 1946, but San Diego fans were accustomed to seeing African-American players in a Padres uniform, although Spanish-speaking blacks were still a novelty. Catcher John Ritchey became the first full-time black player in the Pacific Coast League in 1948 and San Diego's biggest star when Minoso joined the team was giant first sacker Luke Easter.

Minoso replaced another black with San Diego, shortstop Artie Wilson, who was sent to Oakland after a dispute over whether Cleveland or the New York Yankees owned Wilson's contract was decided in favor of the Bronx Bombers. Minoso came to the Indians as part of the settle-

ment.

Minnie grew up harvesting sugar cane in rural Cuba and began playing baseball at 14 on a plantation team. While visiting a sister in Havana in 1944, he joined a candy factory team and moved to Santiago the following season. He became a professional in the Cuban Winter League in 1946, playing third base for Marianao.

A Marianao coach was manager of the New York Cubans in the Negro National League. He acquired Minoso for $150-a-month plus meal money and took Minnie to America. After three seasons at third base, Minoso was sold to Cleveland for $25,000 and sent to Dayton in the Central League, where he batted a dazzling .525 in 11 games.

Minnie looked good in Cleveland's spring camp, but he was shipped to San Diego so he could learn to play the outfield. His inexperience and lightning speed both were evident in his first game on May 21 when he misplayed two singles, but made a sparkling shoestring catch. He got off to a great start at the plate, hitting safely in his first 15 games.

Speed always was a major part of Minoso's game, but when there was talk of a foot race between Minnie and base stealing leader Wilson, Padre manager Bucky Harris rejected the idea on grounds Minoso might pull up lame. "I am in the baseball business, not the Olympics business," said Harris. Minoso was allowed to race 75 yards against Portland speedster Luis Marquez the following year and lost by two strides.

Minoso was an important ingredient in the Padres' drive for the playoffs, batting .297 with 22 home runs and 75 RBIs in 137 games. He had only 13 steals, a fact that might be explained in part by his daring base running and penchant for taking the extra base. Major league teammate Billy Pierce once said that Minnie didn't get many chances to steal, "because he never stopped at first base."

San Diego trailed Seattle by a game for fourth place going into the final day. The Rainiers and Hollywood split, but Minnie led the Padres to a twin bill sweep against Los Angeles, hitting two home runs and driving in four in the opener and winning the nightcap with a two-run blast.

San Diego and Seattle held a special playoff game for fourth place in the final standings. Minoso played the hero's role with four hits, including a double and home run as the Padres won. San Diego beat Oakland in the first playoff round, but lost to champion Hollywood in the finals.

SATURNINO ORESTES ARMAS MINOSO
Born: 11/29/22, Havana, Cuba, BR/TR, 5-foot-10, 175 pounds

		G	AB	R	H	2B	3B	HR	RBI	SB	AVG.
1949	SD	137	532	99	158	19	7	22	75	13	.297
1950	SD	169	599	130	203	40	10	20	115	30	.339
1964	Ind	52	178	22	47	11	0	4	26	6	.264
PCL	3	358	1309	251	408	70	17	46	216	49	.312
Majors	17	1835	6579	1136	1963	336	83	186	1023	205	.298

Minnie Minoso
(left) with
Harry Dorish.

Minoso and Cleveland farmhand Harry Simpson teamed up in 1950 to lead the Padres to a second place finish, four games behind Oakland. Minnie's .339 average was third in the league and he contributed 130 runs, 40 doubles, 20 homers and 115 runs batted in with 30 steals.

Minnie started 1951 with Cleveland but was part of an early season trade with the White Sox, where Paul Richards was the manager. Richards had been with Seattle the year before and was eager to get Minnie, the first black to wear a White Sox uniform in the regular season. Minoso justified the selection by hitting .326 with a league-leading 14 triples to win the *Sporting News* Rookie of the Year Award and finish second to Gil McDougald in the baseball writers' poll.

Comiskey Park negated Minoso's natural power, but it emphasized his other greatest natural attribute, speed. Chicago topped the league in stolen bases annually and Minnie led the "Go Go" White Sox.

Minnie paced the league in stolen bases in 1951, 1952 and 1953 and pilfered 176 sacks before he was swapped to Cleveland in 1958. Batting from a crouch and crowding the plate, Minoso led the league in being hit by pitches a record 10 times and collected a high of 23 free trips to first in 1956.

Minnie came back to the White Sox for two more years and rejoined the team again in 1964 after stints with St. Louis and Washington.

His love for the game was boundless. Minnie was gregarious, always smiling, was popular with fellow players — who appreciated his attitude and hustle — and a great hit with the fans. Over his career, Minnie batted .298 lifetime with eight seasons at .302 or above. He played in six All-Star games and won three gold glove awards.

Upon his release by Chicago in mid-1964, he returned to the Coast League with Indianapolis, hitting .264 in 52 games. Matching the description by Bill Veeck, who once compared Minnie with good bourbon, saying he, "gets better with age," Minoso did not retire. He took his game to the Mexican League, where he performed until 1973 and managed until 1975.

Minnie later was a White Sox coach and closed the ledger on 17 years in the majors with those two pinch hitting appearances in 1980.

ALBIE PEARSON

Albie Pearson was the kind of player universally loved by baseball buffs.

They have great affection for the big power hitters, the guys who can bust one over the fence with a tape measure home run. And they adore the hard-throwing pitchers who send batters back to the dugout shaking their heads because they never really got a good look at "Strike Three!"

But, of all the players loved by fans, no one rates higher than the little guy. At 5-foot-5 and 140 pounds (soaking wet), Albie was one of those they liked the most. It wasn't just his size. His ability and hustling attitude also contributed to Pearson's popularity.

Size — or the lack of it — was what you noticed first about the little outfielder from Southern California's El Monte High School, where he set the school record in the 100-yard dash. Pearson had to be a great one. After all, his dad called him Albie in honor of legendary 144-pound All-American halfback Albie Booth, the "Little Boy Blue" who starred at Yale a few years before Pearson's birth in 1934.

Boston Red Sox scout Joe Stephenson wasn't sure about the breadth of Albie's ability at first. Stephenson saw Pearson playing sandlot ball in Los Angeles, but hesitated to pursue Albie because of his diminutive stature. Stephenson talked to veteran scout Tom Downey, who had no doubts and got Pearson's signature on a contract immediately.

When Albie showed up for his first professional baseball job in 1953 at the San Jose Red Sox camp in Santa Cruz, manager Red Marion shook his head and thought Pearson was applying for the bat boy's job. In fact, the only uniform small enough to fit him at first was the bat boy's.

When Albie pounded a pitch over a distant fence in an early workout, Marion was convinced he had a winner in his 17-year-old outfielder. Later in the season, Red Sox scout Charlie Walgren called him, "pound for pound, the greatest player in the game today."

Albie was hardly the biggest name on the San Jose roster at the start of the California League season. All eyes were on two "bonus babies" on the roster: outfielder Marty Keough and catcher Jerry Zimmerman. Albie wasn't in their league. He hadn't signed for big bonus bucks, just a traveling bag.

But, when the 1953 season was history, Pearson ranked second on the pennant-winning Red Sox in batting (.334), first in walks (108) and was tied with Keough in triples (11). Keough batted .330, Zimmerman .265. Keough was regarded as a better bunter than Albie but in the outfield their fielding records were nearly identical.

Pearson knew he could play, but he was intent on improving. San Jose general manager Bob Freitas drove Albie to Bakersfield after the Red Sox won the post-season playoffs and let him out of the car in front of a relative's house.

"I'll never forget driving away in semi-darkness with

Albie Pearson

Pearson standing in front of the house practicing a swing with his bat," said Freitas. "There was a determined little guy, the day after the close of the season, practicing a full swing at 4 in the morning."

Albie moved on to Albany, hitting .269 in the pitching-rich Eastern League, but leading the circuit with 119 walks. His sharp batting eye won him another base on balls title the following season at Montgomery in the Sally League, where he earned 132 free passes with a .305 average.

Pearson won promotion to the Pacific Coast League's San Francisco Seals, who had just been acquired by the Red Sox after the home-owned Little Corporation went broke.

He surged to a hot start, reaching base 23 of his first 45 trips to the plate and batting .297 in 31 games. In the season opener, Albie reached first base on an error, stole second and scored on a short single to the outfield.

"He'll be in the hair of every rival manager in the league," said Vancouver manager Lefty O'Doul. "I know he's already been in mine."

The Red Sox thought Albie needed more seasoning and assigned him to Oklahoma City. He continued to show potential by leading the Texas League with a .371 batting average.

Pearson returned to the Seals in 1957, a year when no one was certain whether or not it would be the PCL's last season. With Albie batting lead-off, San Francisco won the pennant over Vancouver.

Although he was the smallest player in the league and probably all of baseball, San Francisco manager Joe Gordon said his size actually was an asset because pitchers found it difficult to throw to him. Albie didn't head the league in walks, but his 85 ranked fourth. Albie was an

ALBERT GREGORY PEARSON
Born: 9/12/34, Alhambra, CA, BL/TL, 5-foot-5, 140 pounds

		G	AB	R	H	2B	3B	HR	RBI	SB	AVG.
1956	SF	31	101	18	30	5	2	0	6	2	.297
1957	SF	158	592	89	176	22	11	5	50	9	.297
PCL	2	189	693	107	206	27	13	5	56	11	.297
Majors	9	988	3077	485	831	130	24	28	214	77	.270

		W	L	PCT	G	IP	H	ER	BB	SO	ERA
1957	SF	0	1	.000	1	1	0	4	4	0	36.00
PCL	1	0	1	.000	1	1	0	4	4	0	36.00
Majors (did not pitch in the major leagues)

Harry Simpson (center) with Larry Doby (left) and Jim Fridley.

outstanding bunter and could handle the curve as well as the fast ball without swinging at bad pitches.

In right field, Pearson led the league in assists. He was outstanding at charging the ball, had a quick release and made strong and accurate throws.

On the final day of minor league baseball in San Francisco, Albie pitched in a game in which both the Seals and Sacramento Solons spent as much time clowning as playing serious baseball. Pearson proved he didn't belong on the mound, giving up four runs on two hits and four walks in one inning.

The Red Sox traded Pearson and first baseman Norm Zauchin to Washington for infielder Pete Runnels the following January. It was a great move for Albie, who loved the prospect of playing full-time. He batted .275 in 146 games and won the American League Rookie of the Year Award from both the *Sporting News* and the Baseball Writers of America.

Pearson was sent to Baltimore for outfielder Lenny Green early in 1959 and hit only .216. Baltimore dispatched him to Miami in the International League part-way

> *"Pound for pound, the greatest player in the game today."*
> — *Red Sox scout Charlie Walgren describing Albie Pearson*

through the following season and it appeared his big league career might be finished.

Expansion of the American League in 1961 gave him a new opportunity. Pearson was taken by the Los Angeles Angels and contributed a .288 average and 92 runs. He batted only .261 the next year, but led the league with 115 runs. Albie was at his best in 1963 when he hit .304 and was chosen for the All-Star game.

Pearson closed out his career with two more full seasons with the Angeles, hitting .223 but rising to a .278 mark the following year.

HARRY SIMPSON

Lean and lanky Harry Simpson was the Coast League's rookie sensation in 1950, but he was unable to live up to unreasonably high expectations by others or himself.

Before arriving in the PCL, Harry was touted as a player with, a "50-50 chance to be a second (Ted) Williams." Playing for San Diego, one writer said Simpson was better than Luke Easter, who tore the league apart the previous year before being lost to a knee injury. When he made it to the big leagues, Cleveland officials mistakenly thought he was superior to Minnie Minoso. They kept Simpson and traded away Minoso, who became the *Sporting News* Rookie of the Year in the American League.

While not the equal of any of these stars on the playing field, the soft-spoken Simpson was a skillful and hard-working player during eight major league seasons and 21 years as a professional.

Some reporters called him "Suitcase," which was a take-off on the nickname of another famous black player on the Cleveland roster, pitcher Leroy "Satchel" Paige.

Simpson played ball in his home town in Dalton, Georgia, and continued in the Army during wartime service. Upon his discharge, Harry accepted his first professional contract with the Philadelphia Stars of the Negro National League, playing outfield and hitting .242 in 33 games.

Simpson threw right-handed, but batted from the left side of the plate and often appeared only against right-handed pitchers. Roy Campanella saw Simpson in the winter leagues and wrote a letter telling Stars manager Goose Curry that Harry was too good against all kinds of pitching to be platooned.

After two more seasons with the Stars, Simpson was spotted by Eddie Gottlieb, coach of the Philadelphia Warriors of the National Basketball Association, who thought he knew baseball talent as well as players on the hardwoods. Gottlieb thought that Simpson was a possible Ted Williams. "I'm not going to say that he will hit better than Williams, but he has a chance," said Gottlieb. The appraisal won Harry a tryout by eight major league scouts, but no one gave him a contract.

Cleveland took Simpson to training camp anyway and saw enough to sign Harry and option him to Wilkes-Barre in the Eastern League. A wrist hitter with sufficient power to bang tape measure home runs and the speed to leg out three-baggers, he hit .305 and led the league in runs (125), homers (31) and RBIs (120). His achievements won him promotion to San Diego in 1950.

Simpson's arrival forced the Padres to move Minoso from the outfield to third base. The move was partly because Simpson could only play outfield or first base — where slugger Max West was stationed — while Minoso had played the hot corner before arriving in the Coast League.

Harry started slowly, undoubtedly because of a groin pull that forced him to the sidelines later in the year. But, Simpson was a rookie and didn't ask for time off for fear he'd be branded a loafer.

He was hitting .262 in late April and the *San Diego Union* said his "defensive ability overshadows his comparatively low batting average." Harry put a stop to that kind of talk two weeks later, going 11 for 23 with seven extra base hits to boost his average to .318. At one point, Simpson showed his confidence by boasting there wasn't a Coast League pitcher who could throw the ball past him consistently.

Solid hitting marked his play into June, prompting the *Union* to say that Simpson, "has been the whole Padre team for many weeks now. He no longer bites at bad pitches and with each game he looks more like major league timber. Numerous players and scribes have expressed the opinion he's better than Luke Easter was for the Padres a year ago."

Simpson had expressed the same idea to Hank Greenberg a year earlier when the Cleveland general manager visited him in Wilkes-Barre. It was a poor comparison. Harry had good power and better speed that Easter, but Luke was an awesome slugger with more power than anyone else in the PCL in 1949.

Harry didn't need to be compared with anyone on the San Diego roster, however. He led the league in triples (19) and RBIs (156) and posted the third best average (.323) with 33 homers. If the Padres had a most valuable player, it was Harry.

Only in his third year of organized ball and probably in the need of more experience, Cleveland put him in the line-up in 1951 and sent Minoso off to the White Sox. Harry was shuttled between the outfield and first base and continually experimented with his batting stance. He hit .229 in 122 games with only 14 extra base hits.

After two more mediocre years, Harry wound up at Indianapolis in 1954, where he hit .282 and again showed some power. Back with Cleveland the following year, Simpson was sold to Kansas City in June and finished the year at .300

Simpson made the All-Star team the next season and finished with a .293 average, 105 RBIs, 11 triples and 21 homers. He went to the New York Yankees in a June trade in 1957. After hitting .270, Simpson returned to the Athletics and ended his big league stay in 1959 with Kansas City, the White Sox and Pittsburgh.

Simpson wasn't through. He returned to San Diego in 1960, batting .222 in 90 games, but rallied the following year for a .303 average with 24 four-baggers and 105 runs batted in. Harry wandered for three more years in the American Association and the Mexican League and retired.

HARRY LEON SIMPSON
Born: 12/3/25, Atlanta, GA, BL/TR, 6-foot-1, 180 pounds

		G	AB	R	H	2B	3B	HR	RBI	SB	AVG.
1950	SD	178	697	121	225	41	19	33	156	2	.323
1960	SD	95	284	38	63	11	5	8	40	3	.222
1961	SD	146	515	82	156	23	6	24	105	3	.303
PCL	3	419	1496	241	444	75	30	65	301	8	.297
Majors	8	888	2829	343	752	101	41	73	381	17	.266

LEE WALLS

Occupations ranging from bat boy with the San Diego Padres to slugging star for the Hollywood Stars were on Lee Walls' resume during the years before he left the Coast League for a spot in the Big Time.

Lee began his baseball career lugging bats for the ball club near the Mexican border in 1943 and 1944, not long before he entered Garfield Junior High School, whose most eminent alumnus was a former Padre named Ted Williams.

The Walls family moved to Pasadena, where Lee played

shortstop and pitched for John Muir High School. After graduation, he took his bat and glove along to Pasadena City College. He played there for a year before Pittsburgh thought Lee had the look of a ball player and signed him in 1951.

The Bucs sent Walls to Modesto in the California League where he showed even more promise, playing 91 games at third base and 42 more in the outfield. His .342 batting average was second in the Class C league, which he led with 16 triples. Lee also had 14 homers and knocked in 109 runs.

The Pirates brought him up early in 1952, but he hit only .188 in limited duty and was sent back to the minors. Walls showed his versatility at Waco in the Big State League in 1952, playing infield and outfield while hitting .308 in half the season.

Lee had just turned 20 when Pittsburgh dispatched him to a Coast League city not far from his Pasadena home. He joined the Hollywood Stars and attracted attention in the opener with a score-tying, ninth inning, three-run homer against Oakland.

Lee looked like the rookie of the year early, batting in 21 runs in three weeks before reality set in. He wore glasses to see the ball properly, but hit. 268 with 91 runs scored and 83 RBIs.

Never better than an average outfielder, Lee displayed a strong arm in 1954, throwing out five runners over one span of 18 games. Quiet and self-effacing, Lee looked more confident and after a month was the recipient of the "can't miss" tag from reporters who watched as his batting average soared above .400.

Hollywood won its second straight pennant and Lee contributed 16 home runs, 93 runs batted in and a .290 average. He showed good speed with 18 stolen bases.

The Stars might have made it three pennants in-a-row in 1955, but perhaps their finest team faltered at the end, tying San Diego for first place at 101-67 and then losing to

Lee Walls

the Padres in a one-game playoff. Walls more than did his part, hitting .283 and was first on the club with 24 home runs and 99 RBIs.

Pittsburgh brought Walls to the National League the following season and he had a fine inaugural year with a .274 average, 20 doubles and 11 triples.

Walls and another former Hollywood player, Dale Long, were traded to the Chicago Cubs early in 1957. Lee hit only .237, but rebounded for his best season, a .304 average, 24 homers and 72 runs batted in.

After hitting .257 with diminished power totals for the Cubs in 1959, Lee was sent to Cincinnati and then moved to Philadelphia and Los Angeles. He was a utility infielder and outfielder in his last five seasons in the league, never playing in more than 94 games and hitting between .280 and .179.

At age 31, with a decade of major league service and a .262 career batting mark, the Dodgers released him after the 1964 season. He returned to the American League in 1979, coaching with Oakland and New York.

RAY LEE WALLS
Born: 1/6/33, San Diego, CA, BR/TR, 6-foot-3, 205 pounds

		G	AB	R	H	2B	3B	HR	RBI	SB	AVG.
1953	Hwd	178	593	91	159	15	5	10	83	14	.268
1954	Hwd	162	601	88	174	23	5	16	93	18	.290
1955	Hwd	160	568	81	161	21	3	24	99	10	.283
PCL		3	500	1762| 260	494	59	13	50	275	42	.280
Majors		10	902	2558| 331	670	88	31	66	284	21	.262

BIBLIOGRAPHY

BOOKS

Adomites, Paul, *October's Game*, Redefinition, 1990

Allen, Lee, *The Cincinnati Reds*, G. P. Putnam's Sons, 1948

——, *Cooperstown Corner, Columns from the Sporting News*, The Society for American Baseball Research, undated

Asinof, Eliot, *Eight Men Out, The Black Sox and the 1919 World Series*, Holt, Rinehart and Winston, 1963

Bauer, Carlos, and Robert Hoie, editors, *The SABR Guide to Minor League Statistics*, The Society for American Baseball Research Minor League Committee, 1995

Benson, Michael, *Ballparks of North America*, McFarland & Co., Inc., 1989

Beverage, Richard E., *Hollywood Stars, Baseball in Movieland*, 1926-1957, The Deacon Press, 1984

——, *The Angels, Los Angeles in the Pacific Coast League, 1919-1957*, The Deacon Press, 1981

Brodie, S. Dan, *66 Years on the California Gridiron*, Olympic Publishing Co., 1949

Brown, Warren, The Chicago Cubs, G. P. Putnam's Sons, 1946

Clark, Dick, and Larry Lester, editors, *The Negro Leagues Book*, The Society for American Baseball Research Negro Leagues Committee, 1994

Cochrane, Gordon S. "Mickey," *Baseball, The Fan's Game*, The Society for American Baseball Research reprint of the original 1939 book, Mathews Printing Corp., 1992

Cohen, Richard M., David S. Neft and Roland T. Johnson, editors, *The World Series*, The Dial Press, 1976

Cox, James A., *The Lively Ball*, Redefinition, 1989

Davids, L. Robert, editor, *Great Hitting Pitchers*, The Society for American Baseball Research, 1979

Deane, Bill, *Award Voting*, The Society for American Baseball Research, 1988

Dewey, Donald, and Nicholas Acocella, *Encyclopedia of Major League Baseball Teams*, Harper Collins, 1993

Dickson, Paul, Baseball's Greatest Quotations, Edward Burlingame Books, 1991

——, *The Dickson Baseball Dictionary*, Facts on File, 1989

Dobbins, Dick, and Jon Twichell, *Nuggets on the Diamond, Professional Baseball in the Bay Area from the Gold Rush to the Present*, Woodford Press, 1994

Farrell, James T., *My Baseball Diary*, A. S. Barnes and Co., 1957

Felker, Clay, *Casey Stengel's Secret*, Walker and Co., 1961

Fiffer, Steve, *Speed*, Redefinition, 1990

Fimrite, Ron, *Way To Go, Heroes and Legends of Bay Area Sports*, Tarquin Books, 1978

Finch, Robert L., L. H. Addington and Ben M. Morgan, editors, *The Story of Minor League Baseball*, The Stoneman Press, 1952

Gipe, George, *The Great American Sports Book*, Doubleday & Co., 1978

Graham, Frank, *The Brooklyn Dodgers*, G. P. Putnam's Sons, 1945

Honig, Donald, *Baseball When the Grass Was Real*, Coward, McCann & Geoghegan Inc., 1975

——, *The Man in the Dugout*, Follett Publishing Co., 1977

James, Bill, *The Bill James Historical Baseball Abstract*, Villard Books, 1986

Johnson, Lloyd, and Brenda Ward, *Who's Who in Baseball History*, Barnes & Noble Books, 1994

Kaplan, Jim, *The Fielders*, Redefinition, 1989

Kaese, Harold, *The Boston Braves*, G. P. Putnam's Sons, 1948

Karst, Gene, and Martin J. Jones, *Who's Who in Professional Baseball*, Arlington House, 1973

Kerrane, Kevin, *The Hurlers*, Redefinition, 1989

Lieb, Fred, *Baseball As I Have Known It*, Coward, McCann & Geoghegan Inc., 1977

——, *Connie Mack*, G. P. Putnam's Sons, 1945

——, *The Baltimore Orioles*, G. P. Putnam's Sons, 1955

Lieb, Fred, and Stan Baumgartner, *The Philadelphia Phillies*, G. P. Putnam's Sons, 1953

Lowry, Philip J., *Green Cathedrals*, Addison-Wesley Publishing Co., Inc., 1992

Luhrs, Victor, *The Great Baseball Mystery*, The 1919 World Series, A. S. Barnes and Co., Inc., 1966

Mackey, R. Scott, *Barbary Baseball, The Pacific Coast League of the 1920s*, McFarland & Co., Inc., 1995

Mayer, Ronald A., *1937 Newark Bears, A Baseball Legend*, Vintage Press, 1980

McCarty, Bernie, *All-America, The Complete Roster of Football's Heroes*, self, 1991

Mead, William B., *Low and Outside*, Redefinition, 1990

——, *The Explosive Sixties*, Redefinition, 1989

Meany, Tom, *Baseball's Greatest Hitters*, A. S. Barnes and Co., 1950

——, *Baseball's Greatest Pitchers*, A. S. Barnes and Co., 1951

Moffi, Larry, and Jonathan Kronstadt, *Crossing the Line, Black Major Leaguers, 1947-1959*, University of Iowa Press, 1994

Okkonen, Marc, *The Federal League of 1914-1915. Baseball's Third Major League*, The Society for American Baseball Research, 1989

Okrent, Daniel, and Harris Lewine, editors, *The Ultimate Baseball Book*, Houghton, Mifflin Co., 1979

O'Neal, Bill, *The Pacific Coast League, 1903-1988*, Eakin Press, 1990

Owen, V., *The Adventures of A Quiet Soul, A Scrapbook of Memories*, The Rosicrucian Press, 1996

Patten, William, and J. Walker McSpadden, *The Book of Baseball*, P. F. Collier & Son, 1911

Peters, Nick, *100 Years of Blue and Gold*, JPC Corp. of Virginia, 1982

Povich, Shirley, *The Washington Senators*, G. P. Putnam's Sons, 1954

Powers, Jimmy, *Baseball Personalities*, Rudolph Field, 1949

Reichler, Joseph L., *The Baseball Trade Register*, Collier Books, 1984

Reidenbaugh, Lowell, *Baseball's Hall of Fame: Cooperstown, Where The Legends Live Forever*, Arlington House, 1986

Ritter, Lawrence S., *The Glory of Their Times*, The Macmillan Co., 1966

Ritter, Lawrence S., and Donald Honig, *The Image of Their Greatness*, Crown Publishers, 1979

Snelling, Dennis, *The Pacific Coast League, A Statistical History, 1903-1957*, McFarland & Co., Inc., 1995

Spalding, John E., *John Spalding's Guide to Baseball Guides, Record Books and Registers, 1869-1995*, self, 1996

——, *Pacific Coast League Date Book, 55 Seasons of Strange, Silly and Significant Situations, 1903-1957*, self, 1996.

——, *Pacific Coast League Stars, 100 of the Best, 1903 to 1957*, Ag Press, 1994

——, *Sacramento Senators and Solons, Baseball in California's Capital, 1886 to 1976*, Ag Press, 1995

Spink, Alfred H., *The National Game*, St. Louis Sporting News, 1910

Spink, J. G. Taylor, *Judge Landis and 25 Years of Baseball*, Thomas Y. Crowell Co., 1947

Stein, Irving M., *The Ginger Kid, The Buck Weaver Story*, Brown and Benchmark, 1992

Thompson, S. C., *All-Time Rosters of Major League Baseball Clubs*, A. S. Barnes and Co., Inc., 1967

Thorne, John, and Peter Palmer, editors, *Total Baseball*, Warner Books, second edition, 1991

Walsh, Christy, editor, *College Football and All America Review*, Murray & Gee., Inc., 1949

Zingg, Paul J., and Mark D. Medeiros, *Hits, Runs and An Era, The Pacific Coast League, 1903-58*, University of Illinois, Press, 1994

ARTICLES IN THE SOCIETY FOR AMERICAN BASEBALL RESEARCH PUBLICATIONS

Bauer, Carlos, *The Creation of the Pacific Coast League and the Civil War With the Pacific National League that Ensued During its First Year of Existence, 1903*, The Minor League Baseball Research Journal, 1996

——, *The 1903 Pacific Coast League Season*, Minor League History Journal, 1994

Beverage, Richard E., *Tony Lazzeri: Baseball's First 60-Homer Man*, The Baseball Research Journal, 1991

Blaisdell, Lowell, *The O'Connell-Dolan Scandal*, The Baseball Research Journal, 1982

Cardello, Joseph, *Dazzy Vance in 1930*, The Baseball Research Journal, 1996

Crissey, Harrington "Kit," *The Splendid Splinter's Splendid Finish*, The National Pastime, 1992

Daniels, Stephen M., *The Hollywood Stars*, The Baseball Research Journal, 1980

Etkin, Jack, *An Interview with Frenchy Bordagaray*, The Baseball Research Journal, 1988

Goldstein, Ed, *The Yankee-California Connection*, The Baseball Research Journal, 1990

Hibner, John D., *Last Hurrah for the Seals*, The Baseball Research Journal, 1989

Hoie, Robert C., *The Hal Chase Case*, The Baseball Historical Review, 1981

Langford, Walter, *A Conversation with Willis Hudlin*, The Baseball Research Journal, 1987

Lindberg, Richard C., *Minoso By Any Other Name*, The National Pastime, 1992

Mackey, Scott, *The California Winter League*, The Baseball Research Journal, 1995

——, *The 1925 Seals' Place in History*, The Baseball Research Journal, 1992

Murdock, Eugene, *The Youngest "Boy Manager,"* The Baseball Research Journal, 1975

Noll, Gene, *Pinch-Hitting Pitchers*, The Baseball Research Journal, 1995

Obrand, Rick, *High School Teammates Who Reached the "Bigs,"* The Baseball Research Journal, 1984

Okkonen, Marc, *Harry Heilmann, Voice of the Tigers*, The National Pastime, 1990

Overfield, Joseph M., *Easter's Charisma, Remarkable Slugging Captivated Fans*, The Baseball Research Journal, 1984

Patterson, Ted, *Jack Graney, The First Player-Broadcaster*, The Baseball Historical Review, 1981

Quimby, Allen H., *An Afternoon with Red Lucas*, The Baseball Research Journal, 1981

Schroeder, W. R. Bill, *The 1934 Los Angeles Angels*, The Baseball Research Journal, 1977

Selko, Jamie, *Harry Who?*, The National Pastime, 1995

Simpson, Doug, *The Earl of Snohomish*, The Baseball Research Journal, 1982

Skipper, James K. Jr., *Baseball's Babes — Ruth and Others*, The Baseball Research Journal, 1984

——, *The 1927 Yankees: Great Team, Great Nicknames*, The Baseball Research Journal, 1987

Stout, Glen, *Ted's Titanic All-Star Homer*, The National Pastime, 1992

Williams, Pete, *Stealing First and Fielding with Your Head: Germany Schaefer and Babe Herman as Fools*, The Baseball Research Journal, 1990

Sporting News Baseball Guide and Record Book, 1944-1946

Sporting News Complete Baseball Record Book, 1988

Sporting News Official Baseball Guide, 1947-1958, 1995

Sporting News Official Baseball Record Book, 1942

Sporting News Baseball Register, 1940-1959, 1961-1969, 1971-1973, 1975, 1976, 1988

The Baseball Encyclopedia, The Macmillan Co., 1969

University of California Baseball Media Guide, 1996

ARTICLES IN PERIODICALS

Beverage, Richard, editor, *Memorable Outfields*, Pacific Coast League Potpourri, October, 1995

——, *Memorable Outfields — Continued*, Pacific Coast League Potpourri, December, 1995

——, *Passings, George Metkovich*, Pacific Coast League Potpourri, June, 1995

——, *The Greatest Team of Them All*, Pacific Coast League Potpourri, February, 1994

Fagen, Herb, *Ferris Fain: An Old-Time Star Recalls How It Was in the 1950s*, Baseball Digest, August, 1995

——, *"Go Minnie Go,"* The Diamond, March/April, 1994

Ford, Zak, *Before 40 Big League Seasons, He Spent 4 in the PCL,* Where Are They Now?, March-April 1995

Kelley, Brent, *Baseball's Hard-Luck Losers*, Sports Collectors Digest, Oct. 13, 1989

——, *Irv Noren Played With Mantle and Mikan*, Sports Collectors Digest, June 23, 1995

Sargent, Jim, *Andy Pafko, Remembering the Cubs, the Dodgers and the Braves*, Oldtyme Baseball News, Vol. 7, Issue 4

Sparks, Barry, *Ken Raffensberger, Hard-Luck Hurler Savors All-Star Win and Four One-Hitters*, Sports Collectors Digest, April 25, 1995

Streur, Russell, *The Diamond Road of Bobo Newsom*, Sports Collectors Digest, Feb. 7, 1992

NEWSPAPERS

Arizona Daily Star, Tucson, 1990

Bakersfield Californian, 1976

Fresno Bee, 1978

Los Angeles Times, 1904, 1912-1915, 1917-1919, 1924, 1928-1938, 1940-1945, 1951-1953

Oakland Enquirer, 1909

Oakland Post-Enquirer, 1941

Oakland Tribune, 1909, 1920, 1924, 1928, 1930-1931, 1935-1936, 1940-1942, 1947-1949, 1965, 1969, 1989

Sacramento Bee, 1909, 1922-1924, 1926-1934, 1939-1940, 1946-1948, 1958

St. Louis Post-Dispatch, 1939

San Diego Union, 1949-1950, 1957

San Francisco Bulletin, 1909, 1915, 1919, 1921-1929

San Francisco Call and Post, 1915

San Francisco Chronicle, 1903-1904, 1908-1957, 1964

San Francisco Examiner, 1932, 1936, 1946, 1951, 1964

San Francisco News, 1946-1947

San Jose Daily Mercury, 1904, 1919

San Jose Mercury-News, 1993

Seattle Post-Intelligencer, 1944, 1947-1948, 1983

Seattle Times, 1903, 1904

The Oregonian, Portland, 1909, 1915, 1937, 1941-1942, 1946

The Sporting News, St. Louis, 1903-1957

GUIDES AND RECORD BOOKS

Baseball, Office of the Commissioner, 1943

College Football All-Time Galaxy, National Collegiate Athletic Association, September, 1970

Official Baseball, A. S. Barnes & Co., 1945, 1946

Pacific Coast League Baseball Records; 1903-1940, Helms Athletic Foundation, 1941

Pacific Coast League Official Record Book, 1956

Pacific Coast League Record Book, 1994

Reach's Baseball Guide, 1904-1939

Spalding's Official Baseball Guide, 1904-1939

Spalding's Official Baseball Record Book, 1908-1924

Spalding-Reach Official Baseball Guide, 1940, 1941

UNPUBLISHED MATERIAL

Bauer, Carlos, *A Register of Pre-World War II Coastleaguers & Their Teams (1903 through 1937)*, 1994

——, *Pacific Coast League Rosters: 1903 through 1957*, 1995

Hoie, Robert C., *Batting and pitching statistics, 1918 Pacific Coast League season*, undated

Spalding, John E., *Professional Baseball Death Roll*, 1995

Weiss, William J., *Pacific Coast League Historian's records for players who appeared in fewer than 10 games or pitched less than 45 innings, 1947-1953*